PASSIONATE REASON

The Indiana Series in the Philosophy of Religion

GENERAL EDITOR
Merold Westphal

Passionate Reason

MAKING SENSE
—— OF ——
KIERKEGAARD'S

Philosophical Fragments

C. STEPHEN EVANS

INDIANA UNIVERSITY PRESS
Bloomington & Indianapolis

Manufactured in the United States of America

Library of Congress Cataloging-in-Publication Data

Evans, C. Stephen.
    Passionate reason : making sense of Kierkegaard's Philosophical
fragments / C. Stephen Evans.
        p. cm. — (Indiana series in the philosophy of religion)
    Includes bibliographical references and index.
    ISBN 0-253-32073-9 (alk. paper). — ISBN 0-253-20722-3 (pbk. :
alk. paper)
    1. Kierkegaard, Søren, 1813–1855. Philosophiske smuler.
2. Religion—Philosophy. I. Title. II. Series.
BL51.E858 1992
201—dc20   91-30417
1 2 3 4 5   96 95 94 93 92

To my father and dearly missed mother,
in gratitude for many happy memories that
are blended with the writing of this book.

CONTENTS

Preface

Schopenhauer called the mind-body problem "the world-knot" because he thought that all the problems of philosophy met there; untangle that problem and clear lines could be found to unravel all the others. Kierkegaard's *Philosophical Fragments* is hardly a world-knot in just this sense, and I would not argue that a successful interpretation of it would unravel all the problems of philosophy. However, I am convinced that several of the key problems faced by the contemporary mind, not to mention contemporary philosophy, come into focus when this book is read in a clear-headed way. Two problems have a special significance.

The first problem concerns the place of religious faith—especially Christian faith—in the contemporary world, whether that world be thought of as "modern" or "postmodern." Traditional Christianity believed that the key to human existence was to be found in the life, death, and resurrection of a historical figure. Such faith has had grave knocks in the modern world dominated by Enlightenment rationalism. The historical beliefs about Jesus of Nazareth, bound up as they are with the acceptance of the miraculous and the supernatural, are alleged to be unfounded or even downright irrational. Perhaps even more fundamentally, the Enlightenment mind has had difficulty understanding how *any* historical events could have this kind of meaning for life here and now.

Some theologians and religious thinkers see the postmodern world as more receptive to religious faith, and perhaps it is. The impact of Bill Moyer's PBS program, *Joseph Campbell and the Power of Myth,* shows that contemporary society is still fascinated by religious themes. Perhaps the sociological picture of an increasingly and inevitably secular society is an empty "myth" that fails to recognize the power mythology still holds for us. Many Christian thinkers think we must accept—perhaps even celebrate—the categorizing of the central Christian stories as myths. However, it is by no means obvious that the transformation of the Christian gospel to mythology does not fundamentally change its meaning. Kierkegaard, at least, thought that something distinctive about Christianity, something that distinguished Christian faith from Greek philosophy, would be lost by the elimination of the historical. He thought not only that such a transformation would alter the character of Christian faith in a decisive way, but that the character of *my* history would be altered when the meaning of human existence is no longer centered in something historical. *Philosophical Fragments* pointedly raises the issue of whether history, either the history of a figure of an earlier period or the contemporary history of a living person, can have what Kierkegaard would call "eternal significance."

The second problem that *Philosophical Fragments* brings into focus is one that Kierkegaard confronts in dealing with the first issue. It concerns the place and character of reason in the contemporary world. The Enlightenment urged us to "dare to use your own reason." Reason was seen as an autonomous, objective power, a timeless faculty whose historical character was not taken seriously. This image of reason is challenged by Kierkegaard, who dares to look at what might be called the interested character of reason. For Kierkegaard, reason is not merely influenced by the passions; it has itself become passionate.

Here Kierkegaard anticipates the collapse of classical foundationalist epistemology, and his work has been seized on by postmodern thinkers in a manner quite similar to the way Kierkegaard was utilized by existentialism in an earlier generation. However, I believe Kierkegaard's deepest convictions fit postmodernism as poorly as they fit postwar existentialism. In this book I try to show that Kierkegaard does not leap from the passionate character of reason to relativism or antirealism. He thinks that a reason that *recognizes* its passionate character is a friend to humans struggling to find their place. Furthermore, Kierkegaard thinks there is a place to find and that it is even possible we might find it. Thus, he poses a challenge both to modernism and postmodernism. Both the friends and foes of "reason" are forced to reexamine the actual character of human thinking.

Readers of my earlier work, *Kierkegaard's Fragments and Postscript*, may wonder about the relation of this work to that attempt to engage Kierkegaard. Of course it is a venturesome thing to return to familiar territory. After all, Thomas Wolfe has warned that you can't go home again, and the Johannes Climacus section of Kierkegaard's authorship is in some ways home ground for me. The reasons for returning to this ground are multiple. First, the ground is not wholly or even mainly the same. There is a fundamental difference between the structure of my earlier book and the current work. *Kierkegaard's* Fragments *and* Postscript is a thematic study, organized around the key concepts of both *Philosophical Fragments* and *Concluding Unscientific Postscript*. I there attempted to deal with these concepts in what I took to be a logical order, with more primitive concepts and arguments treated before those which presuppose them. No attempt is made there to look at the order or literary structure of the Kierkegaardian texts.

The present work limits itself to *Philosophical Fragments* and it attempts to give a consistent reading of the book as a whole. It is a kind of philosophical commentary that combines exegesis (though not of the line-by-line type), interpretation, and critical interaction. After some initial orientation, I work straight through the text of *Fragments*, attempting to deal with the major issues that would worry a serious reader. Questions about the purpose, structure, and order of *Fragments* obviously come in for special attention. So the book differs from my earlier one in limiting itself to one of the Climacus books and in attempting to treat that work as a literary whole.

Besides these structural differences, there are differences in problems and perspective as well. As I have continued to read and think about the Johannes Climacus literature, I have seen a number of problems emerge that either were not dealt with or were not dealt with adequately in my earlier book. Secondly, to the degree there is overlap in the books, I believe this book reflects a somewhat new perspective on the ground covered. Though I think the present book is consistent with the main theses of my earlier work, my reading of other authors on the Climacus books has changed my thinking. In particular, I now think a great deal more attention must be paid to the literary form of these works and the irony that pervades that form.

Nevertheless, this book shares philosophical purposes with my earlier one. I have not refrained, therefore, from having my own say on such questions as the relation of human reason to purported divine revelations and the relation between a revealed religion such as Christianity and history, or from presenting my own arguments for the views I wish to defend. I hope my readers will go back and continue to read *Philosophical Fragments* for themselves, but I believe that the best motivation for doing so is gained from hard work on the philosophical issues the book raises.

I must in conclusion express my gratitude to Merold Westphal for convincing me that a book of this sort on *Fragments* was needed, and for his confidence that I was the person to do it. I join that expression of thanks with a hope that he will soon complete his own projected commentary on *Concluding Unscientific Postscript*, which in my mind will serve as a natural companion to my own book. I also owe a heavy debt to Robert Roberts, George Connell, and to Charles Taliaferro, all of whom read an earlier draft of this work and gave me detailed criticisms and suggestions.

The principal work for this book was done at Emory University in 1988–89 with the support of a Fellowship for College Teachers from the National Endowment for the Humanities. Emory University provided me with congenial working conditions and an office in their excellent Candler Library as a Fellow of the Institute for Faith Development. St. Olaf College also provided me with an early sabbatical. I am profoundly grateful to all three of these institutions.

Though this entire work was conceived and written as part of one coherent project, as I worked through the issues, some portions were spun off as articles in order to get some critical feedback. Thus, a section of chapter 7, in an earlier incarnation, was published under the title "Is Kierkegaard an Irrationalist? Reason, Paradox, and Faith," in *Religious Studies*, Volume 25. Similarly, some sections of chapters 8 and 9, in earlier versions, appeared as "Does Kierkegaard Think Beliefs Can Be Directly Willed?" and "The Relevance of Historical Evidence for Christian Faith," in *International Journal for Philosophy of Religion* (Volume 26) and *Faith and Philosophy* (Volume 7) respectively. My thanks to those journals for permission to use that material.

PASSIONATE REASON

CHAPTER

1

ON READING KIERKEGAARD AND
JOHANNES CLIMACUS

Philosophical Fragments is generally agreed to be one of Kierkegaard's most significant works. There is, however, no general agreement about the nature of the book's significance. It is a short book, only a little over a hundred pages in length, attributed to a pseudonym, one Johannes Climacus. It is in one sense a simple book. Though Climacus himself says that it is not a book which every divinity school student could write,[1] this is, I think, due more to a lack of "dialectical fearlessness" on the part of the seminarian than to a lack of knowledge on the part of the student, since the content of the book is for the most part "nothing but old-fashioned orthodoxy with a suitable degree of severity."[2] But in a deeper sense it is a book which is far from easy to understand, one full of irony and satire, with a literary form whose relation to the content is deeply puzzling.

As if the book itself did not present enough difficulties, it is impossible to decide how the book should be approached without seeing it in the larger context of Kierkegaard's authorship. One must decide whether Kierkegaard's authorship does have, as he claimed, a unifying purpose, and if so, what that purpose is. The nature and purpose of the pseudonyms must be decided, as well as the relation between the pseudonymous section of the authorship and that which Kierkegaard published under his own name. Having done that, one must then decide the specific character and purposes of the Johannes Climacus pseudonym and its role in Kierkegaard's overall literature.

I have no illusions that I can answer these questions to the satisfaction of all Kierkegaard interpreters. Nevertheless, I owe my readers some account of the assumptions with which I shall approach the work, and the thinking which lies behind those assumptions. The richness of Kierkegaard's authorship makes the quest for anything like a final, definitive interpretation a hopeless one, and there are approaches to Kierkegaard's literature which differ radically from my own, and yet have shown themselves to be interesting and fruitful. I claim only that my approach is one that is faithful to the text and that it provides an illuminating way of approaching a host of significant problems.

THREE TYPES OF KIERKEGAARD LITERATURE

I find it useful to divide recent literature on Kierkegaard into three broad types. First, there are books which more or less ignore the pseudonyms and read Kierkegaard as a straight philosopher, drawing on Kierkegaard's literature as a whole.[3] I would place in this group philosophers such as Stephen Dunning, Louis Pojman, John Elrod, and the early writings of Mark C. Taylor. Though obviously the philosophical approaches of these authors differ greatly, ranging from the analytic perspective of Pojman to the structuralist, dialectical reading of Dunning, they have in common an approach which emphasizes Kierkegaard as a philosopher and makes the particular character of the pseudonyms unimportant. We might call this the philosophical approach.

The second way of reading Kierkegaard could be called the literary approach, since to some degree it stems from Louis Mackey's important book, *Kierkegaard: A Kind of Poet*.[4] However, the term "literary approach" is not completely satisfactory, since I have in mind here the later writings of Mark C. Taylor and others associated with the series *Kierkegaard and Postmodernism*, of which Taylor is editor. These authors wish to bring Kierkegaard into relation with deconstructionism and other contemporary movements in literary criticism.[5] The term "literary approach" is suggestive, since for these authors the literary form of Kierkegaard's work is decisive. Kierkegaard is fundamentally a poet or literary artist, and in Mackey's words, "Whatever philosophy or theology there is in Kierkegaard is sacramentally transmitted 'in, with, and under' the poetry."[6]

However, the term "literary approach" fails to express the distinctive way the Kierkegaardian texts are approached as literature here. Following Derrida, these authors see Kierkegaard's work as fundamentally subverting its apparent content. The search for any overall "point of view" in Kierkegaard is therefore regarded as hopeless. The pseudonyms must be read on their own terms, and their work is more ironical and destructive than directed toward establishing—or even undermining— traditional philosophical positions through straightforward arguments, dialectical analyses, and so on. Hence I think the best description of this second perspective may be "the ironical approach."[7]

A third category of work is best seen as a synthesis of the first two; I would term it literary-philosophical. Recent books on *Philosophical Fragments* by H. A. Nielsen and Robert Roberts would be excellent illustrations of what I have in mind.[8] Like the second group, Nielsen and Roberts take the pseudonyms seriously, and this leads them to take the literary structure of the books seriously. Also, as is the case with the ironical interpreters, they see much of Kierkegaard's intent as negative, humorous, and ironical subversion of the philosophical and theological status quo. However, unlike the ironical group they do not see this approach as blocking any consideration of the text as primarily philosophical, but, on the contrary, as freeing the reader up for an encounter with the text which will be philosophical in what might be termed a Socratic sense. Though I have learned much from representatives of all three approaches, it is this third approach that I shall attempt to follow most closely in the present work.

The assumption that underlies my approach is that though Kierkegaard does subvert the epistemological tradition of classical foundationalism, he is no friend of historicism and relativism either. Kierkegaard reminds us forcefully of our finitude, and he wants us to recognize the relativity and historicity of our situation, even with respect to what philosophers like to call Reason and Evidence. There is no risk-free method of grasping the truth. Nevertheless, there is truth to be grasped, and what Kierkegaard wants us to see is that our subjectivity is not just a screen that distorts the truth, but may be or become a medium that, when controlled by the right kind of passion, opens us up to an encounter with truth. This encounter cannot produce "the system"; it cannot eliminate the risk that we are mistaken. However, it can allow us to participate in a truth that, provisionally and partially at least, can transform our lives.

A POINT OF VIEW ON THE AUTHORSHIP

I begin by affirming that I agree with Kierkegaard himself that his literature has an overall religious purpose and that Kierkegaard was, as he put it in *The Point of View for My Work as an Author*, "from beginning to end a religious author." In this review of his literature, Kierkegaard views his whole authorship as consisting of two streams, one aesthetic and one religious. The apparently aesthetic writings have, however, as their purpose leading the aesthetic reader to the place where he can seriously confront the religious works. This claim of Kierkegaard has often been attacked on the grounds that it is by no means clear that Kierkegaard understood his purposes at the beginning of his authorship as he did at the end, when he wrote *The Point of View*. Louis Mackey has recently argued that there can be no such "point of view" for Kierkegaard's writings, only points of view.[9] This charge goes in hand with a view of Kierkegaard as deeply confused and even radically self-deceived about his own life and authorship.[10]

I have no wish to endow Kierkegaard with superhuman self-insight or clarity about his life. Like the rest of us, he surely struggled in these areas, though I do think he probably struggled more energetically and successfully than most of us. The readings of his works and life given us by Josiah Thompson,[11] Henning Fenger, and in the later writings of Louis Mackey seem unjustifiably cynical to me; certainly they fall short of the standard of love discussed by Kierkegaard himself in *Works of Love*, where he argues that the lover "believes all things" in the sense of always seeking to discover the most charitable interpretation of another's life.[12] However, for my purposes, it is not necessary to decide the truth of Kierkegaard's account of his own life. For in the final analysis, as Kierkegaard himself would be the first to affirm, the meaning of a body of literature cannot be determined by the intentions of the author, but by what the author realized.

In other words, my justification for seeing a religious purpose as providing a unity to Kierkegaard's literature is not that he affirms that he intended such a unity, but that looking at the literature in this way illuminates it in a powerful manner. Kierkegaard himself admits that he did not have a clear understanding of the plan of the literature at the outset.[13] His own understanding of what he was about changed as he personally developed. He attributed the unity of the authorship to providence,[14] an explanation which many will doubtless discount, but which certainly involves a recognition on his part that the whole thing was not planned out in advance. Whether Kierkegaard intended it or not, the unity is there in the text, in the sense that an honest reading of the authorship beginning with *Either/Or* and continuing through the later explicitly Christian writings can discern a consistent *telos*. Arguments and literary forms work together in an amazing way to draw the reader toward religious issues.

In a sense what I am offering on behalf of this thesis is testimony; I can truly affirm that the literature has taken on a power for me when read in this manner. But I also hope to show my readers how the literature is clarified and illuminated when read in this way, and, ultimately, challenge them to test my claims by going back to Kierkegaard.

TAKING JOHANNES CLIMACUS SERIOUSLY

No area of Kierkegaard interpretation has given rise to more controversy than the pseudonyms. Some have taken as literal fact Kierkegaard's remark at the end of *Concluding Unscientific Postscript*, in which he affirms that though he is the legally responsible author of the pseudonymous books, "not a single word" of the pseudonymous authors belongs to Kierkegaard himself.[15] Indeed, Louis Mackey has even suggested that the books Kierkegaard authored under his own name are simply from another pseudonym, so that "Søren Kierkegaard" is just one more literary *persona*.[16] At the other extreme, some authors have simply ignored the pseudonyms altogether, and have developed an overview of "Kierkegaard's" views by drawing from all the pseudonymous works.[17]

The Johannes Climacus pseudonym has given rise to as much controversy as any. There has been a tendency to view the Climacus pseudonym as a mask for Kierkegaard, even on the part of those who take other Kierkegaardian pseudonyms quite seriously. Niels Thulstrup, for example, argues that because of the similarities between *Fragments* and other works Kierkegaard published at the time, and because there is documentary evidence that the work was originally written under Kierkegaard's own name, with only minor changes when the pseudonym was added, "the work is both thought and written in Kierkegaard's own name and therefore cannot be considered a truly pseudonymous work."[18] Consistent with this claim, Thulstrup's own commentary takes the *Fragments* as a straightforward philosophical work. Thulstrup locates its historical antecedents, tries to discern main theses and arguments, looks at objections, and so on, under the guiding assumption that the text is Kierkegaard's own.

In contrast, H. A. Nielsen's *Where the Passion Is: A Reading of Kierkegaard's* Philosophical Fragments takes the Johannes Climacus pseudonym with great seriousness, or with as much seriousness as one can give to a professedly playful author. Nielsen takes deliberate account of the non-Christian point of view from which Climacus writes in interpreting and assessing the book. For example, at the end of chapter 1, Climacus puts forward what he describes as a "proof" of the truth of the hypothesis he has "invented," a hypothesis which bears a striking resemblance to the Christian story of the incarnation as God's plan to provide salvation for human beings. Since Climacus professes not to be a Christian, Nielsen argues that there must be a difference between accepting the truth of this hypothesis and genuine Christian faith.[19] In a similar manner, Robert Roberts, who also takes the pseudonym seriously, tentatively suggests that some of the arguments in the "Interlude" section of the book are bad arguments which are to be read ironically as parodies of genuine arguments, a conjecture which Roberts partially bases on the humoristic character of the pseudonym.[20]

In this book I intend to follow the policy of Roberts and Nielsen and the precedent of my own *Kierkegaard's* Fragments *and* Postscript, by taking the Johannes Climacus pseudonym as a genuine pseudonym. Thulstrup is undoubtedly right in claiming that *Fragments* was originally written under Kierkegaard's own name, but that fact does not have the decisive importance that Thulstrup gives it. First, as Thulstrup himself points out, there were revisions to the book after the pseudonym was added, notably to the preface. One cannot say in an a priori manner that these changes, however small, may not be significant in altering the thrust of the book as a whole. Taking the pseudonym seriously, for example, allows one to consider the possibility that the tone of the preface alters the sense of the book as a whole.

Even more significantly, taking the pseudonym as a genuine *persona* leaves open the possibility that the transition to a pseudonym was the result of a discovery on Kierkegaard's part about the character of the book. Any creative author, and Kierkegaard was nothing if not creative, makes discoveries about his own work in the process of writing and rewriting. It may well be that the humoristic, non-Christian Climacus pseudonym embodies the standpoint that Kierkegaard found himself to have taken in the composition of the book. In fact, the mere affixing of the pseudonym, even if no other changes in the book had been made, can be seen as a significant act of rewriting on Kierkegaard's part, one which potentially alters every sentence by altering the perspective of the author.

Finally, taking the pseudonym seriously is a strategy which offers little risk. In reading the book as written by Johannes Climacus, I make no a priori assumptions about the character of the pseudonym or its relation to Kierkegaard himself. If the book presents us with serious and sober philosophy, as Thulstrup asserts (and I think it does indeed do this in some sections), we will not be barred from learning things simply because we choose to play along with Kierkegaard and regard ourselves as learning from Climacus. And if Climacus does present views which are substantially in agreement with Kierkegaard's own at the time the book was written, there is nothing to prevent our recognizing that fact. In summary, taking the pseudonym seriously safeguards several significant possibilities for the reader while foreclosing none. At least this will be true for the philosophical reader. If our purpose in reading *Philosophical Fragments* is to construct a history of the development of Kierkegaard's own views, then some potential for loss may be present in attributing the book to the pseudonym. If, however, we read the book, as I wish to do, as forcing us to grapple with a set of significant philosophical questions, then we do well to grapple with Johannes Climacus.

GETTING TO KNOW JOHANNES CLIMACUS

If we are to grapple with Johannes Climacus, we need to get to know him, of course. That task turns out not to be an easy one. Climacus is a somewhat elusive, as well as ethereal, character. We have no real biographical facts to work with, and this is no accident. Climacus wants readers to focus on the issues he discusses; he does not want nosy, curious readers who speculate on his own personal standpoints. Such readers are frustrated by being given nothing to work with.

This is said most clearly in the preface, where Climacus does his best to fend off the reader's curiosity: "But what is my opinion?...Let no one ask me about that, for next to knowing whether I have an opinion, nothing could be more insignificant to another person than knowing what my opinion is."[21] Climacus goes on to say that it is possible that he may find some personal benefit from his work, but if so, it is his business. "Do I get any reward for this, am I like those who, serving by the altar, themselves eat of what is laid on the altar?.. Leave that to me."[22] The same reasons that lead me to take the Johannes Climacus pseudonym seriously lead me to respect this request for privacy, and I shall try to follow this policy, though at times the literary form of the book will force us to think about the perspective from which the book was written.

Still, one can, without a nosy desire to know Johannes Climacus' opinions, want to know more about what kind of an author he is and what kind of literature he is offering us. The literature is evidently philosophy of a sort, which presumably makes Johannes Climacus a philosopher of a sort. It is equally evident from the content of the book that Climacus has a great interest in what some might call religious issues, but which I would prefer to term spiritual issues, since there are a host of issues which come up in what is today termed "religious studies" which do not interest Climacus at all.

Some insight here is provided by the name. Johannes Climacus means "John the Climber." The name is that of a monk from the monastery on Sinai, who is well known for having written *The Ladder of Divine Ascent*, a book which purports to give step- by-step instructions for attaining spiritual perfection. Our Johannes Climacus is obviously a different person, and he shows no interest in or knowledge of the original Johannes Climacus. However, like the monk, he is interested in the question as to how an individual attains spiritual wholeness. Perhaps a remark about Hegel in Kierkegaard's *Journals and Papers* gives us the right clue here. "Hegel is a Johannes *Climacus* who does not storm the heavens as do the giants, by setting mountain upon mountain—but enters them by means of his syllogisms."[23] As a philosopher Johannes Climacus is interested in the question as to the value of thought in attaining spiritual perfection. What role can philosophy, or thought in general, play in becoming what I should become?

Many commentators have explored an early, unfinished work of Kierkegaard's, unpublished during his lifetime, *Johannes Climacus, Or De Omnibus Dubitandum Est*,[24] in order to gain more knowledge about Johannes. In this work Kierkegaard sketches a biography of a young man, Johannes Climacus, who tries seriously to realize the philosophical program of universal doubt. The subject of this biography raises a number of acute questions about the nature of doubt and its relation to philosophy. Kierkegaard evidently intended the book as an indirect critique of contemporary philosophers who wrote as if doubt were an easily attained and easily transcended standpoint. The plan of the book was evidently to have young Johannes enmesh himself in doubt and then discover no way of resolving his doubts, even his doubts about doubt.

While *Johannes Climacus* is a work that is well worth studying for its own sake, I shall not employ it as an intellectual biography of the author of *Philosophical Fragments*. There are several reasons for this. First, we must remember that *Johannes Climacus* is an unfinished work that Kierkegaard decided not to publish. Secondly, we have no real basis for assuming that the subject of the book is identical with the author of *Philosophical Fragments*. Thirdly, *Johannes Climacus* is a book authored by Kierkegaard. Even if we made the unwarranted assumption that the subject of the book is identical with the author of *Fragments*, we would have only the third-person testimony of Kierkegaard about Climacus. Furthermore, the picture given of Climacus is of a young innocent who seems far removed from the mature, self-confident, if somewhat enigmatic, author of *Philosophical Fragments*.

We are not limited to the text of *Fragments* for our knowledge of

Climacus, however, for he is the author of *Concluding Unscientific Postscript to the Philosophical Fragments*, a work which is obviously tied to *Fragments* in a number of ways. The *Postscript* is a sequel to *Fragments* which is half-promised at the end of the first book, and the sequel discusses *Fragments* in a number of places. We have every right therefore to look at *Fragments* in light of that latter work, with the proviso of course that the text of *Fragments* itself remains our primary concern. And we have every right to understand Climacus as the author of *Postscript* as well. With respect to both works, however, we shall keep in mind the fact that Climacus turns out to be an elusive, if not downright devious author, who perhaps cannot always be trusted to say what he means or thinks in a straightforward manner.

In the *Postscript* Climacus describes himself as a *humorist*. This suggests of course that his writings will be funny, and the reader who looks for wit and humor in Climacus' writings will not be disappointed. However, the concept of humor for Climacus is a rich one, which involves much more than just wit. This is not the place for a full account of the concept of humor in Climacus' writings (and Kierkegaard generally).[25] Here I will merely try to sketch a few significant aspects of the concept which shed light on Climacus as an author and character.

Humor for Climacus is not merely amusement, a relief from the important business of life. It involves insight into the human predicament. We find humor in what Climacus calls contradictions, perhaps better termed incongruities. A caricature is comical because of the contradiction between likeness and unlikeness it contains. A comedian who takes a pratfall by falling into a hole while gazing up at the sky is funny because of the incongruity between the upward gaze and the downward ascent.[26]

Of course not every incongruity or contradiction is humorous; often such incongruities are tragic. To qualify as humorous, a contradiction must have the sting removed. We must somehow find the situation painless, by gaining a detached perspective on the contradiction, by having what Climacus calls "a way out."[27]

Everyone is in this situation some of the time; everyone laughs at some things. The person Climacus describes as a humorist is someone who has somehow been able to take this humoristic perspective on life as a whole. The whole of human existence is seen as deeply incongruous.

We human beings have the grandest plans and yet are frustrated by the most trivial of circumstances. Nevertheless, the final word on human life is not tragedy. The existential humorist has somehow found "the way out" which allows him to smile at the contradiction between human aspirations and what life has to offer.

As to what this "way out" is, Climacus is coy, and perhaps it will be different things for different humorists. However, it seems to involve something like a religious perspective for Climacus. The humorist sees a contradiction between our busy striving for meaning and significance and the fact that in the end, "we all get equally far;"[28] we all in fact seem to get nowhere. Nevertheless the humorist finds this funny and not tragic, and in so doing reveals a conviction, however obscure, that what we human beings are seeking is something we possess, at least in the end. The assumption seems to be that what various religions have called "salvation," "eternal life," or "eternal consciousness" is present within us. This allows the humorist to relax a bit, to take an attitude not far removed from that of the speculative philosopher, whom William James described as taking a "moral holiday" from the seriousness of the ethical life. A humorist, says Climacus, has "no seriousness of purpose." Though he may be active, in the end he always "revokes" his action, regards it as having no fundamental importance.[29]

Climacus is careful to distinguish this humoristic religious perspective from Christianity. The religious perspective of the humorist may have come about through an encounter with Christianity; in at least one place Climacus suggests that a humorist is someone who has gained a kind of intellectual knowledge of Christianity that has not been existentially realized.[30] Still, the humorist is far from being a Christian. The religious perspective of the humorist leads, not to the commitment and passion of Christian faith, but to a kind of detached perspective, one which is conducive to philosophical reflection and what Climacus calls psychological experimentation (more on the latter will follow). It is true that Climacus also says that humor can be the outward disguise, the incognito, of a true Christian, and in reading *Fragments*, it is tempting at times to speculate that Climacus may be just such a Christian, who has adopted humor as his outer cloak. This is possible, but we are still better off in such a case respecting the disguise, unless we find Climacus himself taking it off to reveal himself. (There are some passages in *Fragments* that can be read as doing this, as we shall see.) I shall therefore, at least initially, take Climacus at his word when he says he is not a Christian.

Philosophical Fragments, among other things, is a book about the relation of Christianity to philosophy. One can easily see, from the preceding description of the humorist, that someone like Johannes Climacus is an ideal author for such a book. As a humorist, Climacus can be knowledgeable about Christianity and interested in Christianity, as well as other religious perspectives. He can, however, maintain the philosophical detachment necessary to look at the issues fairly. His thinking as a humorist has what one might call an experimental quality to it. By "experiment" Climacus does not mean anything one does in a laboratory of course. Rather, he experiments by thinking hypothetically. The Hongs have chosen to translate the Danish *experiment* by "imaginative construction," and the translation certainly captures an essential aspect of what is meant. The experimenter is a thinker who thinks under the guise of "suppose this were so." *Philosophical Fragments* is just such an experiment, as we shall see, a grand attempt to think out the consequences of a certain assumption, one which is never asserted as true but only entertained hypothetically. In the next chapter I shall try to give an overall perspective on this experiment, before descending to the details of the actual issues and problems discussed.

CHAPTER

2

AN IRONICAL THOUGHT EXPERIMENT

Before examining the details of *Philosophical Fragments*, it will be helpful to have an overall perspective on the book. I shall try to provide such a perspective in this chapter by sketching the book's overall project as I see it and by looking at the book's title page, motto, and preface. Having noted earlier the warring approaches to reading Kierkegaard, it is hardly surprising that any such sketch, including my own, must be controversial. The fruitfulness of my approach will, I hope, be shown by its power to make sense of the particular issues to be discussed in subsequent chapters.

AN INITIAL SKETCH

Philosophical Fragments is, at least on the surface, an extended thought experiment. Climacus begins by posing a Socratic (or Platonic) puzzle about truth. How can the truth be learned? It is very soon evident that by truth Climacus means something very significant. He is not talking about 2+2=4, but the truth which it is essential for human beings to have, the truth whose possession would make human life ultimately worthwhile. We might as well signify the specialness of the concept by speaking of "the Truth" in cases where this special kind of truth is in mind, as the original English translation of *Fragments* did, rather than just truth.

The Socratic puzzle concerns the difficulty of seeking the Truth. How can I seek for what I do not know? If I already know the Truth, I do not need to acquire it, and cannot be said to seek it. If I do not know the Truth, I cannot seek it, for I do not know what I am looking for and could not recognize it if I found it.[1] Socrates (and it is evident that this Socrates is a very Platonic Socrates) solved this puzzle, according to Climacus, by postulating that human beings do possess the Truth in some way and that the acquisition of the Truth is really a recollection of something a person already possesses.

Consistent with this hypothesis, Socrates viewed his own role as a teacher as that of a midwife who helps others give birth to their own ideas.[2] The person who learns from Socrates that the Truth is within himself already realizes at the same moment, if he really has learned the Socratic lesson, that he does not owe Socrates any essential debt. What he has learned he has learned from himself, and Socrates has served only as an occasion for his own self-actualization. The moment in which a person acquires this insight cannot have a decisive importance either, for at the same moment at which the person acquires this Truth, he realizes that at bottom it has always been in his possession.

Climacus thinks that this "Socratic" picture of the Truth and its acquisition is very widely held among philosophers. Indeed, it is more accurate to say that it is taken for granted; most philosophers simply assume some variation of this picture and cannot even imagine an alternative. (What Climacus means by this and why he thinks this will be explored in the next chapter.) Hence, he sets himself the philosophical task of trying to discover an alternative to the Socratic view. He embarks on a thought experiment which consists of the construction of a view which is different from the Socratic view. He does not (with a few apparent exceptions, to be discussed in due course) concern himself with the truth of this alternative, but merely attempts to see if there is any such alternative. In sketching out this alternative, the underlying procedure is simply to ask, "Is this view genuinely different from the Socratic view?" Thus, Climacus will often reject a possibility by arguing that accepting such a view would "return us to Socrates," and just as frequently, he will add a wrinkle to his "thought-project" by merely claiming that the wrinkle makes his constructed view genuinely different from the Socratic perspective. Of course one might think that there are many views which are genuinely different from the Socratic view, and it seems possible a priori that this might be so, but Climacus will be happy if he can think up just one coherent alternative.

Even an unsophisticated first reading of *Fragments* would reveal that the alternative Climacus seems to be "inventing" bears a suspicious resemblance to Christianity. "If things are to be otherwise" than the Socratic view, says Climacus, then "the moment in time" must have decisive significance, unlike the Socratic view, where the moment has no intrinsic importance. With this slim hypothetical foundation, Climacus goes to work. In order for the moment to mean everything, then the preceding state of the learner must be one of being totally devoid of the Truth.[3] The learner must not even have the capacity to acquire or develop the Truth on his own.[4] Such a state of error Climacus decides to call "sin." In such a case the teacher required will be no mere midwife, but someone who will give the learner the ability to grasp the Truth. Such an act amounts to a re-creation of the learner, and therefore only the god could be the teacher on this alternative.[5] The god-teacher who thus makes possible the learner's new birth is no mere teacher, but a savior, deliverer, reconciler, and judge.[6] The disciple of the god cannot regard his relationship to the god Socratically; he owes the god everything, and his new life with the god is so different that he sees himself as one who has been converted, who must look back on his old life with a kind of sorrow described as repentance.[7]

In chapter 2 Climacus imaginatively fleshes out his experiment by a poetic attempt to show that the god could function as such a teacher for human persons only by becoming a human person himself. The divine teacher can carry out his teaching only through an incarnation. The god's actions in becoming the teacher must therefore be actual historical events. Chapter 3 reflects on human philosophical attempts to gain knowledge of God and specifically tries to show the inability of unaided human reason to gain the kind of knowledge of God that such an incarnation would make possible. Here it is argued that reason cannot even gain a knowledge of the god[8] negatively. When unaided by the god's self-revelation, it cannot even adequately understand its own inability to know God, though something of positive significance for the encounter with the god is nonetheless learned from the failure.

Chapters 4 and 5 return to the story of the god's appearance and sketch the kind of historical relationship human beings might have to such an incarnate god, both for immediate contemporaries of the god in history, and for later generations. The thrust of the account is simply that one becomes a disciple of the god, capable of learning the Truth from him, only through a direct relationship. This relationship occurs by means of sensory experience, in the case of the immediate contemporary of the god's appearance, and by means of historical testimony in the case of later generations. However, neither the sensory experience nor the historical testimony is more than an occasion for a direct encounter with the god that establishes the relationship. In neither case is faith in the god a product of rational evaluation of evidence.

The book as a whole thus has a tight, logical structure. The skeleton, a hypothesis about the Truth, is deduced in chapter 1. This hypothesis, which involves the idea that the knowledge of God must be given through a divine self-revelation, is poetically concretized in chapter 2 by imagining the revelation as an incarnation. In chapter 3 the content of the hypothesis is illuminated by contrasting it with rational, philosophical approaches to the knowledge of God. In chapters 4 and 5, the implications of the hypothesis for the question of how a person becomes a disciple of the incarnate God are explained, specifically with respect to the role historical knowledge plays and does not play in the process. The whole thing follows quite closely some of the central teachings of Christianity; one could hardly imagine anyone "inventing" such a tale outside of a culture familiar with Christianity.

IRONY AND MORE IRONY

In *Concluding Unscientific Postscript*, Johannes Climacus has an extended footnote giving his reaction to a review of *Fragments* that appeared in a German theological periodical. Climacus says that the review gives a "plot summary" of the book that is generally accurate but nevertheless gives "as misleading an impression of the book as is possible to give."[9] The reason for this is simply that the review takes the book straightforwardly, with no real appreciation of the irony that pervades the whole project. An attentive reader of *Fragments* will hardly need this external reminder from Climacus in order to see that something funny is going on. Clues abound within the text of *Fragments* itself. The most obvious clues are the "dialogues" with an interlocutor who appears frequently in the text, particularly at the ends of chapters.

For example, at the end of chapter 1 the interlocutor shows up and berates Climacus for undertaking the ludicrous project of inventing something that is already well known. Climacus is like "the man who in the afternoon exhibited for a fee a ram that in the morning anyone could see free of charge, grazing in an open pasture."[10] On the surface the irony is simply that Climacus is pretending to invent something which his Danish Lutheran readers, all baptized and catechized as children, were already intensely familiar with, namely Christianity. No attentive reader could accept the idea that the concepts Climacus explores in his thought-project, concepts such as an incarnate God who functions as Savior and Redeemer, were simply pulled out of the air. Even at the surface level, therefore, Climacus is pulling our leg.

However, the irony goes deeper than the extended joke of pretending to invent something that is well known to everyone. Climacus' exploration of his experiment leads him to the conclusion that his experiment is one that no mere human being could have thought up. That is, the very content of the hypothesis that he pretends to be inventing has as one of its essential features the impossibility of its invention by any mere human! Any concept that could be invented by a human being essentially presupposes the Socratic view that the potential to discover the Truth lies within human nature. The alternative Climacus claims to be inventing presupposes that the capacity for the Truth is lacking in human nature and must be brought to human beings by the god. Climacus argues (how plausibly remains to be determined) that this story is itself one that employs non-Socratic concepts and could only have come from the god himself.

Even this argument on Climacus' part may be part of his borrowing, since it so clearly reflects the traditional Christian claim that Christianity is rooted in a divine revelation, not in human philosophizing. Thus, the interlocutor is angry with Climacus not merely for "inventing" something well known to all, but because, in Climacus' own words, "I falsely attribute to myself something that belongs to no human being."[11] Of course Climacus' cheerful admission of his plagiarism shows that he is merely teasing his reader, not seriously attempting to claim the God's story as his own.

The fact that the *Fragments* is a kind of extended ironical joke in which a thought-experiment is invented, whose content is such that it supposedly could not be invented, is certainly consistent with the portrait we sketched of Climacus as a humorist in the last chapter. Even the specific character of the joke reflects the distinctive character of the humorist as Climacus defines him in *Postscript*. The humorist, he says, always "revokes" or "calls back" his efforts. Just when he seems most serious, he pulls the rug out from under our feet by undermining his own efforts. In a similar way, in *Fragments* Climacus seems to develop a thought-experiment that nullifies itself, at least as a thought-experiment.

It would, however, be very rash to take the humoristic character of *Fragments* as nullifying any serious philosophical purpose. Climacus himself says in *Postscript* that "it is only assistant professors who assume that where irony is present, seriousness is excluded."[12] The fact that the project as a whole is ironical does not entail that particular arguments within the project are not sound or intended as sound. The conceptual distinctions Climacus draws between Christian and Socratic ways of thinking, for example, may be quite sound and important, even if we recognize that they are presented to us in a jesting form. Thus our recognition of the ironical form of the book as a whole by no means exempts us from the philosophical task of examining and thinking through its arguments and claims, even though we recognize that at times Climacus may be pulling our leg. We shall therefore proceed to examine the "details" of the jest.

THE TITLE PAGE

The original title page of *Philosophical Fragments*, whose content is reproduced on page 1 of the Hong translation in *Kierkegaard's Writings*, contains several things worth noticing. First there is the title itself: Philosophiske Smuler eller En Smule Philosophi (*Philosophical Fragments or A Fragment of Philosophy*). The notion of a fragment of philosophy itself has a humoristic ring, or at least it did in Kierkegaard's day, as Hegelian philosophers of the time had practically identified philosophy with systematic thinking. As many commentators have noted, the Danish term *Smuler* is actually lighter than the English "fragments" would suggest. It is an everyday word, not a philosophical term, but a word a person would use at the dinner table to ask for *"en lille smule mere"* (a little bit more) of something. To translate the title as *Philosophical Bits* or *Philosophical Scraps* would not therefore be inappropriate.

By his very title, then, Climacus wishes to distance his philosophical efforts from the Hegelianism which had fairly recently become popular in Denmark. There is little doubt that Hegelianism, particularly as represented by Danish theological Hegelians, is a primary polemical target of *Fragments*, and we will take due notice of the implicit criticisms of this type of view at appropriate places. It would, however, be a great mistake to overemphasize the particular historical circumstances in which *Philosophical Fragments* was written. The book deals with philosophical problems and questions that have a perennial importance, and if Hegelians are attacked, they are attacked for holding views which are very common among theologians and philosophers today as well.

That the book does deal with issues of abiding philosophical interest can also be gleaned from the title page, which poses three related questions: "Can an eternal consciousness have an historical starting-point? How can such a starting-point have more than historical interest? Can one build one's eternal happiness on historical knowledge?"

It is inappropriate to try to answer these questions at the outset, or to suggest Climacus' answers to them, or even to say if he has answers. However, we must have some initial sense of what the questions mean, if we are to read the book with insight. It is clear that the crucial issue here is that of the relation between history and what many religions have called salvation. Most of the world's great religions, though they may be rooted in history in the sense that they may trace their origins to the teachings and life of a historical founder, do not in the end base the salvation of humans on any historical events. Rather, salvation is gained through adherence to a teaching and/or set of practices that have a timeless quality about them. The devout Hindu who realizes his unity with the Divine and understands the Vedic teaching "That Art Thou," whether this is achieved through yogic exercise or philosophical contemplation, has gained an insight into a truth which has no historical datedness about it. The devout Buddhist who has gained release from suffering by attaining selflessness has similarly realized a state of being which seems equally relevant to any historical period. No particular historical facts about the Buddha seem to be necessary conditions for such an achievement.

Traditional Christianity seems markedly different from such religions.[13] According to Christianity the salvation of human beings depends on the life, death, and resurrection of a historical figure, Jesus of Nazareth, who is God incarnate. Here salvation is not premised on some ahistorical doctrine, or merely on some essentially timeless practice of life to be imitated, but is dependent on one's relation to an historical figure. Though many Christians have celebrated this historical rootage, many philosophers and theologians in the nineteenth century, and perhaps even more today, see this historical foundation as a problem. How could the eternal destiny of human beings be decided by events at a particular place and time? How could one's eternal salvation depend on one's awareness of a few contingent historical facts? There seems little doubt that such worries are one of the factors contributing to the continuing attempts by theologians to get behind these traditional Christian claims about Jesus as the Christ and discover a "Jesus of history" who is more like the founders and teachers of other great religions.[14] These embarrassing claims about Jesus as God incarnate could be eliminated if it could be shown that they were creations of the early church which actually falsify the meaning of Jesus' life. If, for example, Jesus essentially offered us a teaching about our relationship to God, or perhaps represented for us a lifestyle characterized by self-giving love, and this teaching and/or lifestyle turns out to be the key to salvation, then there would be no need for the traditional claim that Jesus was uniquely God, a claim that is a deep stumbling-block to those looking for ways to see the great world religions as compatible with each other.

The first of the three questions on the title page, "Can an eternal consciousness have an historical starting-point?" is logically fundamental to the others. The expression "eternal consciousness" here is a preliminary clue to what is termed in the text the possession of the Truth. Climacus simply assumes that human beings are seeking this Truth or "eternal consciousness," whatever it is. An eternal consciousness seems a very close cousin to what Christianity has termed eternal life, but it must be taken in *Philosophical Fragments* in a more formal sense. An eternal consciousness is the fulfillment of my goal as a human being, and Climacus takes it for granted that this is not simply temporal goods. However the Socratic view and Climacus' alternative hypothesis would doubtless specify the content of an eternal consciousness in very different ways, which in turn leads to opposing answers to the question as to whether such an eternal consciousness could have an historical starting-point.

The question essentially is whether what religions have variously termed salvation, eternal life, or nirvana is something that can be acquired (or lost) in time. Could one particular moment, or set of moments, have eternal significance for a person? Old-fashioned Christian orthodoxy had proposed that it did, in a dramatic manner. A person's decisions in this life with respect to Jesus of Nazareth could have the consequences of eternal blessedness or eternal damnation. Such a view makes history decisive in two respects. An individual's eternal destiny is decided by her own historical decisions, and those historical decisions in turn revolve around an historical figure, Jesus of Nazareth.

The second of the questions ("How can such a starting-point have more than historical interest?") is really just the question as to how an affirmative answer to the first question is possible. Assuming that history could be decisive with respect to my salvation, how could this be so? How could an event at a particular place and time have eternal consequences? How could I come to view a particular historical figure not merely as another historical figure, but as the center of my life and the answer to the crucial question as to how I am to fulfill my destiny as a human being?

The last of the three questions again presupposes answers to the ones that precede it. Assuming that an historical starting-point is possible for my eternal consciousness and that an historical event or figure could therefore have more than merely historical interest for me, what role would historical knowledge play in the acquisition of this eternal consciousness? Would I need historical knowledge of the event or figure, and if so, what kind of historical knowledge would I need and how would I get it?

Though these questions obviously are pertinent ones for Christian theologians, they are all properly philosophical ones. That is, they do not presuppose the truth of Christianity or its revelation. They are questions that are logically prior to embarking on a quest for the historical Jesus, or an apologetic attempt to prove the truth of the gospels, or a critical attempt to demolish the gospels as a basis for faith. Before embarking on these historical enterprises, Climacus wishes to ask precisely what one might be able in principle to accomplish through such historical research, by looking at the possible ways salvation might be dependent on history or independent of it.

Besides the title itself and the questions, the title page also contains, of course, the name of the author, Johannes Climacus, and as "*Udgiver*" (editor or publisher), S. Kierkegaard. I have already commented at some length on Johannes Climacus, and will say nothing more about him at this point. The inclusion of Kierkegaard's own name on the title page is doubtless significant, since Kierkegaard did not do this with any of the pseudonymous books which precede *Philosophical Fragments*. Kierkegaard's name appears in a similar way on the title page of *Concluding Unscientific Postscript*, and the significance of the fact is noted when Kierkegaard himself says in *The Point of View* that the inclusion of his name in this way in *Postscript* was a "hint, for those who worry about and have a flair for that sort of thing."[15] My own conviction is that the relationship between Climacus and Kierkegaard himself is a close but complex one. However, putting Kierkegaard's name on the title page as editor by no means implies that the pseudonym is simply a mask for Kierkegaard himself.[16] I think it is fair to say that Johannes Climacus sees things as Kierkegaard himself would see them if Kierkegaard were not a Christian. This means that what Climacus says about Christianity is usually correct, from Kierkegaard's perspective, but it is still the view of an outsider. This, in turn, means that much of the life of faith necessarily remains opaque to Climacus.

THE MOTTO

The motto of *Philosophical Fragments* is "Better well hanged than ill-wed." It is taken, loosely and several times removed, from Shakespeare, since it is a Danish translation of the German translation of a line from *Twelfth Night*.[17] Climacus himself jestingly comments on the motto at the beginning of *Postscript* by noting that the "well hanged author"

of *Fragments* has been "left hanging." However, "better well hanged—
than by an unhappy marriage to be made a systematic in-law of the
whole world."[18]

Niels Thulstrup, in his "Commentary," takes this to be an allusion
to being crucified with Christ.[19] H. A. Nielsen takes exception to
Thulstrup's claim, on the grounds that this reading caters to "the wrong
kind of reader," who is curious about the opinions of Climacus.[20] Presumably, Nielsen thinks that Thulstrup's reading implies that Climacus
is really a "closet Christian," and Nielsen properly objects that this
seems to be an attempt to satisfy precisely the sort of curiosity which
Climacus himself politely asks the reader not to indulge. Nielsen suggests
that the motto is a condensed form of the preface, whose message is that
the book is better left hanging than brought into union with systematic
philosophy.

It seems to me that Nielsen has accurately captured the obvious
meaning of the comment about the Motto in *Postscript,* but Climacus
is jesting in this comment, not attempting a definitive exegesis of his
own motto. And of course part of the power of a literary quote is its
suggestiveness, and I see no reason to think that there was one "correct"
meaning in Climacus' mind (or Kierkegaard's, for that matter). When
read more deeply, one can see the motto as concerned with Christianity,
as Thulstrup thought, without in any way violating the standpoint of
Climacus as non-Christian philosophical observer.

One of Climacus' main concerns in the book is to communicate
to his knowledgeable readers some reminders about what Christianity
really is, a task he accomplishes without so much as even mentioning
Christianity, except once at the very end of the book. He does not
wish to attack Christianity or to defend it, but to increase our understanding of it. As we shall see, one of his main theses is that a natural
human reaction to Christianity is to find it offensive. As a consequence
of this, well-intentioned "defenders" of Christianity are constantly
tempted to alter Christianity in such a way as to eliminate this offense,
by reinterpreting its meaning in terms of more acceptable philosophical
categories. Climacus himself finds such alteration jobs offensive. From
his perspective, honesty demands that one allow Christianity to be
what it is, whether it be offensive or not. So, without in any way
embracing or committing himself to Christianity, he can say that

Christian faith is better off hanged than married off to contemporary philosophy. And of course, as a humoristic thinker who keeps his distance from systematic philosophy himself, it is quite proper for Climacus to apply the motto to himself as well. He too is better off "left hanging" than married off to contemporary philosophical movements, especially if his task is in part to dispel confusions traceable to those philosophical movements.

THE PREFACE

The preface is the section of *Philosophical Fragments* where the personality of Johannes Climacus is most clearly displayed. Paradoxically, what is most visible is precisely the elusiveness of Johannes. The preface tells us what Johannes is not, and it tells us what he is not trying to do. He is not primarily a scholar who wishes to exhibit his historical and textual learning. He is not a systematic philosopher who wishes to make a contribution to the developing (in Denmark) Hegelian movement. There is much jesting and banter about those philosophers who have proclaimed a new era in philosophy, jesting which is directed against H. L. Martensen and his Danish Hegelian followers, rather than against Hegel himself. Climacus himself will have nothing to do with this world-historical self-importance. He writes for personal reasons, modestly and perhaps humoristically describing himself as a "loafer," who has no great justification for his idleness.

As for an overview of his own perspective, Climacus offers us nothing at all. As already noted, he will not tell us his "opinion" or, for that matter, whether he has any such thing as an opinion about the matters discussed. We are, however, given something other than Climacus' opinions, something I would describe as a model of how the issues in the book should be approached. Climacus hints that the book deals with very personal questions, which must be asked by an individual about his or her own life, and cannot therefore be answered by reference to learning. His only contribution to thought is, he says, to stake his own life.[21] He repeats and underlines the seriousness of this remark: "All I have is my life, which I promptly stake every time a difficulty appears."

In coyly offering us a glimpse, not of his convictions, but of what one might term his methodology for approaching the problems, Climacus deepens and alters our understanding of what he means by "eternal consciousness" on the title page and what he will term "the Truth" in chapter 1. His concern is not merely with a concept which has some importance in the history of religion or some other scholarly endeavor, but with the very personal concern a human being naturally shows toward the meaning of her own life. Like other human beings, I will live a relatively short period here on earth. What is the purpose and meaning of this short period? Does my life have any deeper significance, a significance which transcends death itself?

It is the fact that I will die which gives the question of an "eternal consciousness" its poignancy. Climacus hints at this by noting that his own "dancing partner" in thinking through his project is the thought of death.[22] Bringing death into the picture not only personalizes the issues, but makes it clear that disinterested contemplation may not be appropriate. Death approaches, and the luxury of detachment may not be open to the thoughtful reader. Climacus will not take any other person as "dancing partner," neither as objective authority nor devoted disciple. Since no one else can die for me, no one else can decide the meaning of life for me either. It is crucial to see that this is the perspective from which Climacus writes, and it is the perspective from which he hopes to be read.

CHAPTER

3

CONSTRUCTING AN ALTERNATIVE TO THE SOCRATIC VIEW OF "THE TRUTH"

In chapter 1 of *Philosophical Fragments*, Johannes Climacus begins his experiment in earnest. The project, it will be recalled, is to see if there is any alternative to what he terms the Socratic view of the Truth and how the Truth is learned. The Socratic view is characterized as the assumption that the Truth is already present within each person, so that it only needs to be recollected. The teacher on this view will only be an occasion, a midwife who helps the learner discover his or her own self-sufficiency. The moment at which this self-realization occurs thus has no essential importance, for the moment at which I acquire the Truth is also the moment I realize that I did not acquire it, but have always possessed it.

With this baseline firmly in mind, Climacus seeks to create an alternative view, which postulates, as we have noted and shall explore in more detail, that the moment is all-important, that the learner lacks the Truth, and that he must be given the Truth by a teacher who is the god. We have already seen that we have plenty of reason to be suspicious of Climacus' procedure. In chapter 2 I noted that this creation of Climacus is not what it appears to be, since the invention is a curious one that implies its own impossibility as an invention. Climacus' work is ironical through and through.

It would, however, be churlish and self-defeating to allow this realization to block us from playing along with Climacus' game. In order for the irony to have a beneficial effect on us, if that be possible, we must allow ourselves to be taken in and take his invention, initially at least, as what it appears to be. Otherwise, we block ourselves from a close reading of the book at all and have no hope of seeing whether the irony has a serious point, and what that point might be. We shall therefore play along and see how far the game can be pushed.

THE TRUTH

Chapter 1 begins with the question "To what extent can the Truth be learned?" This question raises for us the prior one: "What does Climacus mean by 'the Truth'?" I claimed in chapter 2, without much argument, that this is a special concept in the book, by no means equivalent in meaning to what philosophers usually mean by "truth" in epistemological discussions. Contrary to what the initial question might suggest, *Fragments* is not really a book about how we gain knowledge of various kinds of truths, such as necessary truths or empirical truths, though it touches on such questions now and then and even assumes answers to them at points. The Truth here is closer to what religions have usually termed salvation, and it is also closely related to what Climacus calls the attainment of an "eternal consciousness" on the title page, and an "eternal happiness" at other places in the book.

What justification is there for this unusual if not perverse usage? Part of the justification is the grounding of the book in Platonic thought. The book is in one sense an extended contrast of Platonic and Christian perspectives, and the question with which it begins is of course a central Platonic question. In Plato's own thought, it is fair to say that knowledge of the truth takes on religious significance. Plato assumes that our highest human task is to gain true knowledge, and, as Climacus notes, even bases his own argument for the immortality of the soul on the ability of the soul to grasp eternal truths.[1] Hence Climacus' use of "the Truth" is in part simply a continuation and extension of the sense "truth" takes on in Plato.

Still, one may well ask about Plato's usage here, too. The deeper justification for equating salvation with knowing truth lies in the assumption, not uncontroversial but made by many religions as well as by Plato, that salvation does in the end amount to possessing some kind of insight, some awareness of Absolute or Ultimate Truth. Of course, this must not be taken simply as knowing the truth of some proposition. For example, Christian thinkers have commonly described the ultimate human good as *knowing God*, and such knowledge is certainly thought of as a grasping or encounter with truth. Hindu thinkers have described salvation as involving an understanding of the truth that I am one with God or Absolute Reality. Buddhist thinkers have described nirvana as requiring an understanding of the truth about the illusory nature of the self as an entity and the necessity to escape from the realm of desire. Therefore, though it may be somewhat idiosyncratic to identify knowing truth with salvation, it is not at all unusual to identify salvation with knowing a special kind of truth.

It is for this reason that I think that we must take the definite article seriously, and realize that when Climacus talks about "the Truth" he is not talking about truth in general, but a special kind of truth. The nature of this truth will be conceived differently by different religious perspectives, but in all cases it specifies whatever truth it is that is essential for humans to have in order to obtain the equivalent of salvation. This sense of the Truth is taken up again in the *Postscript* in the discussion of "truth as subjectivity." In an important footnote here Climacus explains that he is talking, not about truth in general, but the kind of truth he calls "essential truth."[2] Essential truth is simply the truth which it is essential for a human being to have. The lack of such truth would mean a lack of humanness.

This becomes very clear in discussing the alternative hypothesis to the Platonic view of the Truth. (I will henceforth refer to this alternative hypothesis, the one with a suspicious resemblance to Christianity, as the B hypothesis.) Climacus claims that the B hypothesis must be one which sees the learner as lacking the Truth. The learner must, however, have had the condition for understanding the Truth at one time; otherwise he "would have been merely an animal, and that teacher who with the condition gave him the Truth would make him a human being for the first time."[3]

We can also discern from this sense of the Truth as that which makes a person human one of the reasons Climacus does not consider the question as to whether salvation is a real possibility for human beings. One might imagine a secular thinker objecting to Climacus by saying that it is possible that salvation is not attainable for humans, and that we should resign ourselves to living in the here and now, satisfying our finite and relative wants as well as we can. The objector in this case may be challenging the assumption of Climacus that salvation consists in eternal life, an assumption he clearly does make.[4] This is a real issue, one that we will consider later in this chapter. However, if the objection is to the concept of salvation in any form, then Climacus' answer is, I think, something like this: To question whether salvation in any sense is possible for human beings is simply to question whether human beings can be truly human. Anyone who is willing to say that there is a *telos* to human life, some way of life that is fulfilling and satisfying that humans ought to enjoy, is committed to saying that salvation in this sense is possible. Not everyone will be willing to say even this, of course, and we shall presently consider the case for giving up the concept of salvation in any form. However, it is clearly the case that even many thinkers who think of themselves as secular humanists do accept such a concept of salvation.

WHAT VIEWS SHOULD BE UNDERSTOOD AS "SOCRATIC"?

This broad understanding of the Truth as the possession of whatever it is that makes a person truly human gives us a broad perspective as well on what Climacus means by the Socratic view. Since his B hypothesis is constructed solely on the basis of its difference from the Socratic view, it is obviously crucial to gain a clear understanding of what that view represents.

Since the Socratic view is defined in terms of the views of a somewhat Platonic Socrates, the most obvious candidate for a representative of the Socratic view is philosophical idealism. Climacus wishes to define an alternative to idealism which resembles Christianity in order to clearly remind people of the logical differences between the two. The point of course is not to show the difference between Christianity and Platonism per se, but to emphasize the differences between Christianity and nineteenth century idealism, represented by Schelling and Hegel. The reminder was needed precisely because nineteenth century idealism, especially in its right-wing Hegelian form, claimed to be Christian. The barbed "moral" at the end of the book makes this clear: "But to go beyond Socrates when one nevertheless says essentially the same thing as he, only not nearly so well—that, at least, is not Socratic."[5] Christianity, Climacus says, does indisputably "go beyond" the Socratic, though he is careful to add that this does not necessarily mean that it is more true. However, to claim to be Christian and "go beyond" the Socratic, while essentially repeating the Socratic, is neither Socratic nor Christian. It is simply muddled.

However, though nineteenth-century idealism is the most obvious candidate for a representative of the Socratic view, it is by no means the only one. If the Truth means the possession of whatever it is that makes us truly human, then the Socratic view in *Philosophical Fragments* must be taken very broadly indeed. Religions such as Buddhism and Hinduism, which assume that the capacity for the realization of the Truth is present within human beings, certainly must be regarded as falling under the designation. Robert Roberts, in his book *Faith, Reason, and History,* has convincingly argued that even such Christian theologians as Schleiermacher, Bultmann, and John Cobb must be regarded as Socratic thinkers, inasmuch as they reduce Jesus in the end to the role of Socratic teacher and deny that human beings are essentially in error in the radical sense of Climacus.[6] Jesus may be a powerful vehicle for the evocation of "the sense of absolute dependence" in Schleiermacher's sense, or Bultmann's sense of radical openness to the future which constitutes authenticity, or he may be a powerful source for creative transformation in Cobb's sense. However, there is nothing about Jesus in such views which makes Jesus uniquely necessary for such things.

Perhaps the concept of the Socratic here can even be extended to purely secular thinkers such as a Carl Sagan, or avowedly this-worldly philosophers such as Karl Marx. Insofar as a secular humanist has a concept of truly human existence, and a conviction that the capacity for achieving this kind of existence is present within human beings, the humanistic view seems Socratic. It is true that a thinker like Marx thinks this capacity is possessed by human beings collectively rather than individually, and this may be a perspective which Climacus does not envision. However, if it is an extension of his concept, it is only a small extension. What all these views—Platonism, Hegelianism, Hinduism, Buddhism, some versions of Christianity, and secular humanism—have in common is a conviction that the capacity for achieving truly human existence is possessed by human beings and does not need to be brought to humans by a teacher who is a divine re-creator of the individual.

WHY ASSUME THAT THE TRUTH CAN BE REALIZED?

Philosophical Fragments constructs a perspective on how the Truth can be possessed by human beings and compares it with the Socratic view as to how the Truth is gained. But why assume that the Truth is attainable at all by human beings? Why assume that salvation is possible, either Socratically or through Christianity? Actually, it is not clear that Climacus makes any such assumptions; however, it is true that he appears to ignore the alternative possibilities they pose for both the Socratic and his Christian-like perspective. I have argued that for Climacus anyone who has a normative concept of true humanness, and assumes that such a state can be realized, falls under the Socratic perspective. Nevertheless, it is certainly the case today that not every-one would be willing to accept these two notions. The idea that there is a normative concept of true humanness flies in the face of the widespread relativism endemic to western culture, including that rela-tivism that is identified with popular conceptions of "existentialism." And not all those who would accept a normative sense of what humans were meant to be have any hope that such a state is attainable. The advice of a Camus to reject hope and embrace the despair of an absurd universe is one prominent example of such a view.[7]

It is striking that Climacus gives no argument against such a view. In fact, he simply gives it no consideration at all. The reason for this is not, I think, that such a contemporary view was utterly foreign to him. Certainly, his creator Kierkegaard was not ignorant of such despair, since he created a striking illustration of it in *Either/Or* I. Rather, I suspect that Climacus does not address such a view because its pro-ponent does not need and will not be helped by philosophical reflection. The despairer needs hope; he needs encouragement. He needs what

Climacus calls in *Postscript* inwardness or subjectivity. He must be helped to recognize that he is an existing being, not identical with Pure Thought. Perhaps he needs therapy. His failings are in any case not cognitive or intellectual.

Climacus is writing as an existential thinker, one who "puts his own life at stake" every time a difficulty appears. From his standpoint, to ask whether the goal of existence can be achieved, or whether there is even a goal, is to opt out of life. It is not that Climacus has up his sleeve some proof that life has a goal and that it can be attained. Rather, he puts aside this option because demanding such a proof would presuppose a detached perspective on life which may be suitable for a being who is Pure Thought, but which is inappropriate for an existing human being.

An analogy may be helpful here. It is often the case, when I play bridge, that in attempting to make a contract I discover that I can only succeed if one of my opponents holds a particular card. In such a case I must play the hand as if that particular opponent does indeed have the card. I do so, not because I have proof that this opponent does have the card, but because I am already in the game. As a player, I do not have the luxury of musing about whether it is possible for me to win. I must assume that it is possible. If I do not do so, what I need is not some argument about the possibility of winning. Rather, I need to care more about the game. I need to understand the point of the game and my own role in the particular situation in which I find myself.

In a similar way Johannes Climacus is writing as a person who is in the game of life and who understands that it is not a game like bridge from which one can abstain and assume the role of kibitzer. He is writing to people like himself who are seeking to become fully human and are committed to that goal. That the quest is a hopeless one is a possibility he ignores, not because it can be proven that such futility is mistaken, but because the existential passion of the individual rules such a view out of consideration.

One further possible objection remains, and that concerns the assumption Climacus seems to make that the possession of the Truth is equivalent to the possession of eternal life or an eternal consciousness. What justification does he have for such an assumption? The questions on the title page make it clear that Climacus does seem to make such an assumption, and at times he makes others equally bold. For example, he seems to assume that both for the Socratic view and for his B hypothesis, knowing the truth is equivalent to knowing God. This is not surprising for the B hypothesis, since on this view, the Truth must be given to the learner by the God, but Climacus also says that the Socratic thinker, who has the condition for knowing the Truth within himself, thinks that God exists, "since he himself exists (*er til*)."[8] Socratic self-knowledge involves a knowledge of God as well.

To conceive of knowing the Truth as equivalent to knowing God and possessing an eternal consciousness would seem to commit Climacus to a fairly specific concept of salvation, one that he certainly does not defend. However, I think there is less to Climacus' assumptions here than meets the eye. We must resist the temptation to read in much specific meaning to the concepts of God and the eternal when Climacus uses these in the context of the Socratic view. Certainly we must not read these concepts as having any recognizable Christian meaning. Climacus is perhaps assuming that true humanness requires a relationship to something ultimate and absolute, but the concept of "God" employed here evidently must be vague and formal enough to be satisfied by Plato's "Form of the Good."

Climacus does seem to assume that true humanness requires an answer to the threat of meaninglessness posed by death and the short-lived character of all human achievements, but such an assumption seems reasonable enough. Humans have always struggled to see their lives as having some significance and meaning that will outlast the grave, and Climacus seems to take it for granted that this will be a component of knowing the Truth in his sense. However, it is by no means clear that this must be taken in the sense of individual immortality, though such a view is certainly one prominent answer to the problem of death in the history of religious and philosophical thought. In the *Postscript* Climacus does raise the problem of the individual's happiness to the forefront of existential thinking, and he is critical of perspectives on immortality which promise only participation in the abstract immortality of impersonal thought. However, these are the perspectives on immortality which Climacus regarded the contemporary Hegelians who were the most prominent illustrations of the Socratic view as holding.

Interpreted in such a minimal way, I think that Climacus' activity in connecting the Truth with eternal life and the knowledge of God requires us to restrict the range of the Socratic view only to a slight degree. Many secular views will still qualify on the grounds that something is still regarded as ultimate and absolute, and some way of giving the individual's life a meaning that can be said to be eternal is still provided. Those who are unwilling to make such assumptions are simply not addressed in the book. Like the relativists and pessimists discussed above, they need a kind of passion and self-understanding that Climacus the ironical philosopher cannot provide. Perhaps Kierkegaard himself would refer them to *Either/Or*.

THE "DEDUCTION" OF THE B HYPOTHESIS

After briefly describing the Socratic viewpoint, with its close-knit group of ideas, centering on the assumption that the Truth is present within humans and including the claim that on such an assumption the teacher and the moment of self-realization can have only vanishing significance, Climacus goes on to construct his alternative B hypothesis. The method of doing this is, on the surface at least, very simple. He simply makes use of the basic principles of logic. If the Socratic view says p, then Climacus makes his alternative say not p. Beginning with the Socratic claim that the moment has no essential significance, he tries to see how things must be if the moment is to have essential significance. If at any point it seems unclear what we are to say, a refresher in the Socratic perspective will help us steer a straight path.

The Condition of the Learner

Since the Socratic view postulated that the learner already had the Truth prior to the moment of self-realization, the B hypothesis must assume that the learner lacks the Truth. To clearly differentiate the B hypothesis from the Socratic view, one must assume that the learner not only lacks the Truth, but also lacks the ability or "the condition" for acquiring the Truth. Here it becomes even clearer that the Socratic view is not limited to a strictly Platonic system of thought. To say that the learner possesses the Truth is not necessarily a commitment to something like the Platonic theory of recollection. Any system of thought, Platonic or Aristotelian, religious or secular, which says that humans possess the ability to gain the Truth will qualify as Socratic.

The learner who thus lacks even the condition for acquiring the Truth is described by Climacus as himself untruth.[9] He is not merely lacking something he might acquire by accident, but his own nature is such that it is impossible for him to acquire the Truth by his own efforts. Climacus expresses this by saying that on the B hypothesis the learner is an antagonist of the Truth.

How did the learner come to be in such a state? Climacus says that the learner's condition of error must be attributable to the learner himself. The learner must originally have had the condition for understanding the Truth; otherwise, given Climacus' sense of the Truth, the learner would never have existed as a human being.[10] We would then be talking, not about how human beings could acquire the Truth, which is what the B hypothesis is supposed to be all about, but about how human beings were originally created. If the condition for attaining the Truth (henceforth just "the condition") has been lost, then Climacus thinks there are three possibilities. Either the god himself took it away, or it was lost through some nonculpable accidental circumstances that the learner found himself in, or else it was lost by the misuse of the learner's freedom.

The first possibility is rejected on the grounds that it would be a "contradiction" for the god to do such a thing. Presumably Climacus is here simply assuming that whatever else God may be, God must be seen as good, as the source of our true humanness, and it would thus be contradictory to think of God as the destroyer of that humanness.

The second possibility is rejected for two reasons. The first reason given, which seems rather flimsy, is that one could not lose the condition by accident, for that would involve the "contradiction" that the inferior (the accidental) would have overcome the superior (the condition). It is not immediately obvious as to what is contradictory about this, since in our experience what is inferior rather commonly seems to overcome what is superior, at least if superior and inferior be given any kind of moral sense, which they apparently bear here.

The second reason given for rejecting the idea of losing the condition by accident seems weightier and in fact may explain what Climacus really has in mind by the first, seemingly flimsy reason. "If he [the learner] could have lost the condition in such a way that it was not due to himself, and if he could be in this state of loss without its being due to himself, then he only possessed the condition accidentally, which is a contradiction, because the condition for the truth is an essential condition."[11]

What Climacus is really doing here is rejecting the coherence of what some philosophers have called "moral luck."[12] He is agreeing with the Socrates of the Apology, who affirms that "nothing can harm a good man, either in life or after death."[13] If one truly believes that what essentially matters in human life is moral character, and if one believes that moral character can only be corrupted by one's own free choices, then Socrates' principle, contrary to common sense as it appears, is correct. Consistent with his own principle, Socrates refused to escape from prison, reasoning that he would not truly be harmed by allowing himself to be unjustly executed, but that he would indeed harm his soul by illegally and immorally escaping from prison.

Climacus is committed to something like this by his claim that one could not possess the condition "accidentally." His argument is really that if you lose the condition through circumstances beyond your control, then your having the condition was at bottom a matter beyond your control. However, this means that you never really had it, since he is obviously thinking of the condition as something which must be integrally linked to yourself. If I seem to have the condition because I have been brought up in a favorable environment, but lose it when my environment is altered, then in a real sense I never really had it. I think it is fair to say that such an argument helps us see better what Climacus has in mind by the Truth and the condition for its attainment, but it is unlikely to be convincing to anyone who really thinks that true humanness is the sort of thing that could be gained or lost "accidentally," or who thinks that one's moral status is a matter of "luck." The argument's chief value is, as someone like H. A. Nielsen or Robert Roberts might say, that it improves our understanding of the "grammar" of these concepts.

If my loss of the condition is due to my own actions, then it might appear that I ought to be able to remedy the damage as well. We can anticipate that Climacus will reject this claim, on the grounds that if the individual can remedy his unfreedom, then he really has the condition and is still in the Socratic position. Nevertheless, Climacus must defend the claim that this denial of the individual's power to overcome his problem is logically consistent with the claim that the problem is due to the individual's own misuse of freedom. Climacus makes this defense by emphasizing the historical character of human freedom. To say that a human being is free is not to say that he always has the power to undo or reverse the consequences of his misuse of freedom, even the consequences with regard to his own nature and subsequent limitations on freedom. In an extended footnote, Climacus makes his case through simple examples—for example, a knight who freely offers his services to one side in a war and then finds he is not free to reverse his offer after his side loses. He also appeals to Aristotle, who notes that depraved and virtuous people no longer have power over their moral condition, though they once did, just as a person has the power to throw a stone or not, but no power to recall it once thrown.[14]

The state of the learner as being in untruth by his own fault Climacus decides to call *sin*. It is fair to say that at this point the ironical character of the whole enterprise of "inventing" the B hypothesis begins to show through rather clearly.

The Teacher

The teacher on the B hypothesis must be, as we have noted, the god. The reason given for this is that in this case the teacher must bring to the individual not only the Truth, but the condition for acquiring the Truth. Giving the condition amounts to a radical transformation of the individual, and according to Climacus, "no human being is capable of doing this; if it is to take place, it must be done by the god himself."[15]

How does Climacus know this? On what basis can he make such a claim? It is tempting at this point to say that here the ironical character of the supposed logical deduction shows through, and that Climacus is helping himself to presupposed Christian understandings of the human situation. While I don't find such a suggestion implausible here, I do not think it is necessary to make such a move either. We must recall my earlier caution about packing too much content into concepts like "eternal consciousness" and "the god" in Climacus. The definite article in the "the god" quite clearly points to the identical phrase used frequently by Plato. Climacus seems to use it quite loosely at times, certainly not in a strictly Christian manner. For example, he says that in the Socratic view the self-knowledge of the individual is a knowledge of God.[16] We could simply defend Climacus here by once more treating his claim as a "grammatical remark," in this case about his concept of "the god." Perhaps for Climacus the god simply designates *whatever it is* that is the source of a person's human character. If that is so, then the claim that only the god could totally transform an individual becomes a necessary truth.

On the assumption that the god is indeed the teacher, as the B hypothesis requires, what will the god do? How will he carry out his activities as a teacher? The answer for the most part is given in chapter 2 of *Fragments*, but the main outline of the answer is already provided in chapter 1. The encounter between the god and the learner is "the moment," or "the fullness of time,"[17] a phrase as fraught with meaning as "the Truth." The moment makes two things possible.

First of all, the teacher is "an occasion" for the learner to "recall" that he is untruth. The teacher does then function in this one respect as a Socratic teacher, and the learner, even if he lacks the condition, is able, with the teacher's help, to make this one discovery on his own, so to speak. Climacus says that this is necessary, because with respect to the discovery of my own untruth, "the Socratic principle applies: the teacher is only an occasion, whoever he may be, even if he is a god."[18] We shall see later that even though this is "the one and only analogy to the Socratic" in the B hypothesis, it is a vitally important point. In chapter 4 Climacus holds that the activity of the god is necessary in order for the learner to come to understand his own error, but it is crucial to see that though the teacher makes this discovery possible, he does not make it inevitable.

Secondly, in the moment, the teacher gives the condition, at least for some individuals. This is not a sure thing; if it were, the decisive importance of the moment would be undermined. In the moment the individual can recollect his own error; "whether or not he is to go any further, *the moment* must decide."[19] Climacus does not spell out here how the condition is imparted; that is the task of the remainder of the book.

The Relationship of Teacher and Learner

The Socratic teacher had, as we saw, only vanishing significance for the learner. The one who had best learned the Socratic lesson that the Truth was within himself learned at the same time that he did not really need Socrates. Climacus says that for the B hypothesis things must be different. Since the teacher is the god who totally transforms the learner, the teacher is no mere midwife, but a savior, deliverer, and reconciler. "The learner will never be able to forget such a teacher."[20] The reason for this is clearly that Climacus thinks that the condition is not acquired in a once and for all fashion, but rather that the learner's continued possession of it is dependent on his relationship to the god.

At this point Climacus' irony does begin to be a bit transparent. The relationship between the teacher who is the god and the learner is now described in a plethora of explicitly Christian terms.[21] The teacher's giving of the condition is a bestowal of something to be held in trust; the teacher will hold the learner accountable for this and hence is properly understood as a judge. The radical change in the learner is described as a conversion, accompanied by a sorrow over his former life properly described as repentance. The outcome of the change is rebirth, and so on. So far as I can see Climacus makes little attempt to show that these qualities can be logically deduced simply by negating the Socratic situation, though the logical clarity and power of the distinctions made earlier has a tendency to beguile the reader at this point into continuing to play along with Climacus and to think he has accomplished more by purely logical reflection than he really has. What is clear, and what still seems sound in the "deduction" is that the relationship between teacher and learner Climacus describes seem to be quite different from the relationship of Socratic teacher and learner.

CAN THIS THOUGHT-PROJECT BE THOUGHT?

Near the end of the first chapter, Climacus poses a question practically guaranteed to throw his reader for a loop. "But can what has been developed here be thought?"[22] In effect, he is asking whether it is possible to think what he has just thought. One is tempted to say, "Of course, you just thought it." Climacus anticipates such a hasty response and warns us not to be in too big of a hurry. Such a hasty response does not do full justice to the question, since it doesn't consider the issue of *who* is supposed to be doing the thinking, and what kind of "thinking" has been going on.

Climacus himself agrees with the "of course" answer in one respect. However, it makes a great deal of difference who is doing the thinking: "This matter of being born, can it be thought? Sure, why not? But who is supposed to think it—one who is born or one who is not born? The latter, of course, is an irrationality that cannot occur to anyone."[23] The obvious suggestion here is that it is only the person who has been reborn by receiving the condition from the god who can conceive of the possibility Climacus has sketched. This, in turn, would imply that Climacus himself must be seen as a Christian writer after all, perhaps one who fits the description of the Christian he himself gives in *Postscript* as one who adopts humor as his incognito.[24]

The suspicion that something like this is going on seems confirmed by the dialogue with an interlocutor at the very close of the chapter. Climacus is interrupted by someone who accuses him of passing something off as his own invention which is common knowledge.[25] Climacus pleads guilty to the charge but uses it as an occasion to pose the question as to who is the real author of the project. Perhaps the interlocutor has himself invented the project? "Or, if you deny this, will you then also deny that someone has invented it, that is, some human being?"[26] This question is evidently rhetorical, for Climacus assumes the respondent will agree that no human being is the true author: "In that case, I am just as close to having invented it as any other person."[27]

Climacus moves from this claim that his project has no human author to an apparent claim that the project is *true*. "This oddity [that the project has no human author] enchants me to the highest degree, for it provides a test for the correctness of the hypothesis and demonstrates it."[28] The ground for this is, I think, the fact that an essential feature of the B hypothesis is its origin in a divine teacher; to go beyond the Socratic, Climacus says at one point, is to reach the concept of revelation.[29] The fact that the B hypothesis is not of human origin, if it is indeed a fact, would appear to be a powerful confirmation that it is indeed not a mere thought-project, but a revelation. Climacus seems to be saying that the very possession and understanding of the ideas of the B hypothesis, which correspond, as we have seen, to Christianity, is a guarantee of its truth. One writer has termed this an a priori proof of the truth of Christianity, or of at least its central idea, that God became a man.[30]

However, this "proof" of the truth of Christianity raises several difficulties. First of all, it appears to contradict the "Moral" at the end of *Fragments*, where Climacus claims to have shown that his project "goes further than" the Socratic—in other words, is genuinely different from the Socratic view—but that one cannot thereby decide the question as to whether the B hypothesis is more true than the Socratic view.[31] Secondly, it would appear to blow Climacus' cover, so to speak, and undermine his own assertions in the *Postscript* that he is not a Christian. Finally, the whole "proof" simply seems most implausible, even incredible. Does Climacus really think that the mere fact that a person has an understanding of Christianity is sufficient to guarantee the truth of Christianity for that person?

The first and last difficulty can, I think, be resolved if we recognize that the "proof," if it is intended to be such, will only be convincing to someone who already has the condition. It must be recalled that Climacus introduces this whole discussion by a claim that the only person who can really understand his project is the person who has been reborn. But this is precisely the person who has received the condition from the god, and it is reasonable that this person will view the consciousness he has received from the god as something he could only have thus received. So Climacus' argument cannot be seen as intended to convince the non-Christian that Christianity is true, and insofar it does not contradict the "Moral," which does not say that Christianity cannot be known to be true, but rather that the question cannot be decided without a "new organ," namely faith.[32] Climacus' remark is not an "objective argument," but one more reminder of how the person who has the condition will see things.

However, this resolution only aggravates the second difficulty, in that the fact that Climacus is one of those who sees the B hypothesis as coming to humans from revelation would strongly imply that he is one of those who have received the condition from the god. Even here, however, Climacus' status remains elusive. Only the believer will be inclined to accept the claim of Climacus that the hypothesis he has spun out is of divine origin. The unbeliever will reject this notion in rejecting the "proof," and properly so. Hence, if Climacus' cover is blown, it will only be for those who share the faith he has allowed to slip out of the disguise. One's decision about Climacus cannot be disentangled from the knot he has tied with respect to Christianity itself.

The reader is here challenged by the claim of Christianity, echoed by Climacus in his B hypothesis, to rest on a divine revelation rather than any human thought. This claim is part and parcel of a view which clearly differs from the Socratic. The reader who nosily insists on penetrating the incognito of Climacus can only do so by disentangling the knot he poses and deciding what he thinks about the claim of Christianity to rest on a revelation.

CAN A NON-CHRISTIAN UNDERSTAND CHRISTIANITY?

But what about the claim of Climacus that only the person who has been reborn can understand his project? Not only does such a claim imply that Climacus himself is one of the reborn, but that his readers must be so as well, if they are to understand him. Perhaps this is correct, and we should see Climacus as directing his book to Christians, reminding them of what they already know. Certainly, Climacus seems to assume that his reader is knowledgeable about Christianity, and perhaps he assumes that his reader thinks of himself as a Christian. This seems to be the case for the interlocutor who shows up at the end of the chapters and a few other places. However, it is hard to believe that Climacus really thought his readers were all genuinely reborn. Furthermore, the claim that only the reborn can understand the project seems too strong. It just does not seem to be the case that only Christians can understand Christianity, and if that were so, it would seem to make it impossible for anyone to accept or reject

Christianity. One cannot accept or reject what one does not understand in any sense.

Furthermore, if we accept this strong claim of Climacus, then his whole project begins to look not merely ironical, but fraudulent. Whether Climacus is personally a Christian or not, he is pretending to invent something that looks like Christianity merely by reflecting on the Socratic view. If, however, one thinks that only the Christian believer can even understand Christianity, then such an exercise must be impossible, and Climacus' deduction must involve quite a bit of sleight-of-hand. We have seen that in its essentials the logical exercise Climacus puts us through seems sound, however, though it is admittedly embellished in the details by the use of Christian language. However unlikely as a matter of fact, it seems logically possible for someone who had the Socratic picture of things to think up something like the B hypothesis. Climacus' own account would seem to show this.

I believe that to disentangle Climacus' comments on the thinkability of his project, we must clarify what we mean by "understanding." Since he says little about this here, it will be necessary to do some thinking on our own about the problems. Climacus himself in *Postscript* makes a distinction between two types of understanding of Christianity: understanding what Christianity is and understanding what it means to be a Christian.[33] The latter is only possible for Christians, but the former must be a possibility for non-Christians as well. It is surely this latter kind of understanding that Climacus has in mind when he says that only the person who has been reborn can understand his project. Given this assumption, it makes sense that he would claim that understanding Christianity is tantamount to seeing its truth, since the conviction of the believer that Christianity is true surely derives from understanding it as a gift from God, an understanding which goes hand in hand with being a Christian.

All this is compatible with the admission that a type of understanding of Christianity is possible for the non-Christian. This would be an "intellectual" kind of understanding, a grasp of the logical relationships the various Christian categories have to each other and to non-Christian ways of thinking. Such an intellectual understanding would make it possible for a non-Christian to read Climacus' book and follow its logical moves, but it would not necessarily make it possible for such a reader to understand the implications of Christianity for his life.

Though I have discussed them together, Climacus poses two distinct even if related issues at the conclusion of chapter 1. The first is the question as to whether the individual who has not been reborn can understand the project. The second is the question as to whether the content of the project could have been invented by a human being, or must rather be traced to divine revelation. The first question I have argued must be answered by specifying further the kind of understanding in question. The second issue must also be further specified if a defensible answer is to be found.

In saying that the project cannot be traced to a human author, Climacus might be taken as saying that it is impossible for the hypothesis to have a human author, because no human who has not received the condition from the god can even understand the project, much less invent it. If we take understanding in the strong sense of "understanding what it means to be a Christian," Climacus probably thinks that such understanding is impossible for the non-Christian. However, as we have seen, the lack of such understanding would not preclude a different kind of intellectual understanding, and it is only this intellectual understanding that would seem to be required to think through the hypothesis. If that is correct, then we should distinguish the claim that Christianity could not have had a human author from the claim that a non-Christian cannot understand Christianity. Perhaps it is true that Christianity would not exist unless it had been revealed, but that is compatible with saying that once revealed it can be understood by someone who is not a Christian.

On this view it might seem that it is at least logically possible for someone to have invented Christianity or something like Christianity, thus undermining the "proof" Climacus finds himself enchanted by. Surely, what I am capable of understanding, I am capable of thinking up, if my imaginative powers are great enough. Certainly, the non-Christian will want to make this very claim, and I do not see that Climacus says anything to prove the contrary. This concession that it is logically possible for someone to have come up with a system of ideas that resembles Christianity is quite compatible with the claim that in fact no human thinker has come up with anything like this, a claim that Climacus makes at the conclusion of the book.[34] And it is equally compatible with the Christian view that no human being could have made such a discovery, not because such an understanding is logically impossible for a non-Christian, but because of the sinfulness that characterizes the human race.

If we take Climacus to be asserting the weaker thesis that Christianity could not have been discovered apart from a revelation, he still seems to claim something which non-Christian readers cannot and will not accept. However, at least this weaker thesis does not commit him to the highly implausible claim that non-Christians cannot understand Christianity at all. It allows him to hold that there is a type of understanding possible for one who has not received the condition, at least for the person who has "heard about" Christianity but not yet accepted it. Such an intellectual understanding would not have much value in itself from a Christian standpoint, but at least it makes sense of the fact that non-Christian readers can understand Climacus' own work. His own deduction is not necessarily spurious or logically flawed. Even if the logical relationships would not have been perceived unless Christianity had been revealed, once Christianity is on the scene, the relationships in question can be understood. Though he may be thinking once more of believers, Climacus hints that understanding of this sort is possible: "Simply because someone knows how to use gunpowder, knows how to analyze it into its components, does not mean that he invented it."[35] Similarly, Christians may understand Christianity without having invented it, and those who have grown up in a Christian culture may also possess a type of understanding, without this implying that Christianity is or could have been a human invention.

The issues raised here about the uniqueness of Christianity, its origin in a divine revelation, and the possibilities for understanding it will all come up again in our consideration of *Philosophical Fragments*. We must now turn our attention to chapter 2, where Climacus continues his thought experiment by speculating about the way in which the god might become the savior-teacher he has postulated in chapter 1.

CHAPTER

4

THE POETRY OF THE INCARNATION

In chapter 2 of *Philosophical Fragments* Johannes Climacus continues his "thought experiment" by sketching the way in which the god might carry out the task of teaching the learner by transforming him. The pretense of a logical deduction is here dropped, and the chapter's efforts are plainly designated "a poetical venture." One might expect from this that the ironical character of the project is thereby lessened, since the notion that a human being might describe something like Christianity by employing her imaginative powers seems less audacious than the idea that the same thing could be arrived at merely by logical reflection on the Socratic view. However, this expectation is incorrect. Climacus himself says that Christianity is no more accessible to the imagination than to purely reflective reason, and the richness and denseness of the biblical allusions in chapter 2 make its ironical character, if anything, even more pronounced than is the case in chapter 1.

THE TEACHER'S GOALS AND MOTIVES

Chapter 2 begins by returning once more to the figure of Socrates. Climacus describes Socrates as possessing a complex, "reciprocal" relation to his social circumstances.[1] Socrates presumably felt a "call and prompting" to be a teacher, and this call and prompting doubtless had a ground in his own upbringing and education. In taking up his vocation as a teacher, Socrates is therefore not simply moved by others' demands or needs, but his own as well. The upshot of all this is that Socrates' behavior as a teacher is not purely altruistic; he meets the needs of others to learn something, but at the same time he satisfies his own needs. Socrates himself understands this and therefore understands that he needs no further reward for his activities, such as money or fame.[2]

The situation of the teacher in the case of the B hypothesis is completely different, according to Climacus. We cannot imagine that the god has the kind of socially conditioned need that he imagines Socrates as possessing, and "the god needs no disciple in order to understand himself."[3] What then could motivate the god to become the teacher? Climacus suggests that only love could be the motive, a pure love for the other which has no element of need for the other or any self-serving quality. Only such a love would allow the god to "move himself" and thus satisfy the situation of Aristotle's unmoved mover, who moves all else while remaining unmoved himself.[4]

The allusion to Aristotle should not, however, fool the reader into thinking that the god Climacus is poetically sketching is in other ways like the remote unmoved mover Aristotle describes. The god Climacus sketches has no need of others, but he is described as having a need within himself to love the other. Far from being remote, the god in this case is a passionate lover who is capable of profound suffering on behalf of his beloved, a suffering which is alien to the impassible God of much classical theology. Climacus says, in fact, that the whole story of the teacher-god is a story of suffering.[5]

If one asks how Climacus knows that the god does indeed love the human beings whom he seeks as his disciples, the answer is simply that he does not know it. It is an assumption that is made to keep the hypothesis going, so to speak. The project, it will be recalled, is to see if any alternative to the Socratic perspective can be conceived. The only alternative, it is argued in chapter 1, is one in which the god is the teacher. Climacus' justification for the assumption that the god loves human beings is simply his claim that he can conceive no other possible motive for the god to become such a teacher.

The assumption about the god's motives provides Climacus with a goal for the god's activities as a teacher as well. In the case of such pure love for the other, motive and goal must coincide, so the goal of the god's activities must be to "win" the learner, to establish and maintain a loving relationship with him.[6] This relationship is variously described as one that is characterized by equality, unity, and understanding. It also becomes clear in the discussion that follows that such a relationship is a voluntary one characterized by freedom on both sides.

Climacus here seems to make some pretty significant assumptions about the nature of love. Are these assumptions defensible? Does genuine love require equality and mutual understanding? Does it require freedom? One might argue the contrary, citing the love of parent and child as example.[7] Do we not here have genuine love which requires inequality and certainly does not presuppose mutual understanding, since neither the child nor the parent can fully enter the other's world?

For his argument to work, Climacus does not have to claim that all love requires equality and mutual understanding, but only that the highest form of love requires this. Such a claim is defensible, I think, even when we consider the case of the relationship of parent to child. Even if we put aside the question, surely very much a live one, as to how much the love of a parent for a child may in the end be mixed with self-interested motives, I believe that the parent-child relationship can reach its fullest potential only when the child is grown. However beautiful and touching the love of a parent for a small child may be, and however lovely the love of the child for the parent may be, there is a sense in which this love must be seen in the context of the child's potential to grow to maturity. A parent who wanted a child to remain a child would not really love that child. The love of parent and child thus potentially, though of course not always in reality, becomes deeper and richer as the child develops. Perhaps such a love only reaches its fullest potential when the child has become a parent herself and can fully understand the sacrifices and love made by the parent. It is only when this stage is reached that an element of mutual freedom is a dominant factor in the relationship, made possible by the greater degree of equality. Even in the relationship of parent and child, then, greater equality and mutual understanding deepen and enrich the love. It seems therefore to me that Climacus is entitled to his assumptions about the nature of a love relationship, at least in the context of such a poetical venture.

THE TRIALS OF LOVE

Given Climacus' assumptions about the motives and goals of the teacher-god, we can see how appropriate it is for him to turn from logic to poetry, for to be in the realm of love is surely to be in the realm of the poet. And as is the case in many a tale of love, the saga Climacus recounts concerns the difficulties love encounters in its quest for fulfillment. Love stories almost always involve difficulties, so the idea that there should be a difficulty is not itself surprising. In most love stories, the difficulty concerns the lovers' inability to be united. They are pulled apart by feuding families or the conflicts of war, or some such thing. Climacus says that these difficulties do not concern him. To begin, it is hard to imagine the god being thwarted by such circumstances, and in any case this sort of problem at most means that the lovers cannot be together in time. Eternity, presumably, will here set things right.

The more troubling as well as more relevant case involves an internal rather than an external difficulty. No environmental obstacle prevents the lovers from being united, but something in their relationship is a barrier to the mutual understanding that love seeks. Specifically, a relationship characterized by great inequality is troubled in this way.

The relationship between the god and the disciple is of course as unequal as one could be. Climacus does not here talk about the metaphysical inequality between God and a human being; the focus is not on God's superiority because of his omnipotence, omniscience, and so on, though he seems to assume that the god is all-powerful. The relevant inequality has to do with the dependence of the disciple on the god. In the case of the Socratic situation the disciple was genuinely autonomous and owed Socrates nothing. The B hypothesis, on the other hand, postulates that the god makes it possible for the disciple to become a new creature. The disciple thus owes the god everything.

Such a situation is fraught with danger, as Climacus sees it. Genuine love wants to build up the lover, but in this case the love of the god threatens to destroy the self-confidence, or, as psychologists today might say, self-esteem of the disciple. The god must then "look with concern" at the human race, "for the individual's tender shoot can be crushed as readily as a blade of grass."[8] The task the teacher-god has set himself out of love is therefore far more difficult than the sheer power required to uphold the created world in existence.[9] It is this difficulty that makes the whole story of the god as a teacher a story of suffering. What agony for the god to find himself in danger of crushing that which he wants to save by the very act of attempting to save.

Climacus seems to be of two minds with respect to the possibility of our understanding the god's sorrows in such a case. On the one hand he says that we human being are so selfish in our own love that we cannot understand such a love and its accompanying sorrow. Human language "does not even have an intimation of such a sorrow."[10] On the other hand, he says that any person who does not have at least an intimation of such a sorrow "is a lumpish soul with only as much character as a small coin which bears neither Caesar's nor God's image."[11] Perhaps he wants to say that though we cannot truly understand the god's position, there are faint analogies in our experience that give us some understanding. That at least is consistent with Climacus' own procedure, for he proceeds to describe an analogous situation in some detail "to awaken the mind to an understanding of the divine," even though he cautions us "that no human situation can provide a valid analogy."[12]

THE KING AND THE MAIDEN

The question as to how the god might actually perform his "teaching" and unite himself to the disciple in mutual understanding out of love is answered by Climacus through his analogy, which takes the form of some musings on the well-known type of fairy tale in which a powerful king falls in love with a peasant maiden. Through this poetic tale we get to see the inequality and the distress it occasions, and we are allowed to explore alternative strategies for overcoming the difficulty.

The king is a powerful one and no external difficulties sully the case. No politicians or foreign powers dare to make trouble, yet the king is troubled by the kingly worry that his love will only make the woman unhappy by reminding her of "what the king only wished to forget—that he was the king and she had been a poor maiden."[13] In such a case how can the love relationship be characterized by the freedom, equality, and mutual understanding that love demands? Will not the maiden always be conscious of her dependence on the king?

To turn for a moment from the fairy tale back to Climacus' own story of the god who is our lover, and to the Christianity which that story is supposed in turn to illuminate, the importance of the issue here cannot be overemphasized. The problem really stems directly from the assumption of the B hypothesis that the learner lacks the Truth. What is at stake might be termed the humane character of Christian faith. Christianity claims to be a faith which restores and fulfills our human-ness, but it has often been perceived, by Enlightenment thinkers and by secular humanists today, as anything but humane. Christianity posits that human beings are sinful and are dependent on God to overcome the problem. Is not such a view of human persons itself degrading and dehumanizing? Certainly it can appear to be, and such a reaction lies at the heart of what Climacus will later term "offense." Whether such a view is in fact dehumanizing and degrading depends on what the truth is about the human condition. From the point of view of Chris-tianity, human beings are actually guilty before God and dependent on God to transform them so as to make a relationship with him possible. Only by recognizing our actual situation can our humanness be fulfilled. Hence Climacus must reproduce this feature of Christianity in his B hypothesis and does so.

As we shall see, the god, even if we presume him omnipotent, has limited maneuvering room in this situation. The actions he must take to avoid misunderstanding make the possibility of offense acute. It is important to see that offense is not something the god wills. On the assumption of the B hypothesis the inequality is real and cannot be simply ignored. To avoid it or ignore it, while it may appear to make the inferior party happier, is ultimately to destroy the possibility of an honest relationship.

The inequality must therefore be dealt with, and to see how we return to the fairy tale. The poet has two possible strategies for removing the inequality. The king must either elevate the maiden to his own level, or else descend to her level. In both cases the king is the agent of change, since to imagine the maiden as capable of elevating herself to his level is to imagine she is more than a maiden, and would invalidate the analogy to the case of the god, where the inequality cannot be abolished by the human disciple without returning to the Socratic position.

Union through Ascent

It might appear that the king could simply bring the young woman to his level by making her his queen. There are several ways this might be accomplished. In each case Climacus claims, however, that his noble king has "seen the difficulties" with such a strategy. What are those difficulties?

That the king might simply order the woman to marry him and expect her to obey out of fear of the consequences is not even considered by Climacus, since such a fearful obedience is far from the loving relationship that is the king's goal. More plausible is the idea that the ascent could be brought about by dazzling the young woman with the splendors of her new position. Climacus switches quickly back from his fairy tale to the situation of the god and describes what this would be like: "The god would then draw the learner up toward himself, exalt him, divert him with joy lasting a thousand years...let the learner forget the misunderstanding in his tumult of joy."[14] What is this "misunderstanding?" Why is it that the girl (to switch back to the fairy tale) would in such a case be "essentially deceived?"

The misunderstanding lies, I think, in the fact that in such a case the young woman's situation is totally a function of the king's good favor. In herself she is nothing, and if she is conscious of this nothingness she cannot possibly have the "bold confidence" she needs to love the king freely. The deception lies in the "diversion" that blocks her from gaining such a consciousness by virtue of the delights that have been bestowed upon her. Even if the young woman would consider herself happy, their relationship would not satisfy the king.

The problem reappears even more acutely if the king appeared "before the lowly maiden in all his splendor...let the sun of his glory rise over her hut...and let her forget herself in adoring admiration." Since he is in love, the king desires "not his own glorification, but the girl's."[15] The king presumably wants the girl to love him, not for his power and riches, but for himself. To lure her by riches and grandeur could not serve his ends, because he could not possibly know she was responding to him rather than the riches and grandeur. This fear of the king's corresponds to the god's worry that should he dazzle the learner with a show of his power, the learner would "love only the omnipotent miracle worker."[16] Furthermore, the king wants a response characterized by freedom and self-confidence, a response that requires the girl to have a sense of her own worth, to understand that she is indeed loved by the king and is not merely his plaything.

In the case of the god and the learner, this difficulty increases to a wholly different order, since the learner lacks the condition. The learner is in fact totally dependent on the god; receives her value and worth in receiving the condition. How can she receive this without being crushed? How can she maintain the self-confidence and boldness to love the god freely?

Union through Descent

The solution must be for the union to be accomplished through the god's descent rather than through the learner's elevation. An analog to this is present in the fairy tale, of course. The king comes to the peasant in disguise, hoping she will learn to love him apart from the distractions of wealth and power. Both the maiden and the king will understand the relationship and will understand that the love is freely given on both sides.

In the case of the god, a disguise will not do. The god must not simply appear to be the equal of the beloved, but actually share the situation of the beloved: "For this is the boundlessness of love, that in earnestness and truth and not in jest it wills to be the equal of the beloved, and it is resolute love's omnipotence to be able to do this, of which neither the king nor Socrates was capable, which is why their assumed characters were still a kind of deceit."[17]

The bottom line is that love does not impose changes on the beloved in an external fashion.[18] The learner must be changed, but the change is brought about by the god changing himself. The difficulty is that there is a real risk that the god will not be recognized, just as the king opens himself up to the possibility of rejection by coming as a peasant himself. If the god's incognito is no mere easily seen through disguise, but his true form, then the risk will be genuine, but Climacus wants to argue that there is no way to avoid it if a real relationship of love is to be established. The ultimate sorrow of the god is that the very course of action that represents the only possible way of satisfying the love relationship can be the very thing that separates the lovers. The ultimate suffering of the god is not the relinquishment of his glory and power to assume the lowly position of the learner, but the realization that this tremendous sacrifice may be all for naught. The very action that is necessary to save the learner may be the action that blocks the learner from responding to the god's wooing. The suffering in the relationship is not reserved for the god alone, however. Toward the close of the chapter, Climacus hints that in some way the learner who becomes the god's disciple must share in the god's suffering.[19] Presumably the individual who does not respond must be understood as miserable as well, since he will continue to lack the Truth, even if this person thinks of himself as happy.

In the appendix to chapter 3 Climacus calls the learner's misunderstanding and rejection of the god offense, and we shall discuss this attitude more fully later. However, it is important to see that the possibility of offense is inherent in this situation of love between unequals from the very beginning. It stems from the god's love for the learner, a love that expresses itself in a respect for the freedom and dignity of the learner.

THE POEM AS THE WONDER

We saw that at the close of chapter 1 a strange dialogue ensued between Climacus and an interlocutor, who objected to Climacus' whole procedure on the grounds that his thought-experiment was something well known to everyone. Climacus' response was to admit that something funny has been going on and to claim that his thought–project was not only not invented by him, but has no human author at all, a claim that raises, as we saw, complex problems about the form of the book and Climacus' own stance as author.

At the close of chapter 2 this strange dialogue is rejoined, at a more intense level. The charge made by the interlocutor is even angrier:

"What you are composing is the shabbiest plagiarism ever to appear." Once more Climacus pleads guilty and this time explicitly attributes his poem to the deity.[20] In chapter 1 the fact that the thought-project is of more than human origin "enthralls" Climacus and becomes a proof of the correctness of his hypothesis. In chapter 2 the contemplation of his poem's divine origin grips his soul with "amazement" and "adoration" and induces him to stand wondrously before the poem, which is not really a poem but *"the wonder"* (*Vidunderet* or "the miracle").[21]

Even more obviously than in chapter 1 Climacus here seems to let his own disguise slip aside and reveal where his heart really is. Though he may seem to be making a highly debatable and dubious empirical claim here, namely that the central core of Christianity is not something a human being could have invented, we must remember to whom he is speaking. The interlocutor, and presumably the readers Climacus is writing for, are evidently people brought up as Christians; they are at the very least knowledgeable about Christianity. The interlocutor accuses Climacus of putting forward as his poem "something that any child knows."[22] It has always been part of Christian teaching that Christianity rests on a divine revelation that is both unique and irreplaceable. Climacus is not so much arguing for this bold claim as reminding his presumably Christian readers of it and what it means. In a culture where familiarity with the Christian message has brought with it dullness if not contempt, he is trying to rekindle a sense of the strangeness of the Christian story, a strangeness that can be taken as a sign of its truth.

It is in fact the case that the analogies to the Christian concept of the incarnation are at best few and far between. Neither Moses nor Abraham nor Mohammed are thought of as divine. Theravada Buddhists say the same of the Buddha. The Hindu notion of a divine *avatar* and the idea of the Buddha as the incarnation of the Buddha-essence both differ significantly from the Christian view of the incarnation in that the Hindu and Buddhist concepts are irreducibly plural. For these religions, there have been many incarnations of the divine, and there can be more. Such a concept is rooted in the Socratic view of things, because its central message is ultimately the possibility of god-likeness within human beings. The uniqueness of the Christian claim lends plausibility to the claim of Climacus: "Presumably it could occur to a human being to poetize himself in the likeness of the god or the god in the likeness of himself, but not to poetize that the god poetized himself in the likeness of a human being."[23] That a culture informed by the Christian story might produce some imitators of the Christian view, such as might be found in the Unification Church, which apparently views the Reverend Moon as an incarnation of God (a reincarnation of Jesus?), does not really undermine this claim.

Despite the reverent response of Climacus himself, the uniqueness of the Christian story, even if it is genuinely distinctive, does little to establish the truth of Christianity. The widespread embarrassment of many contemporary Christian theologians over the belief that Jesus was really divine makes this clear.[24] The uniqueness of the Christian claim is seen as an irritant that makes good ecumenical relations between Christianity and other religions impossible. Despite his seeming reverence at the end of chapters 1 and 2, which in both cases is attributed to a "spell" or an emotion of "amazement" that grips the author, Climacus is not at all ignorant of the double-edged character of this uniqueness claim. It is a major reason why Christianity, both in itself and in Climacus' "poem" version, poses the "possibility of offense" to its hearers.

One of the great ironies of *Philosophical Fragments* lies right at this point. Climacus wants to insist that Christianity lies beyond the human powers of reason and imagination. He will argue in chapter 3 that the incarnation is a paradox that cannot be understood and as such poses the possibility of offense. Yet the net impact of Climacus' reflection is to help us understand the plausibility of the incarnation, given his assumptions about our situation as one in which we lack the Truth and the god seeks to remedy this defect out of love. The incarnation is completely contrary to our natural human expectations, yet something completely contrary to our natural human expectations is precisely what we must have on the premises of the B hypothesis.

It might seem that Climacus is undermining his own case here by his poetic invention. If he has imaginatively invented Christianity, doesn't that show that it is not necessarily of divine origin? But of course Climacus has done no such thing. His "invention" is a transcription of what a Sunday School student today knows or should know.

What he has done through his irony is rekindle a sense of the strangeness of what is thus so familiar. Climacus helps the believer at least to see that his inability to understand the Christian message is itself understandable, and a mark of its truth: a sign that Christianity is indeed what "eye has not seen, ear has not heard," something that has not originated within any human heart.[25]

CHAPTER
5

THOUGHT, PASSION, AND PARADOX

Chapter 3 of *Philosophical Fragments*, entitled "The Absolute Paradox (A Metaphysical Caprice)," is probably the richest and most suggestive chapter of the book from a philosophical standpoint, yet it also is the most puzzling and enigmatic. A central problem that confronts the reader immediately is simply to determine the relation of the chapter to the book as a whole. Chapter 2, with its poetic tale of the god becoming a teacher by taking on the state of the learner, clearly follows and builds on chapter 1. Chapter 4, which begins "So, then (to continue our poem)," clearly takes up where chapter 2 leaves off and continues the tale of the god who becomes a human being. Chapter 3 contains an influential critique of natural theology, a host of provocative claims about human understanding and its relation to various passions, all of which are interesting, but do not seem to be immediately connected to what comes before and after. On the surface, the chapter seems to be a kind of digression, and its purpose and function in the book are far from being immediately obvious.

Chapter 3 begins, as did chapter 1, with Socrates, and I think it is best to see the chapter as a kind of starting-over, a retracing of some of the same ground covered in chapters 1 and 2, though from a slightly different angle. We begin with a Socrates who is puzzled by his own nature, unsure as to whether he is "a more curious monster than Typhon or a friendlier and simpler being, by nature sharing something divine (see *Phaedrus* 229 e)."[1] However, "in order to get started" Climacus immediately shifts from this uncertainty to a type of certainty: "Still, let us now,…make a bold proposition: let us assume that we know what a human being is."[2] With this assumption Climacus has indeed returned to the starting point of chapter 1, for the assumption that we know what a human being is there is said to be the criterion of truth, and this assumption is specifically linked by Climacus to the theory of recollection.[3] Hence the assumption that we humans possess this knowledge is identical with the assumption that we possess the Truth, or at least that we possess the condition for gaining the Truth.

Having made the Socratic assumption, however, Climacus moves away from it even more rapidly than in chapter 1. In an obscure passage, the understanding's postulated self-knowledge is rendered doubtful by an encounter, a "collision" with something. "But then the understanding stands still, as did Socrates, for now the understanding's paradoxical passion that wills the collision awakens and, without really understanding itself, wills its own downfall."[4] This collision, involving a paradox that is "intimated" but not known, is said to be the source of Socrates' own puzzlement about himself. The collision is therefore an event that seems to point the individual in the direction of the B hypothesis by putting the Socratic assumption in question.

I believe that this gives us the clue we need to rightly see the role of chapter 3 in *Philosophical Fragments*. The sense that chapter 3 is a kind of starting-over is correct, but it is not a starting from scratch. The author has some sense of where he has come in the first two chapters, and the issues posed there form an agenda for chapter 3. It is true that the chapter begins once more with the Socratic position, but the hypothesis of chapters 1 and 2 constantly lurks in the background. The central issue of the chapter is, I believe, the various attitudes human reason can take toward the B hypothesis. In surveying these possible attitudes it is proper to begin by exploring how far human thinking can go toward generating the B hypothesis on its own steam. To be precise, we already know from the first two chapters that human reason cannot generate the B hypothesis on its own. Nevertheless, it is proper for Climacus to see if there is any possible point of contact between human reason and the contents of the B hypothesis. In looking at the attempts of human reason to understand what is ultimate, Climacus is beginning with a plausible point of contact: an encounter between human thinking and something it cannot understand, a collision with what he terms the unknown.[5] The closest reason can come to generating the B hypothesis, even if it is unsuccessful, will be an attempt by reason to discover its own limits.

The most plausible attempt along these lines is the fabled Socratic ignorance, in which Socrates, despite the Platonic assumption of recollection Climacus foists on him, comes to a standstill over his inability to fulfill the Delphic injunction to "know thyself." Climacus by no means will concede that his earlier contention about the inability of human reason to generate the B hypothesis is incorrect. The central thrust of the chapter is that human reason cannot by itself conceive of what is "absolutely different."[6] Nevertheless, he is inclined to think that something of significance is present in this Socratic ignorance. Human reason is powerless by itself to discover that with which it "collides." Nevertheless there is in human reason an affinity for this collision. This "point of contact" is not sufficient for reason to dispense with God's self-revelation. Nevertheless, the search for the limits of reason reveals a potential affinity between reason and revelation. The affinity becomes actual only when certain conditions are actualized, but the fact that reason possesses this potential is nevertheless significant. This affinity is the first theme I wish to explore.

REASON'S PASSION: WILLING ITS OWN DOWNFALL

Almost at the beginning of the chapter, Climacus claims that human understanding[7] is gripped by a peculiar passion: the desire for its own downfall. We can recognize right away that Climacus is speaking loosely and poetically here. Strictly speaking, human understanding does not have passions; they are qualities of persons. However persons do think, and their thinking may embody or reflect their passions.

Climacus makes several claims at the beginning of the chapter for which he offers little support or even elaboration. Asserting that "the paradox is the passion of thought" and that "every passion's highest pitch is always to will its own downfall," he concludes that "thus it is the highest passion of the understanding to will the collision, although in one way or another the collision must become its downfall."[8] It is hard to say whether this is intended as argument. In any case, it is clear enough where Climacus wants to go: "This, then, is the highest paradox of thought: to want to discover something that cannot be thought."[9]

That human reason has an enduring fascination with the paradoxical seems right to me; an encounter with the paradoxical does engender something that rightly deserves the name "passion." The psychology involved in the claim that every passion involves something like a Freudian death-instinct seems more dubious to me, but fortunately nothing hangs on this universal psychological claim. We do not need to know if every human passion at its highest point wills its own downfall; it will be enough to see if something like this desire is present in the dominant passions that appear to drive human reason.

Actually, the dubious psychology almost disguises a really decisive move Climacus makes, and that is to view reason as passionate in the first place. In making a controversial and perhaps dubious claim about the ultimate passion of the understanding, we almost do not notice that we have accepted the idea that the understanding is passionate. From Climacus' perspective, human reason is not a disinterested quest for a god-like view of things, but the expression of a very interested human being. It is only in the context of viewing human reason as itself the expression of human passion that the more striking claim begins to make sense.

Climacus tells us that the desire to discover something that thought cannot think "is fundamentally present everywhere in thought." However, we do not notice this "because of habit."[10] Little help is given here to understand these remarks, but I think they make some sense if we take a particular view of reason, a view which I see as implicit though by no means developed. The view is one which could aptly use the title "imperialistic reason." Reason, on this view, far from being a neutral dispassionate faculty, is more like an instrument of control or even domination. A paradox engenders passion in human reason because it is a challenge, a reality that I do not yet know how to control or dominate. The realm of paradox is the realm in which I do not know my way around, and my response reveals a desire to make this realm my own. The response of reason to the paradoxical, and indeed to the unknown generally, reveals a desire for mastery.

It certainly does not appear immediately obvious that all thinking is gripped by the passion to discover something that thought cannot think, but it becomes more plausible if we view human thinking as the expression of this type of desire for mastery. Consider natural science, which many would view as the most important achievement and characteristic expression of reason. Science continually pushes back the frontier of knowledge. The paradoxical, the surprising, the incomprehensible are all incitements to scientific discovery, which continually attempts to understand what is not yet understood. This seems not so much a passion for discovering something that thought cannot think as a passion for understanding everything. However, on close inspection, the latter passion can be interpreted as a disguised form of the first. In seeking to understand what it does not understand, in restlessly seeking to conquer all unknown territory, is not reason seeking to discover if there are any limits to human understanding?

The scientist seems never to find or be content with any ultimate explanation. Molecules are explained in terms of atoms. Atoms are explained in terms of subatomic particles. Subatomic particles are explained in terms of God knows what. What if some ultimate explanation were found? What if reason discovered something that thought cannot think? Two possible responses can be imagined. On the one hand, a feeling of defeat is easily imaginable. The scientist has at last hit on something impervious to imperialistic reason, something that we cannot explain, and therefore cannot dominate or control. Imperialistic reason has failed. On the other hand, we might well take some satisfaction in having reached what could reasonably be termed the goal. We have explained all that could be explained, and if reason could take a somewhat less imperialistic stance, it might see the discovery as fulfilling an ambition that was implicit in reason's activity all along.

The discovery that Climacus envisions as playing such a role for reason does not of course come from natural science, but from the human quest for self-understanding. Nevertheless, the same responses that we envisioned in the case of such a discovery in natural science are possible in the case of the paradox of self-knowledge. Socrates, in his quest for self-knowledge, awakens "the understanding's paradoxical passion that wills the collision." This passion, "without really understanding itself, wills its own downfall."[11] The key point here is that reason has a natural ambivalence about its own limits. Such a limit would be reason's "downfall." However, it could also be seen as the fulfillment or satisfaction of reason's ultimate goal. After an excursion into natural theology and its limitations, Climacus returns to a consideration of this ambivalence, and we will follow his example.

PROOFS OF GOD'S EXISTENCE

After his puzzling initial discussion of Socratic self-knowledge and its "collision" with an unknown which it both fears and desires, Climacus immediately shifts to a discussion of natural theology, the classical attempts to prove God's existence. The transition is made in the following manner:

> But what is this unknown against which the understanding in its paradoxical passion collides and which even disturbs man and his self-knowledge? It is the unknown. But it is not a human being, insofar as he knows man, or anything else that he knows. Therefore, let us call this unknown *the god*. It is only a name that we give to it.[12]

The difficulty, however, is that this does not seem to be only a name, as Climacus himself immediately begins a discussion of the classical attempts to prove that God exists, strong evidence that the name was not exactly chosen at random.

The justification for this procedure lies, I think, in the Socratic viewpoint from which the chapter begins. Climacus has consistently interpreted the Socratic position as equivalent to the claim that knowledge of the divine is bound up with self-knowledge. Insofar as self-knowledge leads to the "collision" with the unknown, it is logical to regard this encounter as itself an encounter with the divine, and since the encounter leads to bewilderment, in turn to interpret the divine as unknown. The ultimate purpose of Climacus is to explore what might be termed negative theology. Can reason by itself come up with a concept of God, precisely by conceiving of God as what is unknown to reason? Or, put in terms of our earlier question, can thought discover something thought cannot think? If it could, would it thereby discover God?

But why does Climacus discuss the proofs of God's existence, which are of course attempts to gain positive knowledge of God? Climacus must first consider these attempts by reason to discover God's reality, and find them wanting. Given their failure, he can then see whether reason can redeem this failure by constructing an understanding of God negatively, as the unknown.

The claim that "the god" is "only a name" seems therefore to be a bit of playful irony on the part of Climacus, since he is taking a serious look at attempts to gain an understanding of what humans have thought of as ultimate or divine. However, the irony is philosophically innocent. If Climacus were trying to show that we human beings do have knowledge of God, then he ought to be able to justify his equation of the divine with the limits of reason. Since his purpose is experimental and hypothetical, and since his conclusion is that we do not have any rational knowledge of the divine, the linguistic sleight of hand in no way functions illegitimately. Climacus looks at the ways positive at-tempts to know God misfire, and this leads naturally to the position he wants to consider, namely whether reason can by itself discover something like the B hypothesis by examining its own failures. This position too is tried and found wanting, but something of interest is nevertheless to be learned from the failure. The discussion of the theistic arguments then, on my reading, is by no means the central theme of the chapter, but it is a discussion that is of interest in its own right and certainly has attracted a great deal of interest from readers. I shall briefly examine his critique.

So far as I can tell, Climacus has two general or a priori objections to the idea of proving God's existence, as well as specific objections to the ontological and teleological arguments. I shall examine the general arguments first, and in that context look at his objection to the ontological argument, and then look at the criticism given against the more empirical teleological argument, or argument from design.

Thought and Being: General Arguments against Natural Theology and the Ontological Argument

The first critical argument takes the form of a dilemma. Either God exists or he does not, says Climacus. If God does not exist, then of course it is impossible to prove that he does. If God does exist, however,

Climacus says that "it is foolishness to want to demonstrate it, since I, in the very moment the proof begins would presuppose it...as decided."[13] This argument of Climacus is obviously not designed to show that sound proofs of God's existence cannot be given, but rather that the project of giving such proofs is somehow pointless.

The idea that lies behind this seems to be simply that I would not try to prove God's existence unless I were already convinced that God did exist. However, if I am already convinced, why should I try to prove it? Although it may be true for psychological reasons that a person would not try to prove God's existence who did not already believe, it is not obvious that it must be true. Could not someone who is simply undecided attempt to discover an argument that would thereby produce a conviction that God exists? In any case, even if Climacus is right about this, it does not imply that proofs of God's existence are pointless. It may be that I would not bother to construct a proof of God's existence were I not already convinced of God's reality on other grounds, but the proof I construct may still have value. It may have value for me in confirming and strengthening my belief, showing me that the belief is reasonable. Even more significantly, Climacus fails to consider the idea that such a proof may have value for other people than myself.

The second general argument offered by Climacus is more promising and certainly more interesting from a philosophical standpoint. The claim is that one cannot really demonstrate the existence of God because existence is not something that can be demonstrated by argument. "I constantly draw conclusions from existence, not towards existence."[14] Here Climacus seems to take a position which is reminiscent of Hume's claim that no "matter of fact" can be demonstrated.[15] The reason Climacus gives for this view, however, is not Hume's argument that no matter of fact can be demonstrated because the contrary of a matter of fact can always be conceived as logically possible, but rather seems to rest on another Humean claim, one echoed in Kant's famous argument that existence is not a quality or property that something can be shown to have.[16] As Climacus puts it, existence is always something presupposed by an argument, or perhaps something added to it, but is never itself established by the argument. As examples, he says that we do not prove that a stone exists, but that some existing thing is a stone, and that in a criminal trial, we do not prove that a criminal exists, but that a person who exists is a criminal.[17] These are supported by another claim that sounds Humean, namely that all that can be accomplished by a demonstrative argument is to develop the consequences of a concept. If we add the Kantian claim that existence is not a concept to this Humean claim that only "relations of ideas" are subject to demonstrative proof, then the conclusion Climacus wants seems to follow.

All of this touches on an issue that is of central importance in Kierkegaard's pseudonymous authorship, namely the relationship of thought to being. In *Concluding Unscientific Postscript*, Climacus argues that to avoid idealism one must hold fast to a distinction between thought and being, a distinction that is undermined if one concedes that being is a concept to be thought. The distinction between thought and being is not a distinction between one thought and another, but a distinction between what is merely thought and what is. Thought deals with possibility; being is actuality. Between a possible X and an actual X there may be no difference at all in conceptual qualities. The difference is not one of content but of mode, and Climacus wants to insist that we understand what it is to be actual not by thinking about a certain quality called "existence" but by being actual, by existing.[18]

This discussion of thought and being in *Postscript* is closely related to the critique of the ontological argument that is given in a footnote in chapter 3 of *Fragments*. Climacus looks at a version of this argument offered by Spinoza, in which it is argued that God, whose very nature is to be the most perfect being, must exist necessarily, since necessary existence is a perfection.[19] On Climacus' view, any success this argument enjoys is due to a failure to distinguish clearly between two senses of "being," ideal being and factual being. To speak of ideal being is to speak of what kind of being a thing possesses; it is to speak of essence. It is possible for things to exist in different ways, including existing necessarily, and it is here appropriate to speak of degrees of being. Factual being, however, is said to be subject to the "Hamlet dialectic, to be or not to be." Here the question is not what kind of being a thing possesses, but whether it exists at all. It cannot be established that a thing exists in the factual sense merely by considering its essence; all that an argument like Spinoza's can accomplish is to explore the nature of God's existence if he does exist. The argument amounts to a profound tautology: "God, who is a necessary being, exists necessarily." In effect, Climacus glosses this roughly as follows: "God, if he exists, exists necessarily." The argument does not establish whether God exists, but what he must be like if he does.

Contemporary defenders of the ontological argument would doubt-less reply that the hypothetical clause in the above proposition makes the proposition incoherent, since it is contradictory to suppose that a necessary being might not exist. God's existence cannot be merely contingent, since if God's existence is possible, then it is necessary.[20] However, Climacus anticipates this reply, I believe. He agrees with Leibniz that it is true that God's existence is necessary if it is possible, but claims that this still amounts to a tautology and "circumvents the difficulty."[21] I think he means by this that we do not really know whether God's existence is possible unless we know that he actually exists. The ontological argument then, on Climacus' view, is a perfect example of what can and cannot be established by conceptual argument. We can elucidate what is contained in a concept but we cannot establish what exists.

Now it must be conceded that in ordinary life we do often regard the existence of things as established by argument. The physicist cites evidence for the existence of a hitherto unknown subatomic particle. The astronomer cites evidence for the existence of a hitherto unknown planet. The neighbor argues that a burglar exists on the block by citing the pattern of break-ins that have occurred recently. On Climacus' view, these arguments for the existence of something are misnamed, and we are speaking loosely in such cases. What we really do is show that a something, assumed to exist, is in fact a subatomic particle, or that a particular astronomical body is in fact a planet, or that an unknown person is in fact a burglar. We are really giving a justification that a particular concept applies to some existing reality.

However, it is not obvious that Climacus is right about this. It does appear at times that the argument is not about whether an existing "X" is rightly described as a planet or not, but about whether "X" exists at all. Whether or not Climacus senses the force of this objection is not clear, but in any case he does shift ground. The analog with respect to God for cases like the subatomic particle and the planet are arguments that the works of God in nature provide evidence for God's existence. Climacus quickly moves from his general, a priori argument against natural theology to a consideration of more specific, empirical arguments such as the argument from design. The criticisms he has of such arguments, as we shall see, are of a wholly different kind.

Critique of the Argument from Design

Climacus does not bother to give a precise statement of what is generally called the argument from design, but that does not matter too much, for he is really criticizing the inspiration behind such arguments in general, not a specific version. He wants to consider whether or not God's existence can be inferred from God's works, "the wisdom in nature and the goodness or wisdom in Governance."[22] Climacus is happy to accept the tautology that the works of god can only be done by the god, but he then goes on to wonder how we identify those works of god. "The works from which I want to prove his existence do not immediately exist."[23] The wisdom and goodness in nature are not *that* obvious to us. The starting-point of the proof is not simply nature as it immediately appears to us, but nature interpreted according to a certain ideal, nature understood as the work of God. Climacus argues that the acceptance of such an ideal interpretation of nature is equivalent to "presupposing that the god exists." Thus, the belief in God which the proof is supposed to support is actually supporting the proof, rather than the other way around. It is only because of this, Climacus says, that I can have any confidence in the argument, daring to "defy all objections, even those that have not yet arisen." If this were not so, if my faith in God really rested on such an empirical argument, then I could not have the kind of confident belief the religious life demands, for I would be continually in suspense, worried that "something so terrible happen [the Holocaust?] that my fragment of proof would be ruined."[24]

So far as I can see, Climacus does not really deny the possibility of a sound argument for God's existence from the works of God in nature. What he denies is that such an argument can be known to be sound, or to be more precise, that it can be known to be sound independently of some subjective faith. His real target is the notion that such a rational proof could be a substitute for faith. Once it is conceded that the recognition of such an argument requires faith and cannot be a substitute for it, he seems to have no objection to such arguments. Socrates, in fact, is taken as a model of the proper way to pursue such things. Socrates, the reputed inventor of the argument in question, "constantly presupposes that the god exists, and on this presupposition seeks to infuse nature with the idea of purposiveness."[25]

I am here using "faith" or "belief" in one of its ordinary senses, not in the special sense Climacus gives it when speaking in chapters 4 and 5 of the positive response of a human being to an encounter with the god who has become human. In speaking of the proofs of God as requiring faith, I mean only that they require the acceptance of a premise that is not self-evident or undeniable, or perhaps the adoption of a way of seeing the world which is equivalent to accepting such a premise. Regardless of the merits of any of the other criticisms of natural theology given by Climacus, his view here seems eminently defensible. Arguments for God's existence may be sound, and even recognizable as sound, but it does not seem true that such arguments depend on premises that any sane, rational person who understands them must accept. Otherwise, why would so many sane, rational persons fail to accept them?

It is worth noting that Climacus does not here conclude that no "natural" knowledge of God is possible. The Socratic position, as we have seen, assumes that a knowledge of God is linked to self-knowledge. Even the B hypothesis does not rule out all knowledge of God. Although from the point of view of the B hypothesis, the kind of knowledge of God that is equivalent to knowing the Truth is not possible for human beings, this by no means implies that it is impossible for human beings to know that God exists and some things about God. The B perspective requires us only to hold that whatever knowledge of this sort that is available is not sufficient for "salvation." Such a knowledge about God does not amount to knowing the Truth. Of course Climacus is not arguing for the truth of the B perspective on this issue, but considering that perspective "hypothetically." Nevertheless, the critique of natural theology given here is quite compatible with the view Climacus develops at length in *Postscript*, which is that a natural religious life, termed Religiousness A, which involves an awareness of God, is possible for human beings, without any requirement of any special revelation from God. The view attacked in chapter 3 of *Fragments* is the claim of reason to develop an understanding of God that can function independently of the individual's subjective participation in the religious life. The target is not natural awareness of God but objective, speculative proofs of God.

The conclusion of the discussion of natural theology is then negative. Human beings, relying on their speculative, rational powers, can explore the consequences of various concepts of the divine, which is in effect to say what would be true if a certain conception of God was correct. Alternatively, they can accept an argument which is not demonstratively compelling by accepting a premise that is not objectively certain. Climacus says that in the latter case "the existence itself emerges from the proof by a leap."[26] This is the only use in *Fragments* of the famous Kierkegaardian concept of the leap. We shall say much more about the notion of the leap later, in connection with the discussion of belief and the will in the Interlude between chapters 4 and 5. Here talk of a leap seems merely to be a way of indicating that the individual has contributed something of a personal nature to the knowing enterprise. Climacus compares this personal contribution to letting go of a doll that rights itself when it is released. He says that so long as I am engaged in proving God's existence, "the existence does not emerge, if for no other reason than that I am engaged in proving it, but when I let go of the proof, the existence is there."[27] This passage is obscure, to say the least, but I think the view that underlies it is something like the following:

Both in *Fragments* and *Postscript* Climacus seems to hold the view that a natural awareness of God's reality is possible.[28] However, this awareness is gained, not through objective speculation, but subjectively, in the course of existing. Proofs of God's existence owe whatever force they have to this natural awareness of God's reality; it is such a conviction as this which is illustrated by Socrates' procedure of "infusing nature with the idea of purposiveness" and thus constructing the argument from design. However, it is Climacus' view that objective speculation and subjective existence are opposite and incompatible movements. Thus, to the extent that I try to speculatively prove God's existence, I make God's reality appear doubtful by removing myself from the existential standpoint which actually offers assurance. Thus, for God's existence to "emerge from a proof," I must "let go of the proof"; that is, remove myself from the indifferent standpoint of the disinterested speculator and take up once more the standpoint of the concretely existing person, replete with interests and passions. Only from this standpoint can I accept the less than objectively certain premise or premises the proof rests upon. This existential movement, this letting go of the proof, is thus what Climacus means here by a leap.

CAN THE UNKNOWN BE KNOWN?

After this extended look at natural theology, we can now return to Climacus' central concern, the quest of reason to discover something that thought cannot think. It looks as if the failure of natural theology might actually be of some positive use to reason in this quest. Cannot reason now define the unknown as that which is absolutely different, and which it is therefore unable to know? And would not such a recognition imply a kind of negative knowledge of the god? Climacus recognizes how tempting this move is, but rejects it nonetheless. He says that "defined as the absolutely different, it [the unknown] seems to be at the point of being disclosed, but not so."[29] The difficulty is that the understanding cannot really conceive of what is "absolutely different."

The understanding in its "paradoxical passion" continually "collides," "reaches," and "is engaged" with the unknown, and yet the unknown remains unknown. The unknown is a "frontier" or "boundary" (*Grændse*) to reason.[30] As such, the unknown is, one might say, a reality in the life of reason, a factor in its activities, but it nevertheless remains unknown. It is like a place-holder in mathematics, an indication that something must exist to fill the space, with no understanding of what that something must be. Having teased us by calling the unknown "the god" and going on to examine the traditional proofs of God's existence, Climacus returns to his serious claim that "the god" is unknown to us, and the name therefore is "just a name."

It appears that the understanding might be able to make some progress toward understanding the "absolutely different," but Climacus says that this is not so. With more than a little echo of Feuerbach, he says that when the understanding tries to conceive of the unknown by itself, the result is idolatry, in that the god is manufactured in our own image:

> The understanding cannot even think the absolutely different; it cannot absolutely negate itself but uses itself for that purpose and consequently thinks the difference in itself,....It cannot absolutely transcend itself and therefore thinks as above itself only the transcendence that it thinks by itself. If the unknown (the god) is not solely the frontier, then the one idea about the different is confused with the many ideas about the different.[31]

The idea here seems to be that the understanding confuses what is absolutely different with what is only relatively different. The content of the "frontier" gets filled in by the reason, selecting from among the many candidates supplied by the imagination for what is genuinely divine, and here Climacus calls to mind the incredible diversity in conceptions of god that are found in various cultures, especially pagan cultures.[32]

Manufacturing god in our own image is in one sense comfortable, in that it allows us to select a god which suits us, but we cannot be really secure in playing this game, according to Climacus. To play this game requires a certain degree of self-deception on the part of reason, because it is at bottom aware of the arbitrariness in selecting one conception of god rather than another.[33] In reality the understanding has become "confused" by its quest for its own boundary, and in its confusion "does not know itself and quite consistently confuses itself with the difference." Climacus calls this situation "the self-ironizing of the understanding,"[34] probably one of the more obscure phrases in the whole of Kierkegaard's authorship. It is not clear, to me at any rate, exactly what this self-ironizing is supposed to be. Is it the activity of reason in manufacturing gods in its own image? Perhaps reason, in becoming so confused that it confuses itself with what is supposed to be absolutely different, makes itself appear ironical to someone who occupies a superior standpoint. A second possibility is that the self-ironizing of the understanding refers to reason's recognition of the arbitrariness of the whole procedure. In this case, the self-ironizing would be an ironical recognition of the problematic character of reason's attempt to transcend itself.

However the phrase be understood, Climacus tries to illustrate this self-ironizing with a "sketch" of a situation that in some respects looks curiously like the B hypothesis that he will focus on in chapters 4 and 5. He supposes that "there exists, then, a certain person who looks just like any other human being, grows up as do other human beings," and so on, and yet "this human being is also the god."[35] How does Climacus know this? He says, "I cannot know it, for in that case I would have to know the god and the difference, and I do not know the difference."[36] I think the point of this is simply to show the impossibility of rationally knowing a particular conception of the divine, but Climacus uses this particular arbitrary conception of the god to underline the fact that reason could not possibly come up with anything like the B hypothesis.

The conclusion of the matter seems to be something like this: Reason in its quest for self-knowledge naturally confronts its own boundary as it falls into perplexity about itself. However, when it attempts to gain any positive knowledge of this frontier, it behaves capriciously and even has an awareness of this capriciousness, at least at a depth level. It is aware that the idea of the "absolutely different" it has formed is not really altogether different. The recognition of this failure on the part of reason is far from actually forming a concept of the unknown, but in the postulated encounter between reason and the god of the B hypothesis, it is not without significance, as we shall see.

THE PARADOX OF THE GOD'S SELF-REVELATION

In the last section of chapter 3 the interlocutor reappears and it finally becomes clear where the whole discussion has been going. The final "sketch" Climacus has made of the god who looks just like an ordinary human being is sufficient to exhaust the patience of the dialogue partner whom we have already met several times, and he bursts in with irritation: "You are a spinner of whimsicalities, that I know full well, but you certainly do not believe that it would occur to me to be concerned about a whim so strange or so ridiculous that it probably has never occurred to anyone and, above all, is so unreasonable that I would have to lock everything I have in my consciousness out in order to think of it."[37] Climacus' response to this is basically agreement. As we shall see, the "whim" he has suggested, resembling the B hypothesis in several key respects, is something that does appear unreasonable to human beings, and is certainly "strange" and even "ridiculous" from a certain perspective. He does make one jab at the interlocutor by noting that the respondent's own assessment of his rational capacities is by no means completely objective. The idea that the interlocutor is offended by the requirement that he "lock everything out of his consciousness" shows that the respondent has presuppositions to which he is attached, despite his presumption "to think about...[his] consciousness without presuppositions."[38] Despite this jab, Climacus wants to say to the interlocutor: "It is exactly as you say; you can't make any sense of my idea."

The reason for this is simple: If the god is truly absolutely different from human beings, then this is not something human beings will be able to figure out for themselves. The god must teach it to them. "If it [the understanding] is going to come to know this, it must come to know this from the god."[39] Climacus goes on, however, to state a stronger thesis. "If it does come to know this, it cannot understand this and consequently cannot come to know this." So the understanding cannot come to know the god as absolutely different by itself nor with the god's help. At this point, Climacus says, "we seem to stand at a paradox."[40]

What is this paradox? If the problem is simply that there is no way to gain any understanding of the god, then there would seem to be frustration of one human desire, but no paradox. The paradox arises, I believe, from the fact that there is a sense in which human beings can come to know the god by revelation. As Climacus puts it, the purpose of God's self-revelation is to allow the learner "to completely understand him."[41] So it is not that the god cannot be known at all. The problem lies in the fact that the god who is known in this way turns out to be one who in a sense cannot be known.

I believe that Climacus is in this second assertion using the word "know" in a special, philosophical sense. To say that the god could be known is to say that he could be assimilated into our previous stock of beliefs and convictions; that one could show that the knowledge of him could be derived from other things we humans claim to know. In claiming that the god cannot be known, even after he has revealed himself, Climacus is claiming that the god's self-revelation is not something that can be appropriated and then dispensed with. Not only could human beings not have discovered the true nature of the god on their own; even after the god has revealed himself, what is revealed is something that is discontinuous with our existing stock of knowledge and beliefs. The god cannot be mastered and domesticated and his self-revelation remains our only channel to apprehend him. In short, the knowledge which the god makes possible bumps up against what I earlier termed the imperialistic character of reason. Insofar as knowledge consists of mastery, the god who is absolutely different cannot be known. This, however, is compatible with saying that in an ordinary, unphilosophical sense of the word "know," when the god reveals himself as absolutely different, the learner, at least when certain conditions are satisfied, can come to know the god as absolutely different.

What is the nature of this absolute difference between the god and human beings? Here much nonsense has been written on the assumption that Climacus has in mind a metaphysical difference. Thus, many have assumed that the problem is that God is supposed to be infinite, eternal, omnipotent, omniscient, and so on, and that these are qualities that are so different from their human analogs that human beings cannot understand them. However, Climacus says very clearly that he has nothing like this in mind at all. The absolute difference does not lie in human finitude per se, but in sin: "But if the god is to be absolutely different from a human being, this can not have its basis in what man owes to the god (for to that extent they are akin) but in what he owes to himself....What then is the difference? Indeed, what else but sin."[42]

It is sin therefore that lies at the basis of the human inability to know God on our own, and at the basis of the paradox that even when we come to know God through God's self-revelation, we still do not "know" God. Climacus obviously thinks that sin has rather profound epistemological implications, or, to take account of the hypothetical form of his work, he thinks that the B hypothesis requires such an implication. It is sin that distinguishes the B hypothesis from the

Socratic view of things, even the Socrates who recognizes his inability to know himself. In beginning his "poem" Climacus distinguished his hypothesis from the Socratic view by supposing that humans are in untruth. Now, after some meanderings, it becomes clear that "we have come to the same point again."[43]

Socrates discovered "otherness" and "difference" of a sort. The discovery made him "almost bewildered about himself." Nevertheless, Socrates lacked "the consciousness of sin, which he could no more teach to any other person than any other person could teach it to him."[44] This is why the paradox with which Socrates collides turns out to be merely "intimated" but not really known or understood.[45] Chapter 3 has explored the closest analogs within the field of human reason to the realization of sin, namely the failure of human beings to gain any knowledge of the god and the resultant bewilderment as the paradox of our own nature is confronted, not knowing whether we are monsters more curious than Typhon or something divine.[46] This encounter with the different, with what is "other," turns out to be, however, only an encounter with what is relatively different and other. When an encounter with what is genuinely different and other occurs, the result will be that what is encountered cannot be mastered or tamed. Imperialistic reason is given a hard knock. Our "presupposition" that we are capable of assimilating what is other is put into question. This hard knock which imparts the consciousness of sin must be imparted by revelation, says Climacus. It cannot be the result of Socratic reflection, at least from the point of view of the B hypothesis.

Thus chapter 3 is an extended "repetition" of chapters 1 and 2. At least it begins where those chapters begin, with the Socratic view of the Truth, and ends where they end, with a sketch of a dramatically different alternative, the B hypothesis. Chapter 3 attempts to describe human reason as not only unable to attain the Truth, but unable to attain an understanding of its inability to attain the truth. Socratic ignorance is the closest approximation to this latter understanding, but it lacks one thing: the consciousness of sin. The interlocutor is quite right to exclaim that he cannot understand the story of the god that is spun out by the B hypothesis. The content of the hypothesis is that the god is what is absolutely different from him and thus it is that which he is unable to understand.

Climacus now begins to refer to the content of the hypothesis regularly as "the paradox." It is a term he uses in several ways. We will postpone a thorough treatment of it until later, but a brief introduction would be helpful at this point. The term is used both for the relation between the god and the learner, and for the god's action in becoming a human being to be our teacher. In both of these contexts, the paradox is said to have a "double aspect." When the term is first used to describe the B hypothesis, at the end of chapter 3, it is the relationship which seems to be the primary focus of concern. The paradox is that a relation to the god is established by an encounter that seems to make any relation impossible, or, to put it in epistemological terms, knowledge of the god is made possible by the discovery that no knowledge of the god is possible. The natural question at this point is whether any sense can be made of such a paradox. It is to this very issue that Climacus turns.

REASON'S AMBIVALENT RESPONSE TO THE PARADOX

The question Climacus poses is whether a "paradox such as this" is "conceivable."[47] (Literally, "does such a paradox allow itself to be thought?") One might think that the answer to this question is obvious, since Climacus has already told us that this paradox is one that reason cannot understand. However, as if he anticipates our quick response, Climacus warns us not to be in a hurry, since "it is not speed that wins but correctness." It is true that there are weighty reasons for a negative response on the part of reason:

> The understanding certainly cannot think it, cannot hit upon it on its own, and when it is proclaimed, the understanding cannot understand it and merely detects that it will likely be its downfall. Insofar, the understanding has much to object to,...[48]

It is evident from this that reason has plenty of grounds for hostility to the B hypothesis, yet it is just as evident that this inability of reason to "understand" the paradox does not settle the question of whether it is possible to "think" or "conceive" the paradox.

On the other side of the coin, Climacus tells us that "yet, in its paradoxical passion the understanding does indeed will its own downfall," which is what the paradox wills also, and thus "the two have a mutual understanding," which is, however, "present only in the moment of passion."[49] Here we have returned to the initial theme of the chapter, which is reason's paradoxical passion to discover its own downfall, a passion that inspires Socrates' quest for self-knowledge, but which the Socratic paradox does not adequately satisfy, at least according to the B hypothesis. At the beginning of the chapter, in looking at the Socratic quest, we saw imperialistic reason as engaged in a quest for its own limit, a limit to which it feels a natural ambivalence. One of the main points of chapter 3 we have discovered is that the quest of reason to discover that which thought cannot think fails; reason cannot on its own discover that which is genuinely other or absolutely different.

Now a further point of the chapter emerges. Understanding this quest of reason helps us to see that there is a possible meeting ground between reason and the different, something in the nature of reason itself that might make a harmonious relationship possible. The "collision" of Socrates with the paradox of self-knowledge is not the B hypothesis; it lacks the consciousness of sin. The true collision is made possible by the god's self-revelatory action. However, by looking at the Socratic analog, an insight into reason's character is gained which is valuable, namely that reason itself is capable of desiring a collision with that which is absolutely different, though it cannot on its own produce such a collision. When reason is gripped by this "passion" then a happy relation between reason and the paradox is possible. When reason collides with the paradox of the B hypothesis, which is not merely "intimated" but actual, the two ambivalent responses we saw in looking at the Socratic collision are still very much in evidence. The negative reaction of reason to the paradox is easy to anticipate and easy to understand, but that is merely one of the two possibilities.

Climacus tries to explain the ambivalence of reason toward the paradox by using what he admits is an imperfect "metaphor," namely erotic love. The happy possible relationship between reason and faith is explicated in an extended proportional analogy, in which reason is said to be related to faith as self-love is to love. "Self-love lies at the basis of love, but at its highest point wills precisely its own destruction.

This is what love wants too, so these two powers are in agreement with each other in the moment of passion, and this passion is precisely love."[50] The thought which lies behind this is, I think, that there is often a tension between self-love and genuine love, but the tension is not a necessary one. When a person falls in love, the initial ground or basis of the love is self-love; people fall in love because they are seeking their own happiness. The paradox is that when they genuinely do fall in love, self-love is transcended, dethroned, as it were. The person gains happiness in sacrificing happiness for the sake of the loved one. Thus, when genuine love is present, love and self-love are united.

Climacus thinks that there is a significant analogy here to the relation between the understanding and faith. In faith the imperialistic understanding is dethroned; it must recognize its limits. "To that degree the understanding will have much to object to," just as a selfish person in the grip of self-love may "shrink from love."[51] Yet Climacus suggests that there is a sense in which the dethroning of the understanding is at the same time what the understanding itself desires; it is a kind of fulfillment of the understanding, just as love fulfills self-love.

The clear implication of this is that the recognition of the limits of reason can itself be rational, at least under certain conditions, those conditions being the presence of a certain passion, unnamed in chapter 3 but soon to be termed "faith." I shall say a great deal more about this passion and its relation to the understanding. Here it is enough to emphasize that when it is present, reason evidently *can* conceive the paradox in some sense, even while it continues to fail to understand it in another. Climacus' analogy also implies that the alternative to this passion that makes it possible for reason and the paradox to get on with each other is not a neutral, dispassionate stance, but a rival passion, a passion analogous to that of the "selfish lover who shrinks from love." This rival passion Climacus will soon term "offense." Both faith and offense seem possible for reason; both are in some sense grounded in its very character. Each in a sense can only properly be understood in contrast with its rival. It is proper then, that Climacus devotes an appendix to chapter 3 to exploring this negative, hostile passion before looking in detail at faith. We shall look at this analysis in the next chapter.

CHAPTER

6

THE ECHO OF OFFENSE

Climacus adds an appendix to chapter 3 that discusses in some detail the nature of reason's passionate rejection of the paradox, a passion he now terms offense. It is obvious that Climacus thinks that this response will be very common. It is important to recognize, however, that offense is not a universal response. Some Kierkegaardian commentators have been so taken with this concept that they have assumed that everyone who truly understands the paradox will be offended, so that offense is even an aspect of faith, or at least that it is something that the person of faith must have passed through and surmounted. However, at the end of the appendix to chapter 3 Climacus describes a group of people, including Tertullian and Hamann, who describe the paradox in the language used by offense, but are not themselves "the offended ones but the very ones who held firmly to the paradox."[1] It is evident from this that offense and faith are mutually exclusive responses, and it follows that if faith is a possibility, offense will not be universal.

Though offense is not universal, it was certainly common in Climacus' day and remains so in our own. There is much talk today about "secularization," and the decline of faith which "modernity" or sometimes "postmodernity" has brought about. Many people seem to believe that traditional Christian faith has become more difficult or even impossible for an educated, thoughtful person today. Similar talk was already common in Climacus' day, though the particular words used varied somewhat. The appendix to chapter 3 is, I believe, an implicit response to this kind of thing. Climacus takes it for granted that Christianity, still presented hypothetically in the guise of his thought-experiment, now briefly summarized as the paradox, will be regarded as absurd by many, perhaps most, people. The thrust of the appendix is that *this* fact is not itself a reason to doubt Christianity, but rather a confirmation of its truth. Recognizing this may be difficult for those who are familiar with the contempt for apologetics often found in Kierkegaard's literature, but a careful reading makes the point emphatically clear, while at the same time explaining why Climacus rejects traditional attempts to argue for the truth of Christian faith.

The answer to those who believe that modern forms of thought have made it particularly difficult to believe in Christianity is that there is nothing particularly "modern" about the difficulty. Climacus thinks that it has always been true that "the understanding cannot get the paradox into its head,"[2] and notes that the paradox fully expects the understanding to regard this fact as a problem, though it is hardly a problem from the point of view of the paradox. Actually, to be more precise, the negative response of reason to the paradox has not "always" been present; to say that is not only to forget the option of faith but to forget the historical character of the paradox. Since offense is a response to the paradox, it follows that offense, like the paradox itself, is a historical phenomenon. It has not always existed, but has come into existence with the paradox.[3] The difficulty of believing the paradox has nothing to do with the nineteenth century, much less the twentieth century, but is inherent in the paradox itself. As soon as we have the paradox we have offense, and as long as we have the paradox, offense remains possible.

The whole of the appendix is presented as a kind of dialogue between reason and the paradox, each personified for literary purposes. It is, however, a peculiar kind of dialogue, in which the claims of one partner, the understanding, are asserted by the paradox to be echoes of what the paradox has already said. The "acoustic illusion" this makes possible is simply that the outbursts that appear to come from the understanding in reality originate with the paradox. The understanding is merely a source of echoes, but it somehow takes itself to be the originator of its assertions, a claim that the paradox indignantly denies.

This "I said it first" argument swiftly degenerates, as Merold West-phal has said, into a name-calling contest.[4] Hence the dialogue is not what one would regard as intellectual discourse on the highest plane.

A certain mutual disrespect marks the encounter, and understanding the nastiness is crucial to understanding the point of the appendix.

It is fair to say that Climacus clearly seems to side with the paradox in the mud-slinging contest and describes the battle from its point of view. At times this strains the reader's ability to hold on to the literary perspective that Climacus is simply engaging in a thought-experiment here, with no concern for truth. We have already seen, however, that there are ample reasons in chapters 1 and 2 for questioning whether Climacus is as detached as he claims, particularly with respect to the "proofs" Climacus offers for the correctness of his hypothesis at the conclusions of those chapters. The appendix has the same flavor, and indeed Climacus speaks of the offended consciousness as "an indirect test of the correctness of the paradox."[5] The reader can continue to play along with Climacus' game, and indeed is invited to do so by occasional reminders of the hypothetical character of the enterprise, but it is increasingly hard not to feel as if one is being ironically teased. Already in chapter 1 we saw a problem with Climacus' literary standpoint, since he seems to understand things which he should not be able to understand unless he is himself one of the god's disciples. In the appendix the irony once more seems a bit translucent, if not transparent. One of the claims Climacus will make about offense and faith is that they are the only possible responses to the paradox. Neutrality and indifference are either impossible or illusory. Since Climacus does not appear to be offended, there are good reasons once more for seeing him as a person of faith, whose literary form is a way of pulling our leg, a serious joke that helps us see some things about Christianity in a new light, or perhaps reminds us of some things about Christianity we have a strong tendency to forget. In what follows, several provocative and controversial claims about offense will emerge, claims clearly made from the perspective of the paradox.

THE PASSIVE CHARACTER OF OFFENSE

The general theme of the appendix seems to be that offense must be understood as *suffering*. Climacus does not mean primarily that offense is a painful condition, though that is certainly part of it, but that it is an essentially passive condition. The term translated as "suffering" in the Hong translation[6] (*lidende*) is not the common Danish noun for painful suffering (*lidelse*), but an adjective formed from the verb *at lide* (to let or allow) that emphasizes passivity. That is, offense is something that the understanding suffers or undergoes as a result of the activity of the paradox.

The sense in which offense is passive is not easy to determine. It is clear that Climacus does not mean that offense is something that simply happens to the understanding, and over which it has no control, for he says that offense is "always an action, not an event."[7] The offended consciousness is not completely inactive, and in fact the differences in degree of activity between various cases of offense allows him to claim that a distinction can be made between active and passive forms of offense, while keeping in mind that all forms are essentially passive.

I think the basic sense of passivity in mind here can best be grasped by looking at the name-calling contest. Reason begins the contest by calling the paradox the absurd. The paradox responds by insisting that these words were taken right out of its mouth. Reason is merely echoing what it has heard. Of course the paradox is the absurd, but reason is a blockhead and a dunce for thinking this is a problem.[8]

In this exchange of epithets it is clear that reason is active. Its passivity consists in the fact that it is the paradox that sets the terms of the encounter. The encounter is initiated by the paradox. The initial response of reason is an imitation of the paradox, something revealed to reason in the encounter. So reason is active, but its activity is unoriginal and lacks spontaneity. Offense is not only a response to the paradox, but a response that is itself learned from the paradox but now turned against its originator.

This claim of the passivity of reason is one that reason itself is likely to deny, Climacus suggests. The understanding wishes to think of itself as the discoverer of the paradox's absurdity, the objective tribunal that has tried the paradox and found it wanting. Alternatively, and just as repugnant from the point of view of the paradox, the understanding "takes pity upon the paradox" and "assists it to an explanation."[9] In both cases the understanding presumes itself to be a judge of the acceptability of Christian faith. From Climacus' perspective, far from the knowledgeable judge, the understanding here plays the role of a mimic, or perhaps a caricaturist, who merely copies in a distorted way what it learns from the paradox.[10] Even worse, the understanding seems to deceive itself, or at least to be unconscious of what it is doing.

IS REASON COMPETENT TO EVALUATE CHRISTIAN FAITH?

The response of Climacus to the claim reason makes to be a competent evaluator of Christianity is interesting but controversial. Insofar as we give the name "philosophy" to human thinking which aims at truth through rational reflection, we could describe the issue as bearing on the relation of Christianity to philosophy. The strength of his position is that it allows him to concede unchallenged the correctness of certain criticisms commonly made against Christianity, by arguing that these criticisms are not really objections. What the critics say is correct, but they are incorrect in thinking that what they say constitutes an objection to Christian faith.

The logic of his position is essentially as follows: If Christianity is true, then human beings lack the Truth, and must have the Truth brought to them by the god. However, since they lack the Truth, the Truth when brought to them must be what challenges and breaks with their established patterns of thinking. Hence the fact that Christianity appears absurd when evaluated by those patterns of thought is exactly what one would expect if Christianity is true. Therefore, the fact that Christianity appears absurd to reason is no reason to think it false; it is in fact a confirmation of its truth.

There is a defensible point in this argument, but I think it is one that must be carefully qualified. In general, I think it is right that one of the characteristics one would expect to find in a true revelation of the god, if it were the case that humans lack the Truth and need to have it brought to them, would be that it would challenge and correct our previous ways of thinking. Hence the fact that Christianity appears unreasonable to us, at least when first considered, is a plus and not a negative, though obviously this confirmation of Christianity's claims is not a proof. It is confirmation, but the weak kind of confirmation in which one of the consequences of Christianity's being true has been shown to hold. If things were otherwise, Christianity would be disconfirmed, and hence it has passed a test of sorts. However, there are obviously many other things besides the truth of Christianity that could account for its appearing unreasonable, and there are many other rival views that may seem equally unreasonable.

The chief difficulty with Climacus' argument, from my point of view, is that it collapses together too quickly different kinds of unreasonableness. There are indeed some ways in which Christianity will appear unreasonable to human beings that are a consequence of our sinfulness. For example, in both *Sickness Unto Death* and *Training in Christianity*, Anti-Climacus, another Kierkegaardian pseudonym, suggests that Christianity appears unreasonable because it postulates a kind of love on the part of God for us that we ourselves lack and cannot comprehend or understand.[11] In effect our own lack of love makes it appear unreasonable to us that such love is a reality. With respect to this sort of unreasonableness Climacus' argument makes sense. The fact that Christianity appears unreasonable in this case is indeed a consequence of our sinfulness, and the fact that it appears unreasonable to unloving people is just what one would expect if Christianity is true. In this case the appropriate response to a critic who makes the charge of unreasonableness would seem to be just the one Climacus recommends: "Of course it seems unreasonable to you and it should." To try to make Christianity acceptable to a "cultured despiser" of this sort by modifying it would be a betrayal.

However, there are other ways Christianity has been alleged to be unreasonable for which this sort of response does not seem quite so evidently right. Suppose, for example, that someone puts forward an objection that is rooted in a misunderstanding of Christianity. For example, imagine that someone has gotten the idea that Christianity teaches that God, who is supremely good and loving, loves some human beings but hates others. Surely in such a case the proper response is not to say that "It is exactly as you say; of course it is unreasonable to say that God is supremely loving and yet does not love some people, but after all, Christianity is unreasonable." Rather, the best response would be to explain to the critic that his objection is faulty because it is rooted in a confusion or mistake of some kind. This sort of response is not so much a matter of putting reason in its place as it is a matter of using reason. The defender of rational scrutiny may well inquire as to why it is legitimate to use reason when it suits one's purposes and then dismiss it as incompetent when it does not. It would appear that some principled way of deciding when reason is competent is needed.

The most interesting case, it seems to me, is one in which the critic claims that Christianity involves a logical contradiction and is thus repugnant to reason. Many commentators have in fact thought that this was precisely what Climacus himself claims when he says that the god's incarnation as a human is a paradox.[12] In the next chapter I will give a full treatment of what Climacus means by calling the incarnation a paradox, and I will argue that this "logical contradiction" interpretation is mistaken. Here I simply want to consider the implications of viewing the paradox as such a contradiction, as well as some implications of an alternative view.

Let us suppose then that Climacus, or someone else, claims that the incarnation is a formal, logical contradiction. Various reasons for saying this can be imagined. For example, it might be maintained that God is essentially eternal, omnipotent, and omniscient, and human beings are essentially noneternal, and finite in knowledge and power. Hence to say that a human being is God is to say that this human being is both eternal and noneternal, limited and unlimited in knowledge and power. The philosopher-critic then appears and objects that one cannot rationally believe a formal, logical contradiction, and that Christianity must be rejected as false. What should the Christian response be? Suppose the Christian admits that the faith is contradictory and therefore absurd from the viewpoint of reason, but maintains that it should be believed anyway, presumably because human reason is distorted by sin and cannot apprehend the truth. The fact that Christianity is logically absurd is in fact one sign of its truth.

Such a response seems a grave mistake to me. Two problems that seem insuperable arise if one admits that Christianity is logically contradictory but asserts that it should be believed anyway. First of all, it is hard to see how an abandonment of the principles of formal logic can be confined to this one area. If both "P" and "not P" can be true, then literally anything can be true. One consequence of this is that the careful thought-experiment of Climacus is invalidated. Climacus' whole work rests on logical principles. He attempts to "invent" a logically coherent alternative to the Socratic position on the Truth and its acquisition. The invention is basically a logical exercise, resting on the policy that where Socrates asserts "P" then the alternative must assert "not P" and thus be genuinely different. The logical principle of noncontradiction, which asserts that "P" and "not P" cannot both be true, underlies this policy.

The fact that the invention is a bit of a ruse, since what is supposedly invented is simply Christianity, in no way invalidates the significance of logic for the enterprise, for Climacus clearly thinks that the logical relations between Christianity and the Socratic view are such that the two views are mutually exclusive. If the logical principle of noncontradiction is not valid, if there is even one exception to it, then there is no reason to think that the B hypothesis is an *alternative* to the Socratic view. Both may be true simultaneously. In short, it is hard to see how Climacus can rely on logic to make his case that Christianity and idealism are mutually exclusive if the Christian alternative he presents rests on the notion that logic is not valid. Climacus himself sees clearly how dependent his project is on traditional logic and vigorously defends the validity of this kind of logic.[13]

However, even more significantly, if belief in Christianity requires belief in a logical contradiction which is recognized as a logical contradiction, then it is hard to see how such belief is even possible. For asking me to believe "P" and "not P" is perilously close to asking me to believe nothing at all. If to say that a man is God is logically equivalent to saying that he is not God, then what exactly is the meaning of the assertion? What exactly am I asked to believe? Suppose I believe that Jesus of Nazareth was God, and I also believe that this belief is logically contradictory because I believe that it is logically impossible for a man to be god. I thus believe it to be a necessary truth that no man is god, and this would seem to imply that Jesus of Nazareth is not god. It is hard for me to see how I can believe all these things simultaneously without confusion or self-deception. Clear-headed belief in a logical contradiction does not seem psychologically possible.

The contrary opinion that is evidently held by many Kierkegaardian commentators who have interpreted the paradox as a logical contradiction seems to me to rest on confusing the idea of believing a logical contradiction with the very different notion of believing something which appears to be logically contradictory. This is, incidentally, as I shall argue in the next chapter, how Climacus' notion of the paradox should be understood. It is not uncommon or difficult for someone to believe that some state of affairs that appears contradictory is a reality. For example, a materialist on the mind-body problem may hold that a thinking physical brain is a reality, even though the idea of such a thing may appear contradictory to a dualist committed to the idea that thought is an immaterial process necessarily carried on by an immaterial substance. But of course in committing himself to the reality of such a thinking brain, the materialist commits himself to the claim that the contradiction in such a state of affairs is only apparent and not genuine. In a similar way, though the incarnation may appear logically contradictory to many people, for a variety of reasons, anyone who actually believes in the incarnation is committed to the claim that the contradiction is only apparent and not genuine. "X appears to John to be P" is logically consistent with "John believes that X is not in fact P."

Now what is the upshot of all this for the claim that philosophy is not competent to pass on the reasonableness of Christianity? The conclusion I wish to draw is that the Christian would be unwise always to take the response to philosophical criticism Climacus proposes. With respect to certain objections, it seems appropriate to say, "Of course Christianity appears absurd to you; it should if it is true." With regard to other objections, it seems better to argue that the critic is just mistaken. When is the first response appropriate and when should the second be followed? In general, I think the answer is something like this: When the critic basically has got Christianity right, but is offended at it, then the first response seems appropriate. In this case the offense, from the Christian point of view, can be traced to sin, either on the part of the critic or on the part of those who have shaped the critic's thinking. However, when the objection is based on misunderstanding, when the critic is making false claims about Christianity, then the appropriate response would be to set him or her straight. If a genuine understanding of Christianity is present, then it can become clear whether the critic is really offended in Climacus' sense. In other words, not every philosophical attack on Christianity constitutes offense, and not every philosophical defense represents a devious selling out of Christianity to make it acceptable to sinful human beings.

I believe that this qualification of Climacus' view on the relation between philosophy and Christianity makes sense of some historical facts that would otherwise be inexplicable, namely, that there have been many philosophers who have defended the reasonableness of revealed Christian faith without thereby altering and distorting that faith. On Climacus' view, it would seem that philosophers who have considered Christian faith should either be opponents or else people who have tried to justify Christianity by altering it to make it acceptable to unbelievers. However, there are of course philosophers such as Augustine and Thomas Aquinas who seem to have done neither of these things.

To claim that philosophical thought may legitimately defuse some objections to faith is to call into question the monolithic character of what Climacus calls "the understanding." Throughout his discussion, he personifies the understanding and therefore implies that reason speaks with a unified voice. There is, I would argue, much danger in such a procedure. It tends to obscure the fact, a fact that Kierkegaard himself helps us to recognize in other contexts, that there is no such thing as "reason" or "the understanding." There are simply a lot of people who reason, and they do not all think in the same way. Many are offended by Christianity, but not all of them.

Why does Climacus assume that the understanding will be offended by Christianity? The question is misleading because, as we have already noted, Climacus does not assume that everyone will be offended by Christianity. Some will believe, and a believer is not offended. So the question must be rephrased. Why does Climacus assume that there is a natural tension between the understanding and the paradox, so that offense is, one might say, a natural if not universal reaction?

I believe that he sees offense as a consequence of two things. One is that Christianity, particularly the incarnation, is something that human reason cannot understand or comprehend. In saying that Christianity is essentially paradoxical, Climacus is not committed to the claim that it is logically contradictory and therefore contrary to reason, but he is committed to the claim that it is something human reason can never master or comprehend, a claim that has been traditionally expressed by saying that the incarnation is above reason. The second factor in explaining the natural tension between reason and the paradox is what I have termed the imperialistic character of reason. If Christianity is something reason cannot fully grasp, and reason insists that whatever is real must be fully graspable, then the stage is set for battle. The claim of Climacus that Christianity is against reason follows from the traditional claim that Christianity is above reason when this is combined with Climacus' thesis that reason is imperialistic and naturally recoils from what it cannot master.

But why should we assume that reason will always be imperialistic? Strictly speaking, Climacus does not assume this, since we have seen that it is not the case for the person gripped by the passion of faith. What he does assume is that reason is naturally imperialistic in people who have not been transformed by faith, and his reason for making this assumption is simply that it is a consequence of sin. The Christian understanding of sin is traditionally that it consists fundamentally in an attitude of prideful autonomy over against God. Climacus sees this attitude as expressed epistemologically in the demand that whatever I accept as true be certified as correct by the standards of evidence and probability that I currently live by. He is, of course, fully justified in making the assumption that humans are sinful because it is a requirement of his thought experiment if the hypothesis "invented" is to be genuinely different from the Socratic position.

One might think that by arguing, as I have above, that reason may in some cases legitimately give a defense of Christianity against the charge that it is unreasonable, I have necessarily rejected the view of Kierkegaard that apologetics is a betrayal of Christianity, a view that Climacus seems to share. In fact I do reject a blanket indictment of apologetics, but I still think that the view I am defending is consistent with the central intentions of Kierkegaard and of Climacus. A distinction can be made between different kinds of apologetics. The central issue is the role played by special revelation and authority. Climacus wants to say that Christianity can only be known to be true by revelation, and hence philosophical attempts to defend Christianity necessarily betray it by making Christianity appear to rest on reason rather than revelation. Certainly, many attempts to defend religious belief, such as those of people like Kant, Schleiermacher, and Hegel fit this pattern. However, Climacus does not seem to consider the possibility of a philosophical defense of Christianity which does not attempt to replace revelation with reason, but argues for the reasonableness of recognizing the limits of reason and the need for revelation.

I cannot see how Climacus can rightly object to that sort of philosophical defense of Christianity, because it seems to be what he himself is doing. He is himself arguing that there is a possible meeting place for reason and the revelation of the god, in that case where reason recognizes its own limits. Climacus would probably respond to this that the kind of philosophical defense I here envisage can only occur when the understanding has been transformed by faith. Perhaps this is so, but it raises one further difficulty for Climacus. Why should it be the case that only the thinking of the "unborn" person who lacks faith deserves to be termed "reason" or "the understanding?" It would appear to be the case that people with faith can think as well, and it is not obvious why reason or understanding is not operative in them also.

It is true that offended people have often tried to appropriate the term "reason" or "understanding" and thus to claim, not just that they find Christianity absurd, but that "reason" does so. Climacus thinks the best thing to do in this case is to make a present of the term "reason" to the opponent, and insist that Christianity is not "reasonable" and should not be made so. Given the variety of senses of "reason" and thus the variety of ways something can be said to be unreasonable, I do not think that Christians can afford to be so polite as to allow the offended person to appropriate the term. Certainly, from Climacus' own point of view, it is not the case that the offended person is reasoning in an essentially objective, neutral manner, while the person of faith is biased and subjective, since offense is just as much a passion as faith. Both offense and faith represent forms of passionate thinking, and it is unclear why the unbeliever's form of thinking deserves the honorific title of "reason," however much the unbeliever would like to appropriate the term.

THE SUPERIORITY OF THE PARADOX TO THE OFFENDED CONSCIOUSNESS

In several respects Climacus views the spat between what he calls the understanding and the paradox as one which is not between equals.

Rather, the paradox occupies a superior position. This is implicit in his characterization of offense as "unhappy love," a love that is analogous to the "misunderstood self-love" discussed in chapter 3. To understand this better, let us return to the analogy with love.

The analogy was, it will be recalled, a proportional equation: faith is to the understanding as love is to self-love. This equation implies that there are formulas for the happy unions of the factors involved. These happy unions will be blocked if the understanding and self-love are in certain conditions. Where a certain kind of self-love is present, then love becomes impossible. Similarly, if the understanding is offended, then faith is impossible and the marriage between the understanding and the paradox cannot be brought about. To understand the force of the analogy for the relations between faith and reason, it would be helpful to understand the romantic situation more precisely. Unfortunately, Climacus says little about the kind of unhappy love he has in mind, so we must largely fend for ourselves.

One comment he does make is that offense, the unhappy love of the understanding for the paradox, "is only like the unhappy love which has its basis in misunderstood self-love; the analogy stretches no further since the power of accident is capable of nothing here,…"[14] I think it is clear from this that he has in mind a case where the unhappiness of love is due to factors internal to the lovers and over which some control is possible. That is, he does not want to consider cases in which the lovers are separated by external factors, such as social conditions over which they have no control, but the case in which something within the lovers make it impossible for them to come together. This means that in the analogous case of offense, what might be termed external factors also must be ruled out. This means that a person who has never had the opportunity to hear about Christianity, or who rejects it because social and cultural factors similarly not subject to his or her control produce a distorted understanding of faith, is not offended in Climacus' sense. Offense must be traceable to something within the offended person.

But to return to the case of romantic love, what is this "misunderstood self-love?" What does it mean for self-love to "shrink from love?" What underlies Climacus' discussion is his assumption on the one hand that self-love is the basis of love, and on the other hand that love represents a dethroning of self-love that is at the same time its fulfillment. People fall in love while they are seeking their own happiness. To find what they are looking for, however, they must be willing to submerge their own happiness and run the risk that is inherent in linking their happiness to that of another. The person who "shrinks from love" out of self-love is the person who is unwilling to run this risk. He or she clings to self-love and fearfully resists caring for the other, worried that such caring will lead to misery. If I shrink from love in this way it is because I think such a commitment may be misplaced and will make me vulnerable. I will no longer be in control. Climacus asserts that this form of self-love is rooted in misunderstanding. It fails to see that in clinging to self-love it blocks self-love from attaining its own goals.

The application of the analogy to the case of faith and the understanding is interesting and sheds much light on the superior position of the paradox. Belief in the paradox represents the dethroning of the understanding, which here must mean something like "human thinking insofar as this can be carried on independently of the god's revelation." Yet Climacus has told us in chapter 3 that "in its paradoxical passion the understanding does indeed will its own downfall."[15] Once more we have a dethroning that represents a fulfillment. The paradox is supposed to satisfy the deepest longings of the understanding.

The superiority of the paradox to offense lies in the failure of offense to grasp this. Offense clings to the security of imperialistic reason that must retain control, just as selfish self-love clings to the quest for its own happiness, blind to the need for commitment to the other in order to find its own true self. Offense misunderstands the need of reason that it is seeking to fulfill, just as selfish self-love misunderstands the need of the self for happiness. The paradox understands this situation while the offended understanding does not. The inequality lies in the fact that the paradox understands the reaction of the understanding, both in faith and offense, but the offended understanding misunderstands its own relation to the paradox. Believing that it must set itself up as a judge in order to defend its own integrity, the offended understanding fails to see that it is not an independent, disinterested party. Rather, the understanding is a passionate responder to the initiatives of the paradox.

The significance of the echo charge made by the paradox lies here. The dependence and lack of originality of the understanding make it plain that the charges it hurls against the paradox are things it has learned from revelation. The fact that it regards these as objections shows that it has misunderstood its position. All the while, Climacus implies, the understanding suffers in the more ordinary sense; its bitterness and resentment reveal an underlying sense of its own need for the paradox, just as the bitterness of the selfish person who shrinks from love may reveal an underlying sense that true happiness lies in the lover who is being rejected.

These claims seem far from an objective view of the situation. As noted earlier, they seem to be made from the viewpoint of the believer. What we have, in fact, is the kind of depth psychology being applied to the religious skeptic that is more often employed by people like Freud and Nietzsche *against* Christian faith. Climacus seems to be saying that the antireligious person in reality wants what he or she is rejecting. The psychology is a bit thin here, though similar accounts are fleshed out in other Kierkegaardian writings.[16] Nevertheless, what is said is probably sufficient to irritate the unbeliever. What then is the purpose of saying these things?

The main one is I think to underline the passional character of reason. Climacus wants us to look through the understanding's self-portrait as a neutral, objective truth-seeker and see the actual character of imperialistic reason. Such a reason will necessarily come into conflict with Christian faith. Pointing this out to someone in the grip of imperialistic reason will probably do little for that person but anger him. However, perhaps the anger will reveal to that person that he is not so disinterested and objective after all. And understanding the situation will at least remove the temptation for the believer to try to alter the faith to make it acceptable to the offended person. The believer, in other words, should acquire a certain boldness and confidence in the face of certain objections. In fact, the believer should regard these objections as a confirmation of the truth of her faith. At the conclusion of the appendix the interlocutor once more appears and accuses Climacus of plagiarism for citing without credit the words of Hamann, Lactantius, Shakespeare, and Luther.[17] Climacus cheerfully acknowledges the plagiarism but claims that one can see from these authors that a clear understanding of the nature of offense can be found in the nonoffended person. Offense is understood by faith but not vice versa.

Analyzing the character of offense reminds the believer of the dangers of substituting reason for revelation. In Climacus' words, it reminds the believer of the "difference" between reason and the paradox,[18] or the difference between a philosophical worldview and ethic that depends on unaided human thinking, and Christianity, which depends on God's revelation of himself. It is interesting to note that the reason the reminder is needed is that in the happy passion of faith, still not named by Climacus, "the difference is in fact on good terms with the understanding." The formula for this happy passion is now given: "The understanding surrendered itself and the paradox granted itself."[19]

It is important to see that the understanding is not totally passive in this happy relationship. The understanding is not rudely shoved aside by revelation, but in faith learns to surrender itself. Here we can see a theme emerging that I will develop more fully in the next two chapters. Despite the reputation of *Philosophical Fragments* as a book that presents and defends a fideism that exalts irrational faith, Climacus in his own way is suggesting that a faith rooted in a revelation that reason cannot fully understand may indeed be rational.

CHAPTER

7

REASON AND THE PARADOX

In chapter 4 Climacus resumes his "poem" and takes up where chapter 2 had left off by imagining the god has "made his appearance as a teacher" by taking the concrete form of a humble human being, a servant, not in the literal sense, but in the sense of being a common, poor, insignificant person.[1] Climacus pauses briefly to worry about whether a god who devotes himself to such a lofty task, with no worries or anxieties about the daily grind of earning a living and the responsibilities of family life, can be thought to be fully human, and answers affirmatively.[2] The servant form is no mere disguise, for the god has really taken on the state of the learner. The task of the chapter is to give a more concrete account of how the god can carry out his task, and how the learner can become the god's disciple, or follower, as the Hongs usually translate the Danish *Discipel*.[3] The formula for how this occurs has already been given at the conclusion of the appendix to chapter 3, and Climacus reiterates the formula with a slight change in wording: "The understanding and the paradox happily encounter each other in the moment, when the understanding steps aside and the paradox gives itself."[4] This encounter occurs when that "happy passion" that is the alternative to offense is present, a passion that finally here receives the name "faith," though Climacus tells us that the name does not matter much. Faith is now explicitly identified as "the condition" for understanding the truth, the condition that Climacus has, in order to distinguish his hypothesis from the Socratic position, assumed that human beings lack and must receive from the god.

To unpack this formula we must now tackle head-on an issue that was raised and skirted in the discussion of offense in the last chapter, namely the nature of the paradox and its relation to reason. What exactly does it mean to say that the paradox is a paradox? What does it mean to say that in faith the understanding must "step aside" or "yield itself?" These questions are crucial ones, not only for understanding the perspective of Johannes Climacus in *Philosophical Fragments*, but for Kierkegaard's whole authorship. For Kierkegaard is often denigrated (or praised) as an opponent of reason, a fideist who gloried in irrationalism, on the strength of Climacus' remarks here. We could of course argue that the pseudonym protects Kierkegaard from any such charge, since one cannot simply assume that Kierkegaard and Climacus think alike here. Such an argument would have merit; at the very least the critic must produce some reason to think that Climacus does represent Kierkegaard to make such criticism stick. What I should like to do, however, is to see whether the charge of irrationalism can justly be directed to Climacus himself. Without assuming anything about the relationship of Climacus to Kierkegaard, I hope thereby to show that this central section of Kierkegaard's literature cannot justly be read as a glorification of irrationalism. It is true that Climacus presents us with what might be termed a critique of reason, one that is in the spirit of the critiques offered by Nietzsche and Marx, but that critique is one that is ultimately in the service of reason. It is not an attempt at reason's destruction.

IS THE PARADOX A FORMAL CONTRADICTION?

Why is it that faith in the paradox requires reason to "set itself aside?" Climacus says that the difficulty for reason lies in the fact that the paradox involves a "contradiction," the contradiction that the same individual is both the god and a human being: "In order for the teacher to be able to give the condition, he must be the god, and in order to put the learner in possession of it, he must be man. This contradiction is in turn the object of faith and is the paradox, the moment."[5] What exactly does Climacus mean when he calls the incarnation of the god a contradiction? Does Climacus think that the believer in the paradox is someone who abandons the universal validity of logical principles by embracing a *logical* contradiction?

Two contrasting traditions of interpretation have emerged over the years as responses to these questions. Many writers, beginning with David Swenson and continuing with such commentators as Alastair MacKinnon, Cornelio Fabro, and N. H. Søe,[6] have claimed that Climacus[7] is not really an irrationalist, because the paradox he discusses is not a formal, logical contradiction. For them Climacus is asserting that Christianity is above reason, not against reason.

Other writers, both purported friends of Kierkegaard such as Alastair Hannay[8] and rabid critics such as Brand Blanshard,[9] have interpreted the paradox as a logical contradiction. For these writers, when Climacus asks for faith in the paradox, he is asking one to abandon the laws of logic and to embrace something which is known to be false, even impossible. Herbert Garelick is typical of many: "This Paradox is the ultimate challenge to the intellect, for all attempts to understand it must conform to the laws of judgment and discourse: identity, contradiction, and excluded middle. Yet the Paradox violates these laws.... Rationally, the statement 'God-man' is a nonsensical statement."[10] Clearly, on this reading, faith is more properly described as being against reason than above reason.

I shall try to give a convincing demonstration that Garelick and others who share his reading of Climacus are wrong. I shall show that Climacus does not mean a formal, logical contradiction when he speaks of the paradox of the incarnation. However, that is only half of my task. I must then explain what Climacus does mean by "paradox" in a manner which does justice to his claims that there is a tension between reason and the paradox. I must account for the tension between reason and the paradox while at the same time showing that this tension is not a necessary opposition. In carrying out this task, I shall keep chapter 4 of *Fragments* as my main focus, but it will be helpful to look at other parts of the book and to look several times at *Concluding Unscientific Postscript*, also by Climacus, to clarify his terminology. Occasionally I shall take note of other works of Kierkegaard that critics have perceived as relevant to the issues.

A case that Climacus does mean a formal, logical contradiction can of course be made. Sometimes the case hinges on the commentator's own belief that the incarnation *is* a logical contradiction. Someone who believes this might naturally assume that Kierkegaard must have discerned this as well. Louis Pojman, for example, says that the paradox is "the uniquely absurd proposition that has the most objective evidence against it."[11] The objective evidence against the paradox is simply that it is or entails a logical contradiction. The argument that this is so relies on Pojman's own view of God and human persons, however. Pojman, not Kierkegaard, says that since God is infinite, eternal, and unchanging, and human beings are finite, noneternal, and changing, "God and man are mutually exclusive genuses."[12]

Support for Pojman's argument here is provided by the fact that Climacus does describe God as unchanging and eternal, and human beings as finite and temporal. One may well conclude from this that God and man *appear* to be mutually exclusive genuses. However, what appears to be the case is not always the case, and there are reasons to be cautious about drawing the conclusion Pojman draws here. One is that two of the qualities Pojman alludes to here, eternality and temporality, in the *Postscript* are described by Climacus as the constituents of human life generally, not just the incarnation.[13] So, Climacus does not necessarily equate temporality with being noneternal, as Pojman illicitly assumes. The paradoxicalness of the incarnation thus mirrors a paradoxicalness which is generically present in human existence, and it is implausible to claim that Climacus understands human existence itself as a logical contradiction, even though he does describe existence as a "contradiction."[14]

Certainly, Climacus claims in many passages that the paradox is a contradiction; the incarnation is even described as a self-contradiction.[15] The logical or formalist reading of "contradiction" is supported by the frequent claims that the contradiction consists in the fact that what is eternal has become historical. The strongest statement to this effect is in the *Postscript*, where Climacus says that the contradiction consists in the fact that the eternal can only become historical by "going against its own nature."[16] A statement almost this strong is found in *Fragments*, where Climacus asserts that the contradiction is that an eternal condition is regarded as something that is acquired in time.[17] The paradox is, moreover, often designated in the *Postscript* as the "absurd," though not, interestingly enough, in *Fragments*.[18]

WHY THE PARADOX IS NOT A
FORMAL CONTRADICTION

Despite this support for the "against reason" view, I think an over-whelmingly strong case can be made for the claim that Climacus does not mean "logical contradiction" when he claims that the incarnation is a paradox. The evidence for this is of two kinds: textual evidence and more general arguments derived from an overall understanding of the project of Climacus.

Textual Evidence

The first point which must be taken into account is that the terms "contradiction" and "self-contradiction" (*Modsigelse* and *Selvmodsigelse*) are not generally used by Climacus to refer to what we would today term a logical contradiction. He does sometimes use the terms in this sense, and when he does, he appears to hold firmly to the principle that a contradiction cannot be affirmed. (I will say more about this later.) Frequently, however, he uses the term contradiction to refer to something that is evidently not a logical contradiction. For example, in the "Interlude" Climacus says that "coming into existence" is a "contradiction."[19] Thus, the mere fact that Climacus often refers to the paradox as a contradiction does very little to support the idea that the paradox is a logical contradiction. Climacus' usage may seem sloppy to a contemporary reader, but he is here, as at so many points, following the Hegelians, who notoriously used the term "contradiction" in a very broad manner.[20] Climacus (and other Kierkegaardian pseudonyms) regularly uses the term "contradiction" to refer to what might today be designated as an "incongruity," with formal, logical contradictions seen as a species of the incongruous.

This can be clearly seen in the discussion of humor and the comical in Climacus' *Postscript*. The comical is defined as a "painless contradiction,"[21] and in a lengthy footnote which follows, Climacus gives numerous examples of contradictions, none of which are formal or logical contradictions. We already noted in chapter 1 the example of a caricature, which is said to be comical because of the "contradiction between likeness and unlikeness" it contains, as well as the case of the man who falls into a cellar while looking up at a window. Here the "contradiction" is between his upward gaze and downward ascent. Seeing the shadow of a man with whom you are conversing is said to be comical because in the shadow you both see the man and yet are aware that it is not him. A fairy-tale character described as seven and one quarter yards tall is said to be comical because the exactness implied by the use of the fraction is contradictory to the distance from reality which is associated with the fairy tale. All of these contradictions are clearly cases of incongruity, not formal, logical contradictions.

Furthermore, on some of the occasions when Climacus does speak of formal, logical contradictions, it is in the context of a defense of the Aristotelian position that the law of noncontradiction must be upheld. In the *Postscript* Climacus' polemic against Hegel is that there are genuine either-or's; not every opposition can be intellectually mediated so that one can reach the position of both-and. This polemic depends on a resolute defense of the principle of noncontradiction and the consequent existence of "absolute distinctions." In *Philosophical Fragments* Climacus says that it is "an unshakable insistence on the absolute and on absolute distinctions that makes a person a good dialectician,"[22] though this has been forgotten in our age because of our failure to take the principle of noncontradiction seriously. Aristotle's argument that one must assume the principle of noncontradiction even to deny it is put forward.[23] In a blast at the theology of his day, which by denying the principle was able to have its cake and eat it too on many crucial issues, Climacus, in alluding to *King Lear*, crisply affirms that saying yes and no at the same time is not good theology.[24]

Not only does Climacus defend the law of noncontradiction. He explicitly distinguishes between a formal, logical self-contradiction and the kind of contradiction which constitutes the paradox. In the course of his discussion of the incarnation, Climacus analyzes how people become believers or disciples. The contemporary generation of believers will obviously receive the condition of faith directly from the God. But what about subsequent generations? Is it possible that they receive the condition of faith from their immediate historical predecessors, who have passed on to them the historical report? Climacus denies this is possible, and the ground of his denial is that this proposal is self-contradictory and "meaningless," *in a different sense than the paradox itself is said to be contradictory.*[25] If the later disciple receives the condition of faith from the earlier generation, this would in effect make the earlier generation the god, which contradicts the supposition that the earlier generation had received the condition from the god, and was therefore *not* itself god.

> That meaninglessness [that the later generation receives the con-
> dition of faith from the earlier generation], however, is unthinkable
> in a different sense than when we state that that fact [the incar-
> nation] and the single individual's relation to the god are unthink-
> able. Our hypothetical assumption of that fact and the single
> individual's relation to the god contains no self-contradiction, and
> thus thought can become preoccupied with it as with the strangest
> possible thing. That meaningless consequence, however, contains a
> self-contradiction; it is not satisfied with positing something unrea-
> sonable, which is our hypothetical assumption, but within this un-
> reasonableness it produces a self-contradiction: that the god is the
> god for the contemporary, but the contemporary in turn is the god
> for a third.[26]

I believe that the same distinction between a formal contradiction and the kind of contradiction which is found in the paradox is implicit in an often-quoted but somewhat obscure passage in *Postscript*,[27] where Climacus attempts to distinguish between nonsense and the incom-prehensible. One can believe the incomprehensible but reason protects one against believing nonsense, says Climacus. A similar distinction between the incarnation as a "contradiction" and a formal contradiction can be found in at least one Kierkegaardian passage from Anti-Climacus.[28]

Arguments from Climacus' General Strategy

Seeing that the paradox is not for Climacus a formal contradiction is not merely a matter of proof-texting. Reflection on his overall per-spective shows how inappropriate it is to think of the incarnation as such a contradiction. One of the key points in Climacus' treatment of the incarnation is its uniqueness. The incarnation is not just a paradox; it is the absolute paradox and as such is absolutely unique. Explaining what Climacus means by this is no easy matter, and he gives little in the way of argument for this uniqueness. Nevertheless, it is obvious that such uniqueness is not served by treating the paradoxicalness of the incarnation as a formal contradiction. Such contradictions are not only not unique; they can be generated at will. Even Louis Pojman sees this and raises it as a criticism of Kierkegaard,[29] who is identified with Climacus by Pojman, but it serves rather to undermine Pojman's assumption that Kierkegaard must mean by contradiction what Pojman thinks he means.

Even more fundamentally, if the paradox is a formal contradiction and can be known to be such, the assumption that undergirds the B hypothesis of *Philosophical Fragments*, which is that human beings lack the Truth, would be undermined. Those who assume that the incarnation is a logical contradiction believe that we have a clear understanding of what it means to be God and what it means to be a human being. God is infinite, eternal, all-knowing; human beings are finite, temporal, limited in their knowledge. Thus we can know that the predicates "God" and "human being" are logically exclusive. All this assumes that we have a reliable, natural knowledge of both God and human beings.

However, as we have seen, Climacus' B hypothesis constitutes a radical challenge to this assumption. The whole of *Philosophical Fragments* is a development of a thought-experiment on the following lines. Socrates had proposed that the Truth, the eternal truth, which for Kierkegaard means the knowledge of God, was present within human beings already. Climacus tries to think through the logical implications of denying this Socratic assumption. He wants to explore the contrary assumption that human beings lack the truth about God and therefore must receive that truth from a revelation which comes directly from God. Thus chapter 3, which develops the notion of the incarnation as a paradox, consistently looks at God as the unknown,[30] that which autonomous, unaided human reason cannot know.

The irony here is clear. In order to know that the incarnation is a formal, logical contradiction we would have to have the kind of knowledge of God which it is the point of the incarnation to deny we possess. One cannot know that a round square is a contradictory concept without a clear concept of roundness and squareness. Similarly, one cannot know that the concept of the God-man is contradictory without a clear concept of both the divine and the human.

WHAT IS THE PARADOX?

We can now understand what Climacus does mean by calling the incarnation a paradox and also lay a basis for seeing why he thinks that there is a tension between the paradox and human reason. A paradox is something that we cannot understand or comprehend. A paradox is something that may *appear* to us to be a contradiction. In general the discovery of a paradox is the result of an encounter with a reality which our concepts are inadequate to deal with, a reality that ties us in a conceptual knot. When we try to understand it we may find ourselves saying self-contradictory things, but of course this does not mean that the reality we have encountered is itself self-contradictory. It means that there is a problem with our conceptual equipment.

If one is convinced that our conceptual equipment is in order, then the natural response to a paradoxical reality will be to dismiss it. For exactly this reason, those who think our natural understanding of God is adequate will naturally resist the suggestion that we can only understand God through a revelation from God. For such people, the paradox is truly "against reason."

To understand this reaction consider again the parallel case, used briefly in chapter 6, of a mind-body dualist who believes that our concept of consciousness logically entails that thinking must inhere in a nonphysical substance which is the subject of consciousness. Suppose this dualist encounters a materialist who believes that the subject of thinking is simply the brain. To the dualist, the notion of a thinking brain is a logical contradiction. The materialist might respond as follows: To you the idea of a thinking brain is paradoxical; it appears to be a contradiction. The problem, however, does not lie in the reality of a thinking brain, but in your constricted concept of the mental.[31]

In exactly the same manner, the believer in the incarnation may respond to the unbeliever: the idea of God becoming a man is paradoxical to you; it may even appear to be a logical contradiction. The problem lies in your constricted conception of God, and more specifically, in your assumption that you understand who God is and what God can and cannot do.

Of course there must be some carry-over between our prior understanding of God and the new understanding which results from our encounter with the God in time, just as there must be some carry-over from our earlier, dualistic concept of the mental to a materialistic concept of the mental. Otherwise, the term "God" in the expression "God-man" would be utterly meaningless, as would "mind" in the analogous "material mind." But this requirement is compatible with rather drastic conceptual transformations. No one today wishes to argue that it is impossible for an atom to be split on conceptual grounds, yet no concept could originally have been more paradoxical than that of an indivisible, smallest unit of matter being divided.

THE TENSION BETWEEN REASON
AND THE PARADOX

We are now in a position to see why Climacus frequently talks of faith in the incarnation as against reason, rather than simply being above reason. Faith is said to be against reason because all of us are in a position in this matter analogous to the dualist who is offended by the notion of a thinking brain. All of us have a strong tendency to think that our ideas about God, or whatever is ultimate and finally important to us, are adequate, or that if they are not, at least that we possess the "condition," the ability to make progress toward such truth.

The B hypothesis must label this confidence in our own rational capacities in this area as sin, since the essence of sin is a prideful assertion of our own independence and autonomy over against God. Since the B hypothesis begins with the assumption that human beings lack the Truth, and therefore are all sinners, it naturally thinks that there will be tension between our human thinking, dominated as it is by an assertion of our own autonomy, and Christian faith, which implies that our intellectual capacities in this area are essentially impaired. Human beings are sinful, and their sinfulness not only blocks them from a proper understanding of God; it is the ground of the natural tension between human reason and the paradox. The difference, the absolute qualitative difference between God and man which makes the idea of the God-man offensive to us is plainly said to derive from human sinfulness,[32] not the metaphysical qualities cited by Pojman as the heart of the paradox. Hence, there is a natural tension between human reason and the paradox, but it is a tension which does not rest on any rational knowledge of the nature of God. It rests rather on what one might call the natural self-confidence of reason.

Note carefully that I am not saying that apart from sin God would be fully comprehensible to human beings. God's nature and the love which God makes evident in the incarnation may surpass the capacities of human reason. However, for an unfallen reason, just as for reason transformed by faith, this unfathomability is not a problem. In this situation reason recognizes the natural "difference" between the infinite and itself and understands its own inability to understand. The "difference" that creates the tension is not this natural difference; it is the difference between the God who unselfishly gives and sacrifices all for the learner and the human being who demands the fulfillment of his own desires, and who, desperately seeking to control and dominate, cannot understand the one who cares only for the other.

We can see now what Climacus means by calling the paradox of the incarnation the *absolute* paradox. One difficulty with the "logical contradiction" view of the paradox is that it cannot explain what is "absolute" or unique about the paradox of the incarnation. Though it is not easy to make sense of what Climacus says here, I believe that the uniqueness of the incarnation is closely related to its capacity to offend us because of our sinfulness. The idea is that the incarnation is naturally shocking to human beings because of sin, so it is not an idea that one would expect any human being to invent. Some paradoxes are relative in the sense that they are paradoxical to some people but not to others. This paradox is absolute in the sense that it is not grounded on some relative intellectual deficit, but on a characteristic that is universally present in human beings. The conceptual inadequacy in question is not one that could be remedied by a little education or hard thinking, as might be the case for other paradoxes, such the paradox of the "material mind."

One could wish that Climacus had said more about the question of why it is that sinfulness makes the incarnation incomprehensible to us. He does suggest in at least one passage that the paradox should be understood in terms of probability, as "the most improbable of all things."[33] This passage supports the idea that the paradox is not a formal or logical contradiction, since such a contradiction is not merely improbable, but impossible. Why does the incarnation appear so improbable to us? Climacus does not really say, but a plausible answer is provided by another Kierkegaardian pseudonym, Anti-Climacus, in his discussion of offense.[34] The answer is roughly this: the incarnation represents the epitome of pure, selfless love. As sinful beings we are incapable of such love and have never experienced it. Hence our sense of what is probable, conditioned by our past experience, is decidedly against the likelihood of such a love being actual. It simply appears to be too good to be true. This answer explains the "infinite difference" between God and human beings as a function of human sinfulness, as Climacus does, and makes the improbability of the incarnation to be a function of that same sinfulness.

CAN REASON HAVE LIMITS?

If I am right in my contentions, then the common view of Climacus (and frequently Kierkegaard, when the two are identified) as an irrationalist rests on a misreading and is not adequately supported, at least to the degree that the charge is grounded in the view that Climacus urges religious believers to violate the laws of logic. Of course it may still be the case that the label "irrationalist" is an appropriate one for Climacus. Whether that is so, on my reading, depends heavily on whether it is irrational to urge that reason is limited, for that claim *is* certainly made by Climacus, or at least it is part and parcel of the hypothesis he is constructing and which he evidently regards as coherent. Is what I have termed the natural self-confidence of reason healthy self-esteem or arrogant imperialism?

An assertion that reason is limited is surely not enough in itself to convict a thinker of irrationalism. Otherwise, Kant and the Wittgenstein of the *Tractatus*, among others, would stand guilty. The answer must surely lie in what the limits are said to be and how they are drawn.

Climacus' writings are often pictured as Kierkegaard's attempt to save religious belief by locating it in an enclave which is marked "off limits" to reason.[35] The assertion that what lies behind the boundary is impervious to reason is itself made dogmatically. This kind of attitude is foreign to Climacus, as well as Kierkegaard, though it is present in many who are allegedly influenced by S.K. Climacus actually stigmatizes the attempt of well-meaning religious people to demarcate a creed, sacred book, or person as an ultimate, unchallengeable authority as "superstition and narrowness of spirit."[36] Though he recognizes the human need for something "really firm" that is impervious to rational reflection, he regards this need as a weakness and says it is incompatible with the kind of subjective concern which he regards as the foundation of the authentic religious life.

Although Climacus argues that the incarnation is something which cannot be rationally understood, he regards this claim as itself one which is subject to rational scrutiny. One cannot rationally understand the paradox, but one can hope rationally to understand why the paradox cannot be understood.[37] In other words, the claim that reason has limits must itself be a claim that reason can adjudicate. Of course reason could be limited in a variety of ways. We have already made a distinction between a possible inability to understand the incarnation that is grounded in finitude and an inability to understand that can be traced to the attitudes and assumptions rooted in sin. It is the latter sort of limit that is relevant, since it is the source of the tension between reason and the paradox, and so it is the kind of limit with which reason must be able to come to terms.

It is crucial to remember that Climacus does not think that the tension between human reason and the paradox is a necessary tension. To maintain its integrity, Christianity must always retain the possibility of offense, but this is only a possibility, not a necessity. For the believer, it is a temptation, but to the degree that one is a believer, it is a temptation which has been surmounted. Faith is described as a happy passion in which reason and the paradox are on good terms. The accord between reason and the paradox is possible in the case where "reason sets itself aside."[38] In other words, there is no conflict between faith and reason if reason can accept the limitations of reason. This claim of Climacus that reason and faith can have a happy relationship means that Climacus' perspective is ultimately consistent with Kierkegaard's statement, often quoted by partisans of the above-reason interpretation of the paradox: "When the believer has faith, the absurd is not the absurd."[39]

In the last chapter we saw how Climacus explicates this happy relationship through an extended proportional analogy, in which reason is said to be related to faith as self-love is to love. This analogy is important enough to be worth reiterating: "Self-love lies at the basis of love, but at its highest point wills precisely its own destruction. This is what love wants too, so these two powers are in agreement with each other in the moment of passion, and this passion is precisely love."[40] There is often a tension between self-love and genuine love, but the tension is not a necessary one. When a person falls in love, the initial ground or basis of the love is self-love; people fall in love because they are seeking their own happiness. The paradox is that when they genuinely do fall in love, self-love is transcended, dethroned, as it were. The person gains happiness in sacrificing happiness for the sake of the loved one. Thus, when genuine love is present, love and self-love are united.

Similarly, in faith the understanding is dethroned; it must recognize its limits. "To that degree the understanding will have much to object to," just as a selfish person in the grip of self-love may "shrink from love."[41] Yet Climacus suggests that the dethroning of the understanding is at the same time what the understanding itself desires; it is a kind of fulfillment of the understanding, just as love fulfills self-love.

The clear implication of this is that the recognition of the limits of reason can itself be rational, at least under certain conditions, those conditions being the presence of the passion of faith, whose formula is repeated several times: the understanding yields itself, the paradox grants itself.[42] What is important here is that the understanding yields *itself*.

HOW IS FAITH ACQUIRED?

What is this condition? How does one acquire it? We have seen that the acquisition of faith is in some respects like the conceptual transformation one might undergo in becoming a materialist with respect to the mind-body problem, so it might be helpful to ask how a similar transformation might be made with respect to that issue. How might a convinced mind-body dualist be convinced that materialism is true, and that his conceptual difficulties with it are rooted in a problem with his conceptual equipment and beliefs, rather than being rooted in problems with materialism? Obviously, no easy answer to this question is possible. The reasons for the change will be complex, but I think one component will be central in any plausible account. There is no guarantee that anything will work, but if such a change is to be made, the central motivation will come from an encounter with reality. Dualism cannot be falsified by any crucial experiment, but if a transformation is to occur, it will be motivated by new factual discoveries about the brain, which show that one's previous assumptions simply are not adequate to deal with reality, or at least that these assumptions are not pragmatically effective any longer.

Of course as Climacus tells the story there is a strong disanalogy between the mind-body case and the case of Christian faith. The dualist is asked to give up convictions which are very important to him, but he is not asked to give up the assumption that he has at least the ability to revise his conceptual structure to make it adequate. The Christian revelation, on the other hand, says to human understanding that it must recognize, not only that it lacks the Truth, but lacks the ability to make progress toward the Truth so long as it proceeds on its own steam. Its conceptual equipment with respect to ultimate religious truth is not only flawed, but irremediably broken, so long as it imperialistically insists on its autonomy and denies its brokenness.

Nevertheless, despite this disanalogy, I believe that the question "How does one acquire faith and arrive at the condition in which reason can understand the reasonableness of recognizing its limits?" can be answered in a way that is quite parallel to the way the corresponding question for the mind-body case can be answered. At least this is what Climacus says. One acquires the passion through an encounter with reality, a first-person meeting with the God himself. The God must grant the condition.[43] Just as one might conceivably learn that brains think by encountering a brain that thinks, so one might learn that God became a man by encountering the God-man. The disanalogy is that in the brain case it is fundamentally my thinking that gets transformed. In the case of the absolute paradox, my thinking is also transformed by the encounter, but this happens via a transformation of myself in which my fundamental cares and attitudes are altered.

Climacus says that this transformation is not an act of will on the part of the believer,[44] even though he clearly thinks that an act of will (or perhaps repeated acts of will) is necessary for it to occur, because it is not an act which the agent can simply carry out on his or her own. The ability to believe requires something which the believer can only receive directly from the god. Faith represents a discontinuity with the past and what one has received through one's natural endowments and experiences.

In a similar way, Climacus denies that faith amounts to knowledge.[45] I think he means that the conceptual transformation which is required here is too drastic to be assimilated to ordinary transformations in the person's intellectual life. Normally, when I come to know something, what is known is certified by standards of evidence and past beliefs. In the case of faith, however, the transformation is qualitatively different, since what is being transformed is precisely my confidence in those standards of evidence and past beliefs. My standards of probability and evidence are themselves brought into question. Furthermore, as we have noted, in this case the intellectual transformation is not fundamental but derivative from a transformation of the whole person that can be described as moral or spiritual.

One way of illuminating the intellectual change that does occur is to employ the distinction Alvin Plantinga has made between evidence and grounds. Plantinga has defended the claim that belief in God may be properly basic for some people.[46] This means that these people do not believe in God on the basis of evidence. Rather this belief is itself one of the basic beliefs in their noetic structure. It might seem that such beliefs would be arbitrary and that there would be no way to determine whether such a belief is justified or not. Plantinga thinks this is not the case. He says that though such a belief is not based on evidence, it may still have a ground.[47] The belief that God cares for me, for example, may be grounded in an experience in which I become aware of God's providential care. Such an experience is not considered by Plantinga to be evidence, for it is not a proposition which has any evidential relationship to the propositional belief it grounds. The experience is not an argument for the belief, and perhaps cannot be transformed into any kind of philosophical argument, and certainly does not need to be thus transformed. Rather, the experience is one which transforms the experiencer. It causes him to be aware of God's loving care for him.

In a similar way Climacus argues that faith in the incarnation may be basic and not the result of historical evidence. Evidence is neither necessary nor sufficient to produce the transformation of the individual.[48] It is the experience of meeting God which produces the passion of faith. This passion transforms the learner and makes possible a new set of beliefs. It is possible, of course, that the believer may be, perhaps usually is, presented with evidence in the course of this encounter, but what is essential is the encounter itself. Such an encounter may properly be said to be the ground of faith without constituting evidence for faith.

Climacus supports his claims here with some thought experiments. He imagines a person who is a contemporary of the god who has "limited his sleep to the shortest possible time" and hired a "hundred secret agents" in order to spy on the god and keep detailed historical records of his every movement. Another contemporary has a similar group of employees to keep track of every word of the god's teaching. No greater historical knowledge can be imagined, but Climacus claims that such knowledge is by no means sufficient to make either of these two characters genuine disciples of the god.[49]

On the other side of the coin, Climacus imagines someone who was out of the country during most of the god's stay and only is able to see the god when the god is dying. This historical ignorance would be no barrier to his receiving the condition "if the moment was for him the decision of eternity."[50] Hence, no special amount of historical knowledge is necessary for faith, either.

Here, Climacus must walk a fine line, for if he removes the necessity for the historical altogether, he is back to the Socratic position, as he himself clearly recognizes. His way of resolving this problem is a claim that though for the disciple the external form of the god is important, the detail of that form is not.[51] The disciple must have a historical point of departure for his or her transformation. Without that we do indeed return to the Socratic position that the Truth is within us already. So the "news of the day is the beginning of eternity."[52] The details of this historical point of departure are, however, insignificant, "so long as the moment still remains as the point of departure for the eternal."[53] The question of how much detail must remain for this to occur is not addressed here, but is in chapter 5, and we shall therefore postpone any discussion of this question until later.

HISTORICAL CONTEMPORARIES AND REAL CONTEMPORARIES

The account Climacus gives of faith as the result of a first-person encounter with the god is, I think, faithful to the experience of many Christian believers. His account of the role played by historical evidence in becoming a disciple implies that historical contemporaneity, which might seem to be a decided advantage in becoming a disciple, turns out to be no advantage at all. Contemporaries may have more historical knowledge, but such knowledge does not necessarily lead to faith; a later disciple may have little historical information, but this ignorance is no barrier to faith. What is crucial is that whatever historical knowledge the person has must become more than historical knowledge; it must become the occasion for an encounter with the god that transforms the learner.

Climacus works this out by distinguishing between a historical contemporary of the god and a "real" or genuine contemporary. The person who has received the condition from the god via a first-hand encounter, whether a historical contemporary or not, is a genuine contemporary. He knows the god and is known by him.[54] The glory of the god is not something like the splendid wedding feast of a great emperor, which anyone would count himself or herself fortunate to have been able to experience. For such a wedding feast a historical contemporary has a real advantage over those who must rely on historical accounts.[55] The glory of the god, however, cannot be seen directly with one's physical eyes, but only with the eyes of faith.

The interlocutor reappears at this point to object that it is presumptuous of the god to claim that his knowledge determines who is a contemporary of his.[56] Climacus patiently explains once more that the god cannot be seen directly with one's physical eyes, but only through the faith that the god himself must provide. Thus, being known by the god is a necessary condition for real contemporaneity. This account of the value of contemporaneity or lack thereof has obvious implications for the case of the disciple of a later generation, implications which the interlocutor claims to have immediately discerned.[57] The interlocutor appears to be a rather dim, if well-read, person, and Climacus seems a bit skeptical of this claim. In any case, testing it allows Climacus to discuss the issue of the later disciple at length in chapter 5, and we will accordingly consider the issue again in due course.

Why do I claim that the account Climacus gives of how someone becomes a believer corresponds to the experience of many Christian believers? It is because most Christians, at least of those who have made a conscious choice, do trace their conversion to something that could be described as an encounter with Jesus Christ. Very few would trace their conversion to historical evidence. While it is not unusual for Christians to be interested in historical apologetics, such an interest is usually the outcome of faith, not the ground of it. The following account[58] from Anthony Bloom, a Metropolitan of the Russian Orthodox Church, who was transformed from a militant atheist to a believer, is typical in form, if not the details:

> While I was reading the beginning of St. Mark's Gospel, before I reached the third chapter, I suddenly became aware that on the other side of my desk there was a presence. And the certainty was so strong that it was Christ standing there that it has never left me. This was the real turning point. Because Christ was alive and I had been in his presence I could say with certainty that what the Gospel said about the crucifixion of the prophet of Galilee was true, and the centurion was right when he said, "Truly he is the Son of God." It was in the light of the Resurrection that I could read with certainty the story of the Gospel, knowing that everything was true in it because the impossible event of the resurrection was to me more certain than any event of history. History I had to believe, the Resurrection I knew for a fact. I did not discover, as you see, the Gospel beginning with its first message of the Annunciation, and it did not unfold for me as a story which one can believe or disbelieve. It began as an event that left all problems of disbelief behind because it was a direct and personal experience.[59]

This account may not seem Climacean in all respects, particularly in its emphasis on the resurrection, which Climacus certainly does not talk much about. (Though I think that the strong emphasis Climacus places on receiving the condition in a first-hand encounter with a living God certainly presupposes the resurrection, when the details of the Christian story fill out the B hypothesis.) However, in its essentials Bloom's story illustrates the points in Climacus I wish to stress. The primary notion is that faith is the result of a first-person encounter with Christ. In Bloom's account, this encounter comes by means of a historical record, rooted in the accounts of contemporaries and passed down frqm generation to generation, but that record is merely the means. This is precisely the formula Climacus gives for the acquisition of faith: "The person who comes later believes *by means of* (the occasion) the report of the contemporary, by the power of the condition he himself receives from the God."[60] Bloom would seem to be a genuine contemporary of Christ, while obviously failing to be a historical contemporary in the ordinary sense.

It is also clear in this account that Bloom's faith is basic for him in the way Plantinga describes, yet it nevertheless clearly has a ground, namely the experience. Bloom clearly does not decide to believe the historical account as a result of evidence for its trustworthiness; rather he comes to evaluate the historical trustworthiness of the account on the basis of his encounter with a living Christ. Notice also the characteristic Climacean perspective on faith as a certainty concerning something which from one perspective appears absurd, or, in Bloom's words, impossible.

Bloom's account may not seem typical of the experience of believers to some. It is perhaps more dramatic, more "mystical" than most conversions. However, these differences do not seem significant to me, and they are not features that Climacus' account requires to be present or absent.

In the Interlude between chapters 4 and 5 Climacus analyzes faith or belief as something that involves the will, an analysis that corresponds nicely with the well-known description of faith in the *Postscript* as a "leap." This term is often thought to express a view of faith as a sheer choice to believe something with no basis for the choice at all. We shall examine the role of the will in coming to faith more closely in the next chapter, but we can already see that the leap of faith is hardly a blind leap into the dark. The believer knows both what he is leaping to and why he is leaping. To anticipate one of the arguments of the next chapter, faith does not require a kind of immoral manipulation of my belief structure, as some have charged.[61] The person of faith is not someone who tries to make herself believe something she knows is not true, or something she has no reason to think is true. Rather, she is someone who now has good reason to mistrust her earlier ideas about what is true, as a result of an encounter with reality that has fundamentally altered the dominant passions that form the core of her being and shape her thinking.

Why then is will necessary? Actually, in the account Climacus gives of the acquisition of faith in chapter 4, there is almost no talk of will, other than the negative claim we have mentioned already, namely that faith cannot be identified with an act of human willing. The whole chapter could in fact be read as preparation for a thorough-going doctrine of predestination, so strongly does Climacus emphasize the primacy of the god's actions and the impotence of human effort. This impression is, however, qualified in the Interlude. There, as we shall see, Climacus allows a role to human will because of a desire to protect human freedom. The transforming encounter with the God in time makes it possible for an individual to recognize the bankruptcy of imperialistic reason, but it does not make it necessary.[62]

If we take seriously the notion that the source of the difficulty in believing the incarnation is sin, then the troubles humans have in believing in the incarnation have very little to do with esoteric meta-physical conceptual puzzles. We have trouble believing because we are selfish and we have trouble comprehending an action which is pure unselfishness. We have trouble believing because we are proud and do not wish to recognize that there are realities which we are unable to grasp. All this may be mostly implicit in *Philosophical Fragments*, but it is quite consistent with the perspective adopted by another Kierke-gaardian pseudonym, Anti-Climacus. In *Training in Christianity* Anti-Climacus gives example after example of offense, and in every case the negative reaction can be traced to moral attitudes on the part of the offended party.[63] In *The Sickness unto Death* the point is made just as clearly: "The real reason people are offended by Christianity is that it is too high, because its goal is not the goal of human persons, because it wants to make a human being into something so extraordinary that he cannot grasp the thought."[64]

CONCLUSION: UNDERMINING NEUTRALITY

So is the paradox above reason or against reason? In a sense it is both. It is above reason in that finite human beings cannot understand how God could become a human person. It is against reason in that our concrete human thinking, permeated by our sense of what is likely and unlikely, which is in turn shaped by our own selfishness and experience of others' selfishness, judges the possibility as the "strangest of all things." However, it is not against reason in the sense of being against the laws of logic. Or at least that is what the believer thinks. For one cannot think that what has actually occurred is impossible, and the believer believes in the reality of the God-man.

Of course the unbeliever does not believe it has occurred, and we have seen that the incarnation is likely to appear to him to be a formal contradiction. So perhaps the answer to the question, "Is Climacus an irrationalist?" will depend on who is answering the question. Such a view corresponds with Climacus' own conclusions on the matter. His main concern is certainly not to argue for the reasonableness of Christianity; nor is it to maintain that Christianity is unreasonable. It is to argue the impossibility of neutrality. When reason encounters the paradox, faith and offense are both possible; what is not possible is indifference.[65]

It is important, however, not to allow offense to disguise its reaction as purely rational, a straightforward logical deduction. Allowing offense to hide behind logic is like allowing a presidential candidate to wrap himself in patriotism and the flag, and thereby evade having to deal with the real issues. The ground of offense is not pure logic, but pride and self-assertiveness, a confidence in the unlimited powers of human reason. Here we see once more the importance of the message of the "Appendix" to chapter 3 of *Philosophical Fragments*, "An Acoustic Illusion," in which it is argued that reason would like to pose as the neutral authority which has exposed the absurdity of the paradox. In fact, the tension between reason and the paradox is a tension which reason has learned about through revelation. Faith and offense are passions, and neither passion—indeed no passion at all—can be derived from the laws of logic.

Perhaps the best way of answering the question as to whether Climacus sees faith as against reason is to say that it depends on what one means by "reason." If one thinks of reason as a timeless, godlike faculty, the answer is that faith is not against reason in this sense, because reason in this sense does not exist in human beings. It is a myth. If one thinks of reason as simply thinking in accordance with the laws of logic, faith is not necessarily against reason either. But if one thinks of reason as the concrete thinking of human beings, shaped as it is by our basic beliefs and attitudes, then there is a tension between reason and faith, one which can be eliminated only at the cost of the identification of Christianity with what Kierkegaard will later call Christendom.

Climacus in this respect resembles a sociologist of knowledge. The term "reason," like "knowledge" and "logic," often functions as an instrument of control. Those with social power attempt to legitimate their ways of seeing and acting in the world by identifying their commitments with abstractions like reason and logic. Climacus says that Christians think that, because of sin, the established attitudes, values, and beliefs which will dominate the designation of what is "rational" will necessarily come into conflict with Christian faith. The possibility of a cultural critique thus stands or falls with the possibility of a critical examination of these established patterns of thinking.

Fortunately, no human being is identical with something called Logic or Reason. We are flesh and blood creatures, finite and temporal, as Climacus in the *Postscript* is constantly reminding the speculative philosopher. It is a constant temptation for us, however, to attempt to evade responsibility for our commitments by attributing them to these ghostly substantives. To interpret Climacus' paradox as a logical contradiction is to give in to this temptation and subvert his reminder that human thinking is always carried on by existing individuals.

CHAPTER

8

BELIEF AND THE WILL

The "Interlude" between chapters 4 and 5 of *Philosophical Fragments* rivals chapter 3 for the honor of being the most difficult and obscure section of the book. The difficulty here, however, is of a different type. In chapter 3 the chief problem lay in determining the overall point of the chapter and its place in the book as a whole. The individual sentences and paragraphs were, with some exceptions, clear enough, but the purpose of the chapter was not. The problem with the Interlude is just the reverse. The place of the Interlude in the structure of the book is not too difficult to determine, and its overall point is likewise accessible. The prose is, however, easily the most philosophically dense in the book.

The alleged function of the Interlude is to give the reader the illusion that some time has passed, so that one can move smoothly from the problem of how the historical contemporary of the god becomes a disciple to the problem of how a member of a later generation might become a disciple. The actual function seems to be to protect the view of faith sketched out against certain possible objections, by analyzing the nature of historical knowledge and belief. In this section Climacus, under the ruse of amusing the reader, "shortening the time to fill it up,"[1] indulges his philosophical, speculative nature and treats a host of profound philosophical issues in a breathtakingly brief compass.

Climacus begins with metaphysics, discussing the nature of possibility and necessity and the character of that kind of change called "coming into existence." This leads naturally to a discussion of the nature of the past and what may properly be described as historical. These metaphysical excursions are, however, undertaken with epistemological ends in mind, as Climacus moves swiftly to a discussion of historical knowledge, which requires in turn an analysis of belief and doubt in general, with important claims about the nature of skepticism and how it can be overcome. Finally, lessons from these discussions are drawn about the nature of faith in the paradox of the god in time.

Climacus makes an important distinction in the Interlude between two kinds of faith or belief. (The Danish *Tro* can be translated correctly by both words; it is the noun form of the verb "to believe.") Faith in the ordinary sense, translated by the Hongs as "belief," is an element in any convictions we have about anything that has "come into existence"; it is part and parcel of all that David Hume called cognition of "matters of fact." Faith in the special or eminent sense is faith in the god who has appeared in history; it is faith in the paradox.

Though it is important to understand the distinction between these two kinds of faith, it is equally important to see that faith in the eminent sense presupposes or includes ordinary faith as a component. This must be the case if the god has truly come into existence, and unless that is assumed, the whole "poem" collapses back into the Socratic position. Climacus says this very clearly: "It [the historical fact of the god's appearance in time] has no immediate contemporary, because it is historical to the first power (faith in the ordinary sense); it has no immediate contemporary to the second power, since it is based on a contradiction (faith in the eminent sense)."[2] I say this at the outset to call attention to the fact that this implies that everything Climacus says about ordinary faith must be true of eminent faith as well, a point some commentators have missed.[3]

POSSIBILITY AND NECESSITY: COMING INTO EXISTENCE

Climacus begins by inquiring as to the character of that kind of change called "coming into existence." This kind of change is said to be different from other kinds of change in two ways. First, all other kinds of changes presuppose that what is undergoing the change already exists, but obviously, something that comes into existence does not exist prior to that change. Second, in other kinds of change, the object changed undergoes some change in quality. However, in a case of coming into existence, if the object coming into existence thereby changes its nature, then it is not *that* object that comes into existence, but some different one.[4]

The key to understanding these differences is to see the change from not existing to existing as a change in being (*Væren*) rather than essence (*Væsen*). What comes into existence must be something, but it is a something that is a "nonbeing." Such a being is, Climacus says, a possibility, and he therefore concludes, in Aristotelian fashion, that coming into existence is a transformation of the possible into the actual.[5] One might say that the change from the possible to the actual is a change in something's mode of being, rather than a change in its essence.

He then raises the question as to whether the necessary can come into existence, and answers the question with an emphatic "no." Some commentators, such as H. A. Nielsen, have been somewhat embarrassed by the robustly metaphysical character of the discussion here and in the following sections and have tried to interpret Climacus as giving us bits of linguistic analysis. Nielsen sees Climacus as providing us with "grammatical reminders" about the use of our concepts, reminders that are unfortunately usually expressed by Climacus in "fact-like" statements that have to be "decompressed" in order to discover their true grammatical status.[6] So when Climacus tells us that "no coming-into-existence is necessary," all he is really saying is that the two concepts of necessity and coming-into-existence "do not go together in our discourse."[7]

It is of course perfectly true that the points Climacus is making are deeply embedded in our language and thus may rightly be described as grammatical. However, it seems to me a mistake to think that these points simply reflect the way we talk, as if they would no longer hold if we talked some other way. There is no reason to think that Climacus regarded them that way. When Climacus gives his points a "fact-like" expression instead of simply making remarks about "our concepts" I do not see this as "unfortunately obscuring" his point.[8] Certainly the fact-like statements he makes do not express empirical facts, but it is clear that Climacus does not think they do. But why should one assume that there are no other kinds of "facts" than empirical ones?

It is Nielsen, I think, who tends to obscure the point, by making it appear that Climacus only wants to make some inoffensive remarks about the way we talk. Climacus himself is clearly trying to talk about necessity and possibility, not as features of our language, but as features of the way things are. He is focusing on what logicians call *de re* necessity, the necessity of things themselves, rather than *de dicto* necessity, the necessity of propositions or statements. The nature of things is reflected in our statements; our statements do not dictate how things must be. Climacus seems closer in sensibility to a Greek or medieval philosopher here than to contemporary Wittgensteinians. His claims, while they may well be in accord with what could be called "common-sense metaphysics," are not uncontroversial, but fly in the face of metaphysical convictions held by many philosophers.

Briefly, Climacus claims that what is necessary cannot undergo the change of coming into existence because the realm of necessity is the realm of the unchangeable. This same point is made in a number of different ways: "All coming into existence is a *suffering* (*Liden*), and the necessary cannot suffer."[9] The thinking here seems to be that whatever necessarily is what it is cannot change, for if it can change, then it is not necessarily what it is. "The necessary cannot be changed at all, because it always relates itself to itself and relates itself to itself in the same manner."[10] A necessary being would have to be something that was completely independent of the actions of anything else, for if it is dependent on something else, then again it would not necessarily be what it is.

So vehemently does Climacus hold necessity apart from actuality, that he rejects Aristotle's claim that there are two kinds of possibility in relation to necessity.[11] Aristotle reasoned, plausibly enough, that whatever was necessary was surely possible, since it cannot be impossible.[12] However, what is *merely* possible may not exist, so his view seems to imply that what is necessary and must exist is also possible and thus also may not exist. Aristotle deals with this by positing two different kinds of possibility, mere possibility and the kind of possibility which necessity includes, but Climacus rejects this solution and says his mistake lies in accepting the idea that the necessary was possible.[13]

Climacus moves from his claim about necessity to some very sweeping claims about the nature of the actual: "All coming into existence occurs through freedom, not by way of necessity. Nothing coming into existence comes into existence by virtue of a ground, but everything by a cause. Every cause ends in a freely acting cause."[14] Nielsen again finds this claim to be embarrassingly metaphysical, and what is worse, it sounds like Christian or at least theistic metaphysics.[15] It seems natural indeed to understand here a reference to a world that is contingent, and whose contingency reflects its status as one created by a free action of God. Nielsen says that we must resist the temptation to read this passage in that way, since Climacus has rejected natural theology in chapter 3 and cannot appeal to the authority of revelation without violating the hypothetical character of his experiment.

I think Nielsen is right to insist that we must not read Christian convictions into Climacus at this point, and indeed, his language sounds more Greek than Christian. Every cause ends in a freely acting cause, but Climacus does not identify this freely acting cause with God, and indeed, does not even claim that all causes end with one freely acting cause. However, though this may not be Christian metaphysics, it is difficult not to see this as metaphysics. In claiming that everything that happens does so ultimately because of a freely acting cause, Climacus does seem to adopt a view of the world as rooted in personal agency, for the word "freedom" simply does not apply to anything other than actions. Though these comments are not explicitly Christian and do not even by themselves constitute a commitment to theism, they certainly seem to be congenial to a theistic view of things.

Does this contradict the attack on natural theology in chapter 3? I cannot see how it does, since, as I have said, there is no attempt to identify this freely acting cause, even if we assume there is only one, with God. Certainly this freely acting cause seems miles away from "the Truth," that truth that gives human beings their humanness, which is the real subject of chapter 3. Even if speculative metaphysics rightly thinks of the world as requiring a "first mover," that hardly would constitute the Truth that Climacus thinks is bound up with self-knowledge.

In any case, we must remember that the attack in chapter 3 is focused on attempts to *prove* that God exists. Even if Climacus is thinking of God in the Interlude, he is certainly not attempting to prove that God exists. His claims come closer to being bald assertions than proofs; they are quite compatible with the view of chapter 3 that a type of knowledge of the God can be gained, not through a proof, but through a "leap."

That, however, raises a different sort of question, namely what sort of justification Climacus can give for these claims. As I have said, he really gives nothing that could be called an argument for his view that everything that comes into existence does so ultimately because of a "freely acting cause." Why does he think he is entitled to make such statements?

The outrageousness of his procedure here may be partly attributable to the whimsicalness of the literary structure at this point. We must recall that Climacus purports only to be killing time, giving the reader the illusion that 1843 years have passed. Such a project may entitle him to a few bald claims, thought-provoking but not established.

However, the claims in the context are not all that outrageous. The audience Climacus is addressing consists of people who are at least nominally Christian, even if they do not fully understand their own Christian commitments. As such they could be expected to be familiar with and accept the standard Christian view of the world as created by God in a free action. In any case, since Climacus' purpose is to explore the conceptual differences between Christianity and philosophical idealism, it is not so outrageous for him to take for granted the broadly theistic picture of things that Christianity presupposes.

In the final analysis, as we shall see when we get to the epistemological issues, what Climacus is really interested in is providing support for the view that all judgments about things that have come into existence are contingent, and thus can never amount to necessary truths. Since many philosophers who reject the quasi-theistic metaphysics Climacus seems to espouse will accept this claim, the underlying metaphysics may not be all that important to his argument.

NATURE AND HISTORY

In the second and very brief section of the Interlude, Climacus extends his analysis of "coming into existence" by distinguishing between two different senses of "history." In one sense anything that has come into existence has a past and therefore has a history. The whole natural world can therefore in one sense be said to have a history, and one properly speaks of natural history.[16] In another sense, however, Climacus says that nature "does not have a history" because "it is too abstract to be dialectical, in the stricter sense of the word, with respect to time."[17] Nature thus must be contrasted with that which is "dialectical with respect to time" because it is historical "in the stricter sense." The historical in the stricter sense is that which "contains within itself a redoubling (*Fordobling*), that is, a possibility of a coming into existence within its own coming into existence."[18]

One could hardly ask for denser philosophical prose than this. In talking about being "dialectical with respect to time" I believe that Climacus is talking about the same thing another Kierkegaardian pseud-onym, Vigilius Haufniensis, discusses in *The Concept of Anxiety* in making a distinction between mere time and temporality.[19] Haufniensis there says that temporality differs from mere succession by virtue of tense. Past, present, and future are qualitative features of experienced or lived time that cannot simply be regarded as objective features of a successive universe, but arise when that universe is lived by a being who has the power to reflect on possibilities and act on them. Such a being makes time "dialectical" by understanding the present as the moment in which what he necessarily is (the past) is projected into what he could possibly be (the future).

In a similar way, Climacus suggests that history in the stricter sense, the kind of thing that is meant when we speak of the history of a person or a nation, only comes into being when we have a self-conscious being or beings on the scene, whose lives contain possibilities. Human beings are obviously natural creatures and share in the biological "his-tory" of the planet. However, their nature as creatures is not fixed; they are constituted by possibilities, not merely in the sense in which there are various possibilities for an animal or a plant, but in the stronger sense that humans have possibilities of which they are con-scious and can freely choose. History in the strict sense concerns the use made of those possibilities.

Climacus thus seems to commit himself to human freedom in a rather strong sense. Human beings are "relatively freely acting causes." To be sure, they are creatures, which is why their freedom is only relative, and must be placed within the context of "an absolutely freely acting cause." Nevertheless, human history is a process which is doubly characterized by contingency. It reflects first the contingency of nature, since history is a part of nature, but secondly, it reflects the contingency of human freedom itself. Human beings are creatures who have been freely brought into existence, but as part of their nature, they possess the power to bring actions into existence.

In all of this Climacus once more seems to help himself to a healthy dose of metaphysics, and the quasi-Christian character of the metaphysics seems even more pronounced. H. A. Nielsen once more tries to whitewash this, as if it were something to be ashamed of, and suggests that the second "coming into existence" is the coming into existence of the self, and that all that is meant by this is that the individual thereby gains the power to speak a language. The relatively freely effecting cause is identified with those who taught the individual to speak.[20] It is certainly correct to connect being able to use language with the reflective power that Climacus is focusing on, but Nielsen seems to miss the fact that the emphasis here is not on language but on freedom. History in the strict sense is made possible by the fact that I can apprehend my past as providing me possibilities for action, not merely by the fact that I have a language by which to recount that past. It is my freedom and the necessity for decision that makes my life into a narrative by making my past not merely a succession of events but the first part of an on-going story.

THE UNCHANGEABILITY OF THE PAST

In the next two sections Climacus begins to reveal his agenda in making his speculative claims. The paradox of the god in time is a historical event. If it is possible to understand historical events as necessary, then reason might be able to remove the paradoxicalness of the paradox by coming to understand it as necessary. This would be a disaster for Climacus' hypothesis, so he swiftly moves to block any such attempt by arguing that what is historical is not necessary and therefore cannot be known as necessary.

The claim that what has happened can be understood as necessary was one that Hegelians had made. Hegel had taught that the movement of history as a whole was necessary in some sense, only we cannot understand the necessity of what occurs at the time it occurs, but only in retrospect. This is expressed in one of Hegel's most memorable lines: "The owl of Minerva takes flight only when the shades of night have fallen." It seems quite obvious that this Hegelian view is incompatible with the metaphysics of freedom that Climacus has so boldly adopted and assumed as true, but Climacus nevertheless takes the time to deal with one confusion that makes the Hegelian view seem more plausible than it is.

This confusion is a failure to distinguish between historical unchangeability and metaphysical necessity. It is quite true that the past is past and as such, cannot be changed. However, this unchangeableness is not the same thing as metaphysical necessity. Roughly, the difference seems to be this. What is metaphysically necessary cannot be conceived to be otherwise than it is; in such a case we can reasonably hope to attain absolute certainty concerning the matter once we have fully understood the issue, since no alternative state of affairs is possible. What is historically unchangeable lacks this characteristic. The historical, since it involves what has come into existence with freedom, remains contingent. It may be that what has happened cannot now be changed and thus cannot become otherwise, but it remains true that it could have been otherwise. It cannot lose this contingency without losing its historicity. Thus anyone who claims to understand the necessity of a historical event in effect is claiming to have a knowledge of something historical that would transform it into something nonhistorical, a curious kind of knowledge indeed.[21]

Climacus buttresses his argument here by some interesting claims about the relationship between the past and the future. He says that if one concedes the necessity of the past, then it will follow logically that the future is inevitable as well.[22] His thoughts here are supported by an interesting and well-known argument for the truth of fatalism that has been developed by contemporary philosopher Richard Taylor. Taylor precisely expresses a view of the past and future that is the alternative to Climacus':

> Yet, there is one thing I know concerning any stranger's past and

the past of everything under the sun; namely, that whatever it might hold, there is nothing anyone can do about it now. What has happened cannot be undone. The mere fact that it has happened guarantees this.

And so it is, by the same token, of the future of everything under the sun. Whatever the future might hold, there is nothing anyone can do about it now. What will happen cannot be altered. The mere fact that it is going to happen guarantees this.[23]

The crucial issue here concerns the reality of freedom. Does the future contain real possibilities? Or, as Taylor claims, is it the case that "nothing *becomes* true or *ceases* to be true; whatever is truth at all simply *is* true."[24] Climacus would say that the error of Taylor is that he has confused the unchangeableness of the past with metaphysical unchangeableness. Having stolen the contingency of the past, Taylor quite consistently robs the future of its openness as well. From Climacus' point of view a philosopher who claims to be able to understand the necessity of the past is the mirror image of a prophet who claims to be able to predict the future with inevitability.[25]

THE NATURE OF HISTORICAL KNOWLEDGE:
BELIEF AND THE WILL

With a bit of metaphysics securely in place, Climacus can now focus on his primary epistemological concern, namely our cognitive relationship to past events. He has ruled out any understanding of the past as necessary, but what type of understanding of the past is possible? Climacus' discussion here is complex; his main thrust seems to be to emphasize the uncertainty of historical knowledge and the role of the will in overcoming this uncertainty. His comments have been widely read as rooted in skepticism, and his claims about the role of the will in the formation of belief have been taken as irrationalism par excellence, since he seems to many to embrace the absurd view that with respect to historical matters it is up to the individual to decide to believe whatever he or she wants, regardless of the historical evidence that may bear on the matter. I believe that a careful reading of the text will show that these criticisms are rooted in misinterpretations of what Climacus actually says.

A good example of the sort of criticism I have in mind here is provided by Louis Pojman. In his book *Religious Belief and the Will*,[26] Pojman has analyzed and criticized what he terms volitionalism, which is a position that regards beliefs as under the control of the will. Pojman distinguishes several kinds of volitionalism.[27] First, he distinguishes prescriptive from descriptive volitionalism. Prescriptive volitionalism is a normative doctrine that holds that it is permissible, perhaps even obligatory, to will to hold certain beliefs. Descriptive volitionalism is a psychological theory that holds that the will actually does have the power to do this.

Pojman also distinguishes direct from indirect volitionalism. Direct volitionalism treats the action by which a belief is formed as a basic action which can simply be willed. Indirect volitionalism regards the formation of a belief as an outcome of doing other actions. Both prescriptive and descriptive volitionalism can be either direct or indirect.

In his book Pojman analyzes Kierkegaard as a classic example of volitionalism, basing his analysis primarily on the writings of Climacus, whom he identifies with Kierkegaard. (For literary consistency I shall henceforth speak of Climacus where Pojman discusses Kierkegaard, since it is the Climacus literature that is mainly at issue and it is that literature that is my concern.) Pojman sees Climacus as a direct voli-tionalist who accepts both descriptive and prescriptive volitionalism. Climacus and volitionalists in general are strongly criticized by Pojman on several counts. Direct, descriptive volitionalism is said to run afoul of psychological laws and to involve a conceptual confusion as well.[28] While Pojman allows that we can and do modify beliefs indirectly, and thus concedes the truth of indirect, descriptive volitionalism, he claims that prescriptive volitionalism, even of the indirect sort, is subject to censure. A plausible ethics of belief must see truth-seeking as a strong, prima facie duty,[29] but forming a belief through an act of will, which Pojman insists must mean forming it independently of evidential con-siderations,[30] shows a lack of concern for truth. It is in fact a kind of lying to oneself.[31]

I shall not here challenge Pojman's arguments against volitionalism, though in my judgment they fail, due to overly restricted and tendentious definitions of the positions attacked. What I want to do is challenge his reading of Climacus as a direct volitionalist.

It should be noted that Pojman's reading of Climacus is by no means unusual. Terence Penelhum, for example, in his fine book *God and Skepticism*, gives such a reading of Kierkegaard, whom Penelhum identifies with Climacus. According to Penelhum, Kierkegaard saw all belief as grounded in an act of will, though in the case of Christian belief the act of will can only be carried out with divine assistance.[32] Penelhum also regards this direct volitionalism as untenable, though he is somewhat more sympathetic to indirect forms, and thinks Kierkegaard's position can be reformulated in these terms.

One way of defending Climacus' analysis of faith against this charge of volitionalism would be to trade on the distinction Climacus makes between faith "in the eminent sense" and faith or belief in the ordinary sense. Even if ordinary belief is treated as subject to the will, this would not imply that the same is true for faith. Faith, it might be argued, is a miracle that resists philosophical analysis, the result of a divine act that humans cannot fathom.[33]

Even if this line of thought were sound, I would still be concerned as to whether Climacus has given an adequate account of ordinary belief, and I see no reason to concede the claim that he has adopted an untenable volitionalism in his view of belief. However, the claim that genuine faith has nothing to do with ordinary belief does not stand up to critical scrutiny.

In fact, this claim makes it mysterious why Johannes Climacus should invest so much energy analyzing the concept of ordinary belief. Even more significantly, Climacus says very clearly, as we have already noted, that faith in the eminent sense includes faith in the ordinary sense as a component.[34] Climacus analyzes the concept of belief in the ordinary sense because he sees eminent faith as a special kind of belief. Eminent faith is ordinary historical belief which has the absolute paradox as its historical content and which is acquired, not through considerations of evidence, but through a life-transforming encounter with the god.

One cannot then insulate Climacus' concept of faith against philosophical scrutiny by claiming that it has nothing in common with ordinary belief. If volitionalism is an objectionable view, then anyone who wishes to see if Climacus' project has merit must challenge the assumption that Kierkegaard is a direct volitionalist in his view of belief.

Why do philosophers like Pojman and Penelhum attribute direct volitionalism to Climacus? Climacus does say in the Interlude that "belief is not a piece of knowledge but an act of freedom, an expression of will."[35] He maintains that the "conclusion of belief is not a conclusion but a resolution," and that the opposite of belief, doubt, is also dependent on the will.[36]

We must look at the context of these remarks. The polemical target in view here is the claim we have analyzed in the last section, made by Hegel and employed by some religious Hegelians in the defense of Christianity, that historical events can be understood as necessary. If historical assertions could be converted philosophically to necessary truths, then Christianity could retain its historical foundations, while at the same time gaining a kind of invulnerability to the ravages of historical critical scholarship. Climacus' argument is directed against those who would avoid risk and claim to attain a kind of final knowledge, in this case of human history. Climacus' counter-position is the Humean view that all matters of fact are contingent, historical matters of fact being doubly so, and thus no knowledge of history can attain the certainty of a necessary truth.

SKEPTICISM AND DOUBT

We have seen that Climacus thinks metaphysical truths rule out any understanding of history as necessary, but he underlines the point with some epistemological reflections that draw heavily on classical skepticism, particularly Sextus Empiricus. It is important to recognize, however, that Climacus does not embrace skepticism himself. He borrows arguments from the skeptics, but he says very clearly that he assumes that there is knowledge of the past; he only wants to analyze the nature of this knowledge.[37]

The account given of historical knowledge is not easy to interpret, but the main points seem to me to be as follows. First, Climacus claims, in agreement with both classical foundationalism and classical skepticism, that there is a category of truths, "immediate sensation and cognition," which can be apprehended with certainty, and which "cannot deceive."[38] Climacus does not spell out the nature of this immediate knowledge, which seems similar to Hume's knowledge of impressions, and it seems to me in many ways a dubious position to hold. However, the realm of objectively certain knowledge Climacus here concedes turns out to be vanishingly small. He gives two examples to clarify his meaning. The first is that of perceiving a star; the second is perceiving an event.

In the first example, Climacus says that "when the perceiver sees a star, the star becomes dubious for him the moment he seeks to become aware that it has come into existence."[39] "Thus faith (*Tro*) believes (*troer*) what it does not see; it does not believe that the star exists, for that it sees, but it believes that the star has come into existence."[40] This is obscure, and some have interpreted Climacus as saying that one can have immediate knowledge of the existence of a star, but not of the genesis of the star, since it occurred in the past.[41] Against such a view one can rightly object that even our present awareness of the star is an awareness of a past object, since the light being perceived has taken years to arrive, and it is even possible that the star no longer exists. However, I do not think this can be Climacus' intended meaning, and this becomes clear when we look at the second example, that of perceiving an event.

Here Climacus says that "the occurrence can be known immediately but not that it has occurred, not even that it is in the process of occurring."[42] This may seem even more obscure than the case of the star, but I believe what Climacus has in mind is simply this. Both in the case of the star and the event, there is a something, a *content*, of which I am immediately aware. This something has been articulated by different philosophers in different ways, but he surely has in view what some have labeled "sense data," and what others have thought of in terms of what might be left after a phenomenological *epochē* has been performed. Whatever this something is of which we are immediately aware, it cannot be identified with an object in the space-time world which we think of as "objective," out there, so to speak. To affirm the existence of a star as an object which has "come into

existence" is to affirm the existence of something more than the immediate content of my experience. It is to affirm the existence of a public
object with a public history. Similarly, to affirm of an occurrence "that
it has occurred," is not simply to utter a tautology. The affirmation
that the event has occurred entails that one is committed to affirming
a "transition from nothing, from non-being."[43] Here the event is again
not simply a content in one's consciousness but a part of the public
world, and such an affirmation carries with it for Climacus inescapable
risk. The risk is grounded in the logical gap between my experience,
when that experience is construed as giving me certain knowledge, and
the world as I ordinarily perceive it and act in it.

Note that even if one rejects the implied inner world of certainty,
this does not damage Climacus' main thesis, which is the riskiness of
judgments about matters of fact. One may well find doctrines of sense
data and their like dubious while still agreeing that human judgments
about stars and events are contingent and fallible.

But now to the main issue, which concerns the implications
Climacus sees in the riskiness of affirmations about matters of fact. He
argues that it is the uncertainty of these judgments which makes skepticism possible. The Greek skeptics "doubted not by virtue of knowledge
but by virtue of will."[44] This in turn implies that "doubt can be
terminated only in freedom, by an act of will."[45] The nature of doubt
in turn illuminates the true nature of faith or belief, which must be
seen as the "opposite passion of doubt."[46]

Pojman reads these passages as a commitment to an extreme form
of volitionalism. As he sees the matter, Kierkegaard is saying that all
beliefs are under the direct and immediate control of the believer. Thus
if I believe that I am looking at a computer screen as I type these
words, or that I was born in Atlanta, Georgia, this is the result of a
decision I have made, and I could easily have willed to believe the
opposite of these things, regardless of the evidence. Such a position is
implausible, to say the least. It does not appear that beliefs are normally
under direct, voluntary control in this way.

I believe that Pojman's reading rests on a faulty understanding of
what Climacus means by such terms as "will" and "freedom." First, in
tracing belief to will, Climacus by no means necessarily implies that
beliefs are consciously chosen. Climacus does not tell us very much

about the psychological theories he holds, but it seems fair to assume that he would accept the general psychological convictions that Kierkegaard and other Kierkegaardian pseudonyms hold. This assumption is especially reasonable in the context of responding to criticisms like those of Pojman, who identifies Kierkegaard with Climacus.

If anything is evident about Kierkegaard as a psychologist, it is that he is a depth psychologist. While Kierkegaard certainly assigns will a central place in the human personality, he thinks that human beings hardly ever make choices with full consciousness of what they are doing. In *The Sickness unto Death*, for example, though both despair and sin are traced to the will, the pseudonym Anti-Climacus says that most people are in despair and sin unconsciously. Lack of clarity about what one is doing is the rule, not the exception, in the Kierkegaardian picture of the personality.

This point is just as evident in the discussion of skepticism in *Fragments*. The Greek skeptic would agree and understand that his skepticism is rooted in will, according to Climacus, *to the degree that he has understood himself*.[47] [emphasis mine] This implies, of course, that the skeptic may not understand himself, may not realize that he doubts because he wills to doubt. Thus, to say that belief is grounded in the will by no means implies that belief is always or even usually the result of a *conscious* act of willing.

Secondly, Climacus nowhere says that beliefs can be controlled by the will *directly*. Pojman's reading implies that beliefs can be produced or annihilated willy-nilly, but this is simply not present in the text. Pojman simply does not consider the possibility that Climacus, in speaking of the human power to will to believe something, may have in mind the well-known fact that beliefs can be modified indirectly, in the course of doing other things. That it is the latter possibility that Climacus has in mind is strongly suggested by the fact that he calls both belief and doubt passions.[48] Passions are not things that can be created by an immediate act of will, and neither Kierkegaard nor Climacus conceives of them as that sort of thing. Passions are things that must be slowly cultivated and constantly renewed. Acts of willing play a role in this cultivation, and Kierkegaard regards the higher ethical and religious passions as things we are responsible to achieve. However, by and large, passions are formed on a long-term basis, and they are not simply willed into existence, but formed indirectly through a process of willing to do other things.

Strong support for this interpretation is found in the discussions of skepticism in the *Postscript* and in *Fear and Trembling*. A major theme, which parallels a familiar refrain in Hume, is the difficulty of skepticism. Contemporary Hegelians, who claim to have overcome skepticism through a universal doubt which overcomes itself, are mercilessly attacked, primarily on the grounds that universal doubt cannot possibly be achieved, much less overcome if it could be.[49] What the ancient skeptic regarded as the task of a lifetime, an infinite goal which he could only hope to approximate, since life continually elicits belief from us, is accomplished by the contemporary professor in his opening lecture. It is the fact that doubts—and beliefs—are not always under our voluntary control that makes such a professor a comic figure for Kierkegaard. The difficulty of doubt is also a major theme of the unfinished *Johannes Climacus*.

And of course the same is true of other passions discussed in the Kierkegaardian literature, especially the passion of faith. The polemic against "going further" than faith, for example, presupposes that faith is not something one can acquire simply by fiat.[50] Once more, it is said to be a task for a lifetime.

A plausible reading of Climacus' discussion of the role of will in the life of the skeptic must first focus on the skeptic's goal: tranquility of mind. It is the attainment and sustaining of this state of mind which is the primary object of the skeptic's will. To this end he wills to refrain from drawing conclusions. A hasty reading may suggest that Climacus thinks that the skeptics can do this by a direct act of will: "By the power of the will he (the skeptic) decides to restrain himself and hold himself back…from any conclusion."[51] Climacus emphasizes that it is the will that is decisive here, not rational argument: "Insofar as he (the skeptic) uses dialectics in continually making the opposite equally probable, he does not erect his skepticism on dialectical arguments, which are nothing more than outer fortifications, human accommodations."[52]

Though the emphasis is on the will, since Climacus wishes to claim that the skeptic is a skeptic in the final analysis because he wills to be a skeptic, there is no claim here that belief states are always or even ever under the direct control of the will. On the contrary, there is the clear statement that at least in some cases the control exercised by the will is indirect. Though the ultimate source of doubt is the will, doubt is achieved through cognitive *means*. Because of the facts of human psychology, the skeptic must make use of dialectics, "outer fortifications." These may be denigrated as "human accommodations," but it is nonetheless important that such accommodations are necessary. Climacus also says that the skeptic "used cognition to preserve his state of mind."[53] This suggests that the control exercised by the skeptic was at least not complete, and that it was achieved by such techniques as looking for evidence on the other side of a belief toward which one is inclined, constructing arguments which are equally balanced on both sides of an issue, and so forth.

So Climacus' point is not the indefensible claim that beliefs are always simply willed into being, regardless of the evidential situation of the believer. It is rather the subtler claim that there is a logical gap between whatever totally objective, certain evidence we have for matters of fact, and our beliefs about these matters. It is this gap which makes skepticism as a willed life-stance possible. It provides room, as it were, for the skeptic to do what he needs to do to arrive at a state of suspended judgment, though this is not necessarily easy and will certainly not be successful in all cases. What exactly the skeptic will need to do is not spelled out, and there is no reason it should be, since that is a matter of empirical psychology. Climacus evidently thinks that what must be done to be a skeptic will include familiar cognitive strategies such as focusing on arguments for both sides of a position. Since most of us are not skeptics, it follows that we nonskeptics must differ from the skeptic in a crucial respect. We do not will to achieve that state of suspended judgment that the skeptic longs for. We have different ends and consequently do not embark on the activities which the skeptic employs to achieve his ends. Climacus may or may not think that particular beliefs are sometimes under the direct control of the will, but he certainly does not think this is always or generally the case. What he does think is that what we want to believe and think ultimately plays a decisive role in what we do believe and think.

This claim may point to a fact of human psychology which many philosophers find regrettable, and not to be welcomed, but so far from being implausible, I find it utterly undeniable. Who can observe the comments of hearers after a so-called debate between the presidential candidates without realizing that the beliefs of the hearers about who won the debate, who had the strongest arguments, and so on, are heavily shaped by their commitments to one candidate or the other? It is a plain and evident fact of human psychology, like it or not, that how we interpret evidence, weigh evidence, even what we consider to be good evidence, is heavily shaped by our desires. Of course this influence is generally mediated by my whole noetic structure. In reflecting on a presidential debate I recently saw, I believe that one candidate was much more sincere and concerned about important problems than the other, not simply because I want that to be true, but because I was already convinced that the second candidate was an unprincipled opportunist. However, the past beliefs which I brought to bear on the situation were equally colored by my past desires, emotions, and values. So will still played a significant factor in shaping the belief.

When we come to what Climacus calls the historical in the strict sense, the logical gap between totally objective, certain evidence and belief becomes even greater. Here we have not only the contingency of all matters of fact, but the double contingency introduced by free human actions, which always must be interpreted and understood. Climacus seems to be right in maintaining that there is even more room for disagreement and uncertainty with regard to human activity, and hence more room for skeptical stratagems, as is shown by the status of such disciplines as history and sociology as compared with physics and chemistry.

Notice that Climacus does not seem to adopt a radical relativism or historicism on the basis of his assertion of the significance of subjective factors in the formation of belief. That is, he does not say that there is no objective truth about nature or history. Nor does he claim that our beliefs cannot be true in some objective sense. All he wants to maintain is that our beliefs always contain an element of risk, because the objective evidential situation always contains an element of uncertainty which we resolve in the formation of our beliefs. This resolution is made possible by our desires, hopes, and fears, and so on, which in turn reflect themselves in our behavior and choices. Climacus' general term for this "subjective" factor in belief formation is "will." It may be in many ways a poor choice, but it reflects Climacus' desire to maintain personal responsibility. He does not see this emphasis on "subjectivity" as alien to or incompatible with a concern for truth.

When human beings resolve their beliefs in certain directions, they certainly are not motivated solely by "objective" evidence, but there is no reason to assume that they think that "subjective" factors necessarily lead them away from the truth. On the contrary, we generally think that subjective factors can help as well as hinder the search for truth. Hence it is not surprising that Climacus seems quite realistic in his assumptions about truth and cheerfully combines an emphasis on subjectivity with a realism that may rightly be termed "Greek," since it follows Plato and Aristotle very closely. In the next section I shall explore in more depth the question of whether this emphasis on subjectivity is indeed compatible with a concern for truth.

EMINENT FAITH AND THE ROLE OF WILL

I believe that I have cleared Climacus of the charge that he holds to an untenable form of descriptive volitionalism, which ascribes to humans the power to form their beliefs willy-nilly, independently of cognitive considerations. However, a new criticism is suggested by my defense. Suppose that it is true that human beliefs are frequently shaped by our desires, hopes, and fears. Surely that represents a melancholy fact to be derided, not a goal to be emulated. However, Climacus seems to think a prescriptive volitionalism that accepts willing to believe is praiseworthy. Pojman and others who share a commitment to an ethics of belief regard this as wrong; they say we ought to form our beliefs on the basis of evidence to the extent that we can. Is it possible for will to play a role in the acquisition of belief without the abandonment of a concern for truth? I shall try to argue that it can, at least for the acquisition of faith in the eminent sense. I shall restrict my discussion to faith in the paradox because that is the main concern of Climacus, and in any case he says very little about just how the will operates in other cases to shape belief.

Actually, he says little enough about how the will operates in the case of eminent faith as well, but I believe he says enough to enable us to construct a plausible account of the role will plays in coming to faith in the paradox. On the typical picture given of Climacus' account of faith and the will, a concern for truth seems totally absent. The typical picture given of eminent faith is that it requires a "leap of faith." (Though the discussion of faith as involving a leap comes from *Postscript* rather than *Fragments*.) The leap is necessary because Christian faith requires belief in the reality of the incarnation, the absolute paradox, which the critic perceives as a logical contradiction. Assisted by divine grace, the believer manages, through a heroic act of will, to get himself to believe what he knows is absurd, for what is logically contradictory could not possibly occur.

In the previous chapters I believe I have shown that this picture is fundamentally flawed. Here I shall briefly recapitulate some of my conclusions. The paradox of the incarnation cannot be known to be a logical contradiction. It is a mystery to human reason, one which appears to be a contradiction to us when we attempt to master it and make it our own. Relative to our experience and expectations, it is totally incongruous. It appears to us to be a contradiction, not because we know that God and man are mutually exclusive genuses, but because our sinfulness makes it impossible for us to understand an act which is a manifestation of pure, unselfish love, and our pridefulness demands that we dismiss what we cannot dominate and master.

To know that the incarnation is a logical contradiction, we would have to have a clear grasp of what it means to be God and to be human. The message of the B hypothesis, as Climacus spins it out, is that we lack any such knowledge. The truth about God is not something we possess; it must be brought to us by God himself. The person who comes to see the limitations of her own knowledge in this area is a person who can respond to God in faith. This faith is *not* produced by an act of will on the part of the believer, but rather is a gift of God, given in a first-person encounter.[54]

Just as a convinced mind-body dualist might be convinced that the paradoxical notion of a thinking brain is a reality if he should encounter one, so the believer might be convinced that the paradoxical notion of the God-man is a reality by a personally transforming first-person encounter with the God-man.[55] The belief is a response to the transforming encounter with reality, not of some arbitrary act of will. Far from being an abandonment of any concern for truth, the believer has changed her mind about what is true as a result of an encounter with the Truth in which she has acquired the Truth.

Does this account leave any role for the will at all? When we consider the explicit statement of Climacus that "faith is not an act of will," it is tempting to say that human willing plays no role at all in the acquisition of faith. Such a view of faith could easily be completed in accord with well-known Christian doctrines of predestination. Such a doctrine is not for Climacus, however, who does leave some "room" for human agency to play a role. Early on in the book he has already informed us that there is one point of analogy between the Socratic position and the B hypothesis; the one thing that the god in time can teach me Socratically is that I am in untruth. "To this act of consciousness [discovering my untruth] the Socratic principle applies: the teacher is only an occasion, whoever he may be, even if he is a god, because I can discover my own untruth only by myself."[56]

Even my sinfulness is something that must be revealed; on Climacus' view I cannot discover it by myself. However, when it is revealed to me in the encounter with the god I have a choice as to whether to accept this insight. This choice turns out to be decisive for whether I acquire faith or not, since it in turn is decisive for whether I can come to understand the limitations of my reason and its natural reaction to the paradox, since that reaction is itself shaped by my sin.

We can now understand something of the role of will in the acquisition of faith. It remains true that faith is not an act of will; it is a gift of the god. However, an act of will is necessary if the gift is to be received, necessary if the encounter with the God-man is to be a transforming one. The recognition that my own ideas about God are irremediably flawed and that I must accept my dependence on a divine revelation is not easily attained. Such a recognition runs counter to my natural, sinful tendency to assert my own autonomy. If God is to change me, what is required is a humble acceptance of my need to be changed. Humility is a moral quality which it is quite proper to see as something which must be willed. What is required in the leap of faith is not an immoral attempt to manipulate my beliefs so as to make myself believe what I know is untrue. Rather, I am asked to transform myself so that I can be open to an encounter with the truth which will totally transform my life.

What is necessary is the relinquishment of imperialistic reason and the acquisition of humility. Climacus saw it as necessary to see the individual as retaining some natural, intellectual ability, namely the ability to recognize its inability, just as Socrates' wisdom consisted in his honest recognition of his ignorance. Even this recognition is made possible by the encounter with God, but it is not a recognition which God forces on anyone. Such a transformation from pride to humility is essentially moral and practical, however vast its intellectual consequences, and its attainment requires no sin against any plausible ethics of belief. In seeing the passion of faith as grounded in the leap of the will, Climacus is not endorsing manipulation of beliefs, but recognizing the essential role moral character plays in the quest for truth, especially with regard to religious truth.

Eminent faith turns out to be triply contingent and therefore triply uncertain for Climacus. Since its content is the god who has come into existence, it shares with all matters of fact the contingency that coming into existence introduces. Since the god's appearance is historical, it shares with other historical truths the uncertainty that attaches to the freedom involved in human history, which is constituted by a "coming into existence within a coming into existence." Finally, it has its own unique uncertainty, since the god's appearance in time is the absolute paradox, the event that absolutely goes against my natural, sinfully shaped expectations of what is probable.

The first two kinds of uncertainty get resolved by the human will, according to Climacus. If I decide not to follow the strenuous path of the skeptic, I have, consciously or unconsciously, chosen to believe, though this choice is not necessarily a conscious, datable decision. It is more like a long-term fundamental project that I may discover myself to be committed to in retrospect. For me, there really is an external world and I can know something about it. If I decide to believe that the Roman Empire fell because its moral toughness was undermined by Christianity, then I have successfully resolved the greater uncertainty that pertains to human history.

The uncertainty that attaches to the paradox cannot be resolved in the same manner. It can only be resolved as a result of the encounter with the god through one of the two passions that ensue from that encounter: offense or faith. Will does play a role, however, in determining which of these passions ensues from the encounter.

Nevertheless, faith in the paradox shares the other two kinds of uncertainty, and Climacus views this as significant, since it implies a barrier to anyone who would try to substitute objective factors for subjective factors in the acquisition of faith. This cannot even be done successfully for ordinary faith. It is utterly impossible for eminent faith, which involves all the uncertainty of the other kinds as well as its own unique uncertainty. In all of these cases, however, the uncertainties do get resolved. Existing human beings do arrive at beliefs, and when they encounter the incarnation they also arrive at faith—and offense.

CHAPTER

9

FAITH AND HISTORY

In chapter 5 Climacus returns to the question of how the members of a later generation might become disciples of the god. The question is posed ironically in the chapter title, "The Disciple at Second Hand," since chapter 4 has already forcefully argued that there can be no disciple at second hand. A person becomes a disciple only by a first-person encounter with the god in which the god grants the condition of faith. Thus every disciple, of whatever generation, is a contemporary of the god in the significant sense, and historical contemporaneity becomes unimportant.

In essence, then, the problem posed in chapter 5 has already been answered in chapter 4, which leads Climacus to hope that the interlocutor, who has already claimed to have immediately discerned the far-reaching consequences of that chapter, perhaps perceives the impossibility of asking about a "disciple at second hand." Alas, the interlocutor, whose dimness is becoming a bit tiresome, does not get the point. Instead of seeing that the whole question of a disciple at second hand is based on a confusion, the interlocutor, befuddled by the 1843 years that have supposedly passed during the Interlude, wonders if it is correct to lump all the subsequent generations together. Should one not consider whether the situation of the people of the third generation might differ from the people of the fifth generation, and so on?[1]

Climacus patiently humors the interlocutor by embarking on a detailed comparison of the two extremes within the class of later generations, the first generation after the god's appearance and the last generation. We can be confident that the differences between the two will turn out to be relative and inconsequential, since if there is no essential difference between a historical contemporary and a later disciple, it would be surprising indeed if within the general category of "later disciples" some later generation turned out to possess an essential advantage over earlier ones in the acquisition of faith.

THE FIRST AND LATEST GENERATIONS OF "SECONDARY" DISCIPLES

The comparison between the two extremes within the general category of later disciples is executed briskly. The first generation has the advantage of being closer in time to the god's appearance. This makes it easier for them to obtain accurate historical information about the event. Of course even this generation must deal with the uncertainty that is inherent in the historical realm, according to the Interlude, and thus cannot gain absolute certainty, especially with regard to the details. Climacus argues that contradictions with respect to minor details is what one would expect from the most truthful witnesses, since complete agreement would probably be the result of a concocted story.[2]

However, the really decisive problem for the first generation is that the fact in question, the paradoxical entry of the god into time, is not a "simple historical fact." The divinity of the god, since he is present in human form, could not be directly observed, even by the eyewitnesses, so it could hardly be directly inferred from the testimony of those witnesses to their immediate successors. Even the miracles or signs performed by the god are of no value to those who lack faith.[3]

The only genuine advantage possessed by the first generation, according to Climacus, is that they are closer in time to the "jolt" that the god's appearance is sure to bring. This jolt is valuable in that it will certainly attract attention and raise the awareness of the people who hear the news. Unfortunately or fortunately, this heightened awareness, according to Climacus, is by no means partial to faith; it can just as easily lead to offense.[4] The only advantage is that it is clearer to the person that a decision is called for.

The later generation has the apparent advantage of being able to observe the consequences of the god's appearance. If perchance the fact in question has "completely transformed the world, has penetrated even the most insignificant trifle with its omnipresence,"[5] then this provides those who come later with a "probability proof."[6] Climacus has several reasons for thinking this advantage to be an illusion. First, he argues that the consequences of a fact cannot change the character of the fact, any more than a son can change the fact of who his father is.[7] If the fact in question is a paradox, then no consequences can alter this. Secondly, he argues that if this fact has indeed transformed the world in such a manner, it has come about through the power of the faith it has inspired.[8] If those consequences make faith unnecessary, then presumably the consequences may well undo themselves. Most important, however, is the fact that historical significance is no guarantee of truth, since misunderstandings can also have consequences, and untruths can be powerful. In fact, Climacus says that human history is full of this phenomenon.[9] This last point throws a significant light on how Climacus understands "truth." Kierkegaard's writings are often read as developing a "subjective" concept of truth, in which truth simply is identified with the existential power of an idea. Climacus in this argument seems to me to hold onto a concept of truth that has an element of objectivity to it, since he here claims that a falsehood can be existentially powerful.

So neither the greater historical accuracy of the first generation with respect to the original fact nor the long-range historical perspective of the later generation, who can see the original fact as the beginning of a process, has any real value for Climacus. The basic insight Climacus clings to in both cases is that the evidence available to each generation could only serve to make faith more probable, but "faith is by no means partial to probability—to say that about faith would be slander."[10] This low estimate of the value of probability is something that we will consider in some detail later, for it is crucial to Climacus' rejection of historical apologetics.

It is clear that of the two types of historical apologetics, it is the argument from the consequences that draws Climacus' greatest ire. Someone who thinks that the first generation is better off because of their greater historical information is mistaken, and the mistake has as a practical consequence a romantic delusion that it would have been better to have lived near the time of the god's appearance. However, the delusion of the later generation is more pernicious. The idea that the consequences of the fact qualitatively alter the situation of the later believer is tantamount to the notion that faith might become "naturalized."[11] Clearly, Climacus has in mind here the idea that someone born in a "Christian land" might simply possess faith automatically; it is the same idea that he skewers in *Postscript* in his discussions of whether a person might gain faith automatically by being baptized as an infant, and which becomes the target of Kierkegaard's final attack on "Christendom."

The notion that faith might become naturalized in this way is the ultimate in lunacy, according to Climacus, since it amounts to the claim that one can be born with one's second nature. Birth and the second birth are identified.[12] Climacus says that he can make some sense even of the doctrine of reincarnation, but the idea of being born with faith "is just as plausible as being born twenty-four years old."[13] Climacus' venom here is instructive, as is his criticism. First, the criticism makes it clear that logical clarity and the avoidance of contradiction are things that Climacus prizes very highly. He can make no sense of a first birth that is simultaneously a second birth that presupposes a first birth. This confirms our earlier contention that the paradox cannot properly be understood as something that contains a logical contradiction.

The ground for the venom of the attack is perhaps harder to discern. I think the right clue here is that the naturalization of faith amounts to its *domestication*.[14] The evil of Christendom is that it eliminates something of surpassing value in Christianity, its discontinuity with the existing order of things. It is this discontinuity that makes it possible for Christianity to subvert and transform things. To naturalize Christianity is therefore to deify the established order, to rob Christianity of its power to call into question established values, attitudes, and institutions.

THE IRRELEVANCE OF HISTORICAL
EVIDENCE FOR FAITH

Having dealt with the quibbles of the interlocutor concerning the differences between later generations, Climacus returns to the central issue, which concerns the situation of the later disciple. Before answering the question, which he actually has already answered in chapter 4, he makes some "observations for orientation" concerning the possibilities.[15] Essentially, he describes three possible categories under which the fact of the god in time might fall.

First, the fact might be a simple historical fact. In this case being a historical contemporary is an advantage, but in that case the fact could only have relative value and significance. Secondly, the fact might be an "eternal fact." This concept is not immediately transparent. He says of such a fact that "every age is equally close to it."[16] Perhaps an example of the sort of thing Climacus has in mind would be an alleged philosophical insight such as the Hindu conviction that every human being is divine: "That art thou." The claims of Buddhists that suffering stems from the desires of the ego might be another example. Such insights have no intrinsic connection to any "datable" event. They may have been first propounded by some historical figure, but their truth does not depend on any knowledge of the propounder's life, or any other historical event. They are pure "Socratic" truths.

Eternal facts are then equally available to every historical period, but Climacus says that such truths are not grasped by faith, for "faith and the historical correspond perfectly to each other."[17] It is obvious here that Climacus is using the term "faith" in a somewhat technical sense. People often do speak of someone's commitment to some "Socratic" principle as a faith commitment, and Climacus himself admits in *Postscript* that his usage is a bit fastidious here and that one can speak of Socrates as possessing a kind of faith.[18] Nevertheless, Climacus is quite justified in his main point, which is that there is a big difference between a faith like Christianity, which involves belief in genuine historical events, and the "faith" that is involved in accepting some Socratic principle. The historicity of the former type of belief involves possibilities for being mistaken that are absent in the latter case.

The third possibility is that the fact in question is "an absolute fact."[19] This category, which is of course the one Climacus says his hypothesis belongs to, is a kind of hybrid of the first two. Its content is historical, as in the case of the first category, but it is absolute like an eternal fact in being equally relevant and available to every generation. "If that fact is an absolute fact,...then it is a contradiction for time to be able to apportion the relations of people to it."[20] So, although the historical is essential if his hypothesis is not to collapse back into a Socratic position, the historical aspect must not "be accentuated in such a way that it becomes absolutely decisive for individuals."[21] Following this line of course requires that Climacus adhere to the view he has already announced, that there is no advantage to either the contemporary generation or any later one in the acquisition of faith. The reason this is so is that faith is always acquired in a first-hand transformative encounter. For the historical contemporary, his perceptual experience of the god provides the occasion for this encounter, while for the later generation the report of the contemporary provides the occasion. What is essential is the transforming encounter itself.

There is clearly a kind of egalitarian assumption lying behind the claims Climacus makes about the necessity for an "absolute fact" to be equally available to every generation. It is difficult to put it precisely, but the idea is roughly that whatever it is that is essential for human life must be equally available to every age of human history. Put so baldly and in isolation, it is difficult to see how such an assumption might be defended, but later in the chapter Climacus suggests a plausible line of defense. If we assume the kind of God that Christianity accepts, would it not be fair and just of God to operate along the lines of such a principle, and would we not expect God to operate fairly and justly? "Would the god allow the power of time to decide whom he would grant his favor, or would it not be worthy of the god to make the reconciliation equally difficult for every human being at every time and in every place..."[22] When Climacus' egalitarian principle is linked in this way to the concept of God it acquires great appeal, though it is by no means self-evidently true.

This egalitarian principle is clearly a large part of the reason that Climacus sticks strongly to his formula for the later generation's acquisition of faith: "*By means of* the contemporary's report (the occasion), the person who comes later believes by the power of the condition he himself receives from the god."[23] Since the historical records are only an occasion, the accuracy and completeness of the records are completely insignificant. "Even if the contemporary generation had not left anything behind except these words, 'We have believed that in such and such a year the god appeared in the humble form of a servant, lived and taught among us, and then died,' that is more than enough."[24]

If this is right, then Christians and those considering Christianity who worry about the strength of the historical evidence of the gospels in the New Testament are misled. The historical records do not function as evidence, but as occasion for an encounter with the god, and their ability to do that is unrelated to their quality as historical evidence. In any case Climacus says that the content of the alleged fact, being a paradox, is not the sort of thing for which any evidence would be adequate. "Lawyers say that a capital crime absorbs all the lesser crimes—so also with faith: its absurdity completely absorbs minor matters. Discrepancies, which usually are disturbing, do not disturb here and do not matter."[25]

There are several different kinds of issues that are tied together in Climacus' dismissal of the relevance of historical evidence. First, there is the egalitarian principle we have identified. Secondly, there is the claim that the encounter with the god is unaffected by the quality of the historical records, which function solely as an "occasion." Thirdly, there is the contention that the paradoxical content of the belief in this case is such that no historical evidence would be sufficient to warrant belief, and hence it makes no difference whatsoever if the actual evidence available is poor in quality. I shall focus first on the egalitarianism, and then deal with these other issues in the next section.

CLIMACUS THE EGALITARIAN

The egalitarian principle Climacus seems to accept is appealing. Something like this principle is, I suspect, a chief reason why many modern theologians reject the idea that historical beliefs are necessary for salvation, which converts their brand of Christianity into a Socratic view, according to Climacus.[26] Climacus, however, thinks that the principle is compatible with the traditional Christian understanding of faith as including historical beliefs, such as the belief that Jesus rose from the dead after suffering under Pontius Pilate.

However appealing, this principle is problematic for Climacus. It is hard to see how a Truth that is historical can be "equally available to people in every time and place." Even if Climacus is right in his contention that the contemporary generation has no essential advantage over later generations, that hardly amounts to the equality he demands. Many people in both the contemporary and later generations cannot possibly have faith in Climacus' sense, for the simple reason that they live in places where the story has not reached, even in a fragmentary way. Such people may not be excluded from the Truth by being members of a particular generation, but they are surely excluded by being part of a particular region, and as Climacus himself affirms, discrimination by geography seems no better than discrimination by time. And with respect to the generations that lived before the god's appearance, time would appear to decide whether faith is a possibility for them.

Perhaps Climacus would be better off weakening his egalitarian principle to something like the claim that among those who have been confronted by the news about the god's appearance, there is equality of opportunity. The quality of evidence then will be irrelevant for this class of people. Something like this principle may be salvageable, but it faces problems too, in light of what we know about the sociology of knowledge. It does not appear obvious that those who have heard of the event are on an equal footing, for they have all not heard in the same way. Does a young Marxist who has only heard the story of the god's appearance from those who describe it as superstition have the same opportunity as those who have heard from believers? Climacus' account would seem to imply an affirmative answer, but that seems dubious, to say the least. In any case, if the principle of equality is weakened to take into account accidents of time and geography, it is hard to see why it should not be further weakened to take into account other sorts of "accidents of upbringing."

An alternative to weakening the principle would be to abandon it altogether. A convinced Calvinist, for example, full of confidence in the sovereignty of God and full of suspicion of our human moral intuitions about how God should behave, might simply reject the idea that people in different ages and places should have an equal opportunity to obtain the Truth. Perhaps the selectivity involved in historical faith is simply part of God's will. Alternatively, and less Calvinistically, one might argue that such selectivity is a necessary evil, something that God must accept if he chooses to reveal himself to human beings historically.

Still another alternative for Climacus, and the one I personally find most appealing, is to "save" the principle of equality in its strong form by an "auxiliary hypothesis" which implies that those who had no opportunity to hear about the incarnation of God, or those who have had no fair opportunity to hear, will nevertheless have an opportunity to obtain faith. The trick here is to form such a hypothesis in such a manner that it does not amount to a reversion to the Socratic position. The danger is that if the Truth is available to all people, regardless of their historical situation, it will be construed as a Socratic truth which has no essential relation to history. If, for example, one simply said that everyone who existentially commits herself to the most adequate idea of God or other moral ideal available to them is thereby in the Truth, then we would clearly be back to Socrates.

There are several possible auxiliary hypotheses that might avoid this fate, however. For example, one might hold that those who do not have an opportunity to encounter the god in this life will have the news of the god's appearance proclaimed to them after their death. People in this situation would be excluded from the Truth during their temporal existence, but would not be excluded eternally, and their situation would not seem to differ much from those who only heard about the god at the end of their lives and were thus similarly excluded from faith for much of their lives.

Of course it must be acknowledged that the Socratic position may indeed be the correct one, and if that position is accepted, the contortions we are exploring are unnecessary. Climacus himself, it will be recalled, is not trying to argue that the Socratic view is wrong, but only experimentally attempting to develop an alternative. In view of the difficulties with that alternative, it is fair to ask, "Why bother?" The answer surely lies in whether human beings possess the Truth. If so, there is no reason to bother with the alternative. If human beings lack the Truth, if they are in fact sinful as Climacus' hypothesis assumes, then there is every reason to bother. It is part of the hypothesis, of course, that human sinfulness is something that is itself revealed as part of the encounter with the god. Therefore, those who have not had the encounter, or who have in offense refused to believe they are sinful, will naturally think the whole business a waste of time. Such a reaction, according to Climacus, is completely natural and to be expected but by no means entails that the alternative hypothesis is false.

IS FAITH INDIFFERENT TO THE QUALITY OF HISTORICAL EVIDENCE?

Let us assume for the moment that Climacus' thought-experiment is presented in order to illuminate the nature of Christian faith, as Climacus himself clearly says at the conclusion of the book. When this assumption is made, Climacus' thoughts on the relationship between faith and historical evidence are quite unusual when compared with most Christian thinkers, and their oddity seems to stem from a deep internal tension.

On the one hand, Climacus wants to maintain there is an essential difference between Christianity and Greek modes of thought, a difference which depends on the historical component of Christianity. Either Christianity is something essentially different from what Socrates could have come up with, or else Christianity does not exist, "precisely because it has always existed,"[27] to borrow the words of another pseudonym, Johannes de Silentio. He locates this essential difference ultimately in the historical entrance of the God into history. A real alternative to Socratic immanence requires that we deny that the Truth is in us, even in the form of a potentiality for recognizing the Truth.[28] The Truth as well as the capacity to recognize the Truth must be brought to us by a God who enters history. So any attempt to replace the Jesus of history with a mythical figure whose real significance lies in the existential meaning of the narrative or in the content of the teaching must be rejected.[29] The objectivity of the historical is required in order to get "the God outside yourself,"[30] as Climacus says in *Postscript*.

This emphasis on history is, however, coupled with a depreciation of historical knowledge as in any way necessary or sufficient for becoming a disciple. Climacus seems to make historical knowledge virtually irrelevant to faith:

Even if the contemporary generation had not left anything behind except these words, "We have believed that in such and such a year the god appeared in the humble form of a servant, lived and taught among us, and then died"—this is more than enough. The contemporary generation would have done what is needful, for this little announcement, this world-historical *nota bene,* is enough to become an occasion for someone who comes later, and the most prolix report can never in all eternity become more for the person who comes later.[31]

The unusual nature of Climacus' ideas is now clear. More commonly, those who have held that the incarnation was a genuine historical event in something like the traditional sense, however varied that sense may be, have also held that it was important to have good historical evidence for that event. Those who believe we do not have such evidence, but still wish to affirm a faith in Christ as the divine lord, have tended to reinterpret the incarnation as a symbol whose power does not rest on its objective historicity.

The question I wish to pose is whether the conjunction of the claim that the historical is essential with the claim that historical evidence is unimportant makes sense. If not, the question of which to modify would still be open. Both traditional Christians as well as those more liberal Christians still engaged in the quest for the historical Jesus would argue that what must go is the cavalier dismissal of historical evidence. These groups have been suspicious of Kierkegaard for what they perceive as his irrationalism. Many contemporary theologians, on the other hand, convinced that making faith dependent on historical evidence is a recipe for disaster, would argue that what must go is the assumption that faith must be grounded in factual historical events.

I believe that Climacus has strong reasons for wishing to avoid both of these recommendations. Whether those reasons are ultimately decisive, and indeed whether there is really a coherent alternative to the revisions his critics would urge upon him, remains to be determined. There are several reasons why he wishes to avoid making faith dependent on historical evidence. First, there is the egalitarian commitment we examined in the last section. Secondly, there is what might be called the incommensurability between authentic religious commitment and matters of intellectual evidence. This theme, which is more developed in *Postscript* than in *Fragments*, focuses on the character of Christian commitment, which has about it an absoluteness and finality. A person of faith is someone who is willing to risk her life and stake everything on what she believes. The evidence for a historical event can never be more than probable and tentative, subject to revision in light of new findings. Climacus thinks that if faith were based on evidence, it would necessarily share in this tentativeness. He wants to see faith as a life-transforming passion but does not see how such a passion could be engendered by calculation of evidential probabilities.

On the other hand, Climacus wishes to resist giving up the objective historicity of the incarnation because it is the actual historicity of the incarnation that makes possible a revelation that can confront and correct my deep-rooted assumptions about God and myself. If I am indeed sinful, and if those deeply rooted assumptions are wrong, then this is not a possibility to be dismissed in a cavalier way. The incarnation makes Christianity what is termed in *Postscript* a religion of "transcendence." Transcendence is important here not only for its possible value as a corrective and challenge to my individual errors and pride, but represents as well the foundation of any genuinely human social order. The established social order constantly attempts to deify itself; that is the secret of Christendom, which is merely the attempt to employ Christianity to do what human societies always do. To foil this human attempt at self-deification, epitomized in the Hegelian political philosophy, we need a God who is truly transcendent, so that the established order can be seen in its relativity, and the possibility of critical dissent be kept open. Despite Kierkegaard's own political conservatism, there is a radical element to his social and political thought, an element that is tied to transcendence. Without a transcendent God in time, we humans will manufacture God in our own image, and we will do so to buttress the status quo.

Despite these good reasons for holding both to the historicity of the incarnation and the irrelevance of historical evidence, Climacus' view is problematic. Is it possible to believe that Jesus Christ lived and died for me as the Son of God, and be indifferent to critical questions about the factual character of my beliefs? Suppose, to push things to the extreme, that it could be shown that there was no first-hand evidence at all, and that overwhelmingly powerful evidence appeared that the New Testament was concocted in the fourth century. In such a situation would a person not naturally doubt whether Jesus had lived at all, and *a fortiori* doubt that he was indeed divine?

One could at this point retreat to the view that the object of faith is simply that the god has appeared somewhere, sometime. However, the content of faith would in that case seem distressingly vague, a blank canvas that will have little power to jolt and overturn our current Socratic ideas. Does such a vague notion really differ much from a Socratic myth? M. J. Ferreira puts the point by pointing out that historical events have identity conditions if we are meaningfully to refer to them.[32] If we want to say that something occurred in history that is the foundation of our faith, but how it occurred can be left to the historians as unimportant, the question arises as to whether what occurred can be completely divorced from how it occurred. Ferreira claims that we need at least some information about an event in order to identify the event.

Think, for example, of Moses. Moses is the individual who confronted Pharaoh, led Israel out of Egypt, inscribed the ten commandments, and so on. Some or much of this information may be inaccurate, but, according to the view of historical reference I find most plausible, if we had no reliable information about Moses whatsoever, then it is hard to see how we could have any true beliefs about Moses, because we could not use the symbol "Moses" successfully to pick out a historical figure. In the same way, it would appear that to speak meaningfully about "Jesus" as the historical incarnation of God, we need some accurate historical information about Jesus. And if it is important for our information to be historically accurate, how can we avoid a concern for the quality of the historical evidence?

Climacus' answer to this problem lies in the view of faith we analyzed in chapter 7, which sees faith as properly basic, in Alvin Plantinga's sense of the term.[33] Faith is grounded in a transforming encounter with Christ. Historical records function as the occasion for this encounter, but the encounter is itself the ground of faith, which is not based on evidence. No amount of historical evidence is sufficient to guarantee that the encounter will occur or that faith will be its outcome, and no specific amount of historical evidence is necessary in order for the encounter to occur or faith to ensue. To answer Ferreira

Climacus must steadfastly maintain that objectivity in the content of one's beliefs is compatible with subjectivity in the grounds. It is undeniable, I think, that meaningfully to believe in Jesus as God one must have some true historical beliefs about Jesus. But why must those beliefs be based on evidence? Why couldn't the beliefs be themselves produced as part of the outcome of the encounter?

To refer successfully to Jesus of Nazareth, some of my beliefs about Jesus must be true, but it seems possible that a person might believe in the historical record because of her faith in Jesus, rather than having faith in Jesus on the basis of the historical record. Of course if the beliefs are false, then they are false, and the person is mistaken, but that risk is unavoidable, and Climacus does not think one should try to avoid it. Nor does the fact that the belief in question is not based on evidence mean that the belief is arbitrary or groundless, since it is *grounded* in the first-person encounter with Jesus.[34] What is required is that this encounter be an experience of Jesus in which true knowledge is given. The situation is analogous to a case of ordinary sense perception in which I come to believe that there is a flower before me because I directly perceive the flower. In such a case I do not normally regard the existence of the flower as something that I infer or conclude on the basis of evidence.

One objection to Climacus' attempt to rest so much on an experience of Jesus as God is that any interpretation of such an experience necessarily rests on a host of background assumptions. Surely a person cannot simply directly come to perceive Jesus as forgiving her, commanding her to do something, or inviting her to faith in the pages of the gospels without assuming that the gospels are indeed an accurate representation of Jesus and that they provide a reliable means for becoming aware of Jesus at work in one's life. In a similar way, ordinary sense perception also depends on background beliefs. For example, I would not believe there is a flower in front of me as a result of my perception if I did not believe that the light was normal, that my eyesight was functioning normally, and so on. So some would argue that to know that there is a flower in front of me I must know these other things. Similarly, some might argue that to know that Jesus as God is speaking to me, I must know other things as well. So, in both cases, it may be argued, my belief still rests on other evidence, namely the evidence I have for these background beliefs.

William Alston has argued that this kind of objection rests on a confusion of levels.[35] We should distinguish between *having* a ground for a belief and *knowing* that one has a ground for a belief, between being justified and knowing that one is justified. For my belief that there is a flower before me to be properly grounded, it is necessary that the light be of a certain sort, that my eyesight be functioning normally, and so on, but it is not necessary for me to know these things, or to have evidence that they are so. It is sufficient that they are true and that I believe them. To know *that* my belief is properly grounded I may need to know such things, but that is another matter. In a similar manner, in order to have a properly grounded belief that Jesus is God, the individual may need to believe that Jesus reveals himself in certain ways, and those beliefs have to be true. But it is not necessary for the individual to know these other things, or have evidence for them, though that may be necessary for the individual to know *that* her belief is properly grounded.

I conclude that Climacus' position is philosophically defensible. There is nothing incoherent in the notion of a historical belief which is grounded in a transforming experience, rather than in historical evidence. Whether that is in fact how Christian faith is produced is another matter, of course. To decide that one must decide whether Jesus is indeed God and whether experiences of Jesus of the appropriate sort are possible.

To revert to the language of the "thought-experiment," Climacus is probably right in saying that the "scrap of paper" with the words "we have believed that the god appeared among us" would be "more than enough" to be an occasion for faith, should the god choose to use that scrap of paper as an occasion to reveal himself. And he is clearly right in saying that no amount of evidence will necessarily produce faith in someone. So strong, historical evidence is neither sufficient nor necessary for faith. Nevertheless, it is difficult to accept the further conclusion he seems to draw, namely that evidence is irrelevant to faith.

My worry can be expressed as follows: Certainly God could use a scrap of paper to produce faith. Perhaps he often does produce faith in ways that make evidence irrelevant. But is this always or even normally the case? If I have a belief in Jesus of Nazareth, that is a belief with historical content, and it cannot be isolated from my other historical beliefs. Unless God produced my belief by overriding my normal thought processes, it is hard to see how I could regard massive evidence that Jesus never existed, or never said any of the things attributed to him, as utterly irrelevant to my faith. Even a belief which is "properly basic" and grounded in direct perceptual experience is subject to being over-ridden by contrary evidence. Similarly, even though I believe that Jesus has revealed himself to me, is it not possible that I am mistaken, and is not the liveness of that possibility affected by the quality of the evidence I have for Jesus' historical reality?

I believe that the basic worry Climacus has about admitting the relevance of historical evidence for faith is that he does not want the question of faith to be a scholarly question. He does not want to leave the ordinary person who is deciding whether to be a Christian or not in the clutches of the historical scholars, with their endless debates and never-decided controversies. After all, the individual who must decide whether or not to become a Christian is making a decision about how her life should be lived. She does not have the luxury of waiting for the scholars to reach agreement, which will never happen in any case.

I sympathize with Climacus' worry on this point, but I believe that this concern can be met without the drastic claim that historical evidence is irrelevant for faith. The actual situation with regard to historical evidence seems to be this. For orthodox Christians, the historical accounts of Jesus' life are regarded as reasonably accurate at least, plenty sufficient for faith, and the evidence for this conclusion is regarded as adequate. For others, the account is much less accurate, and the evidence accordingly less powerful. In extreme cases, skepticism extends to almost all the details of Jesus' life. However, all parties would agree that in reality there is far more evidence than the "scrap of paper." How much more is a matter of dispute.

Now why is it that the evidence seems adequate to one party and inadequate to the other? Doubtless each side will have its own preferred explanation. Perhaps skeptics will say that wish fulfillment is at work in the believer. Perhaps believers will follow Climacus and say that their own experience of Jesus is the deciding factor.

What I wish to maintain (and here it should be plain that I am speaking for myself and not Climacus or Kierkegaard) is that it is possible for the believer to say that the encounter with Jesus is decisive, just as Climacus maintains, without claiming that historical evidence is irrelevant. That is, it is possible for a believer to claim that it is significant that we have as much evidence as we have, and even to admit that if we did not have evidence of some type, faith would not be possible, while still properly believing that the decision is not in the end one which scholarship can settle. Though the evidence by itself would never be sufficient to produce faith in *anyone*, it is possible that evidence of a certain type might be necessary for faith for some people, though not everyone, since not everyone will have the reflective bent or cognitive capacities to appreciate the force of various possible problems.

To go back to the level distinction we employed earlier, for those of a certain reflective bent, being justified in believing may not be adequate. They want to know that they are justified, and if they lack such knowledge, their faith may be troubled by crippling doubts. Or, more modestly and more plausibly, I think, they at least need to rule out the possibility that their beliefs can be shown to be false. Perhaps they may have this need because they have encountered people who claim to be able to show their beliefs are false. Such a believer might admit the relevance of historical argument, while still holding to the Climacus-inspired view that what is finally decisive in settling the argument is first-hand experience of Jesus.

Such a person is not necessarily thrown back into the clutches of the scholars, even though he may not ignore the work of the scholars altogether. To avoid the specter of an unending scholarly inquiry which never leads to commitment either way, he may only need to believe that there is enough evidence to make the truth of his beliefs possible, and it is hard to see how that weak conclusion could be threatened by scholarship. What the believer holds is that the evidence is good enough for one whose belief has the ground of a first-person encounter, or perhaps even that the evidence is seen in a different light for one who has had such an encounter. In the latter case the encounter could be understood as transforming the individual, giving her the proper perspective from which to view the evidence, or even as giving her the capacities she needs to appreciate its force.[36] A view such as this one seems to me to make more sense of the way committed believers actually respond to disturbing historical evidence. The usual stance is not dismissal of the evidence as irrelevant, but confidence that the contrary evidence will not be decisive.

EVIDENCE FOR A PARADOX: MAKING THE IMPROBABLE PROBABLE

Climacus has one further reason for treating historical evidence as insignificant, which might be called the "capital crime" argument. Just as a capital offense "absorbs all lesser crimes," so the paradoxicalness of the incarnation makes minor historical problems insignificant.[37] The idea is that the incarnation, being a paradox, is so improbable as to appear absurd. The viability of belief in such a paradox cannot be affected by petty details of the historical records, such as divergencies and contradictions of various witnesses. Its antecedent probability is so low that it cannot be made meaningfully lower; nor could resolving such problems make the probability meaningfully higher. Climacus goes so far as to argue that to try to make the incarnation probable is to falsify its character. The paradox is by definition the improbable, and one could make it probable only by making it into what it is not.[38]

These arguments are strikingly reminiscent of Hume's famous critical attack on miracles. In *An Enquiry Concerning Human Understanding* Hume argues that it could never be reasonable to believe that a miracle has occurred, because a miracle, which is by definition an exception to the laws of nature, is necessarily as improbable an event as can be imagined, since the laws of nature describe what normally happens and therefore what one can reasonably expect to occur.[39] Even the best and strongest evidence for a miracle imaginable would only serve to balance and could never overcome this strong a priori improbability.

It is worth inquiring, both for Climacus and Hume, what concept of probability and what assumptions about probability seem to underlie the arguments. The term "probability" is used in both objective and subjective senses. Objectively, to say that an event is probable is to say that it is objectively likely to occur. Thus the probability of a certain outcome when cards are dealt or dice are rolled can be calculated with some precision. We often say that an event is probable, however, when we know nothing about the objective probabilities of the matter. In these cases we mean that it seems likely to us that the event will occur. For example, I may think it is probable that I will receive an exceptionally large raise in salary next year, even though I have no statistical data on which to base such a claim. It is simply rooted in my belief that my work will be recognized and rewarded by the proper authorities. Such a claim is more a statement about my expectancies than it is a statement about statistical frequencies in the objective world, and such a probability claim is no stronger than the beliefs on which it is based.

Hume's argument appears at first glance to be rooted in objective probability, since it is the infrequency with which laws of nature are violated which makes a miracle improbable. Critics have pointed out, however, that if this is Hume's argument, then it seems to rest on a shallow understanding of how the probability of historical events is estimated. The probability of a historical event cannot be estimated simply from the frequency with which an event of that type occurs, since history is replete with unique types of events. A French emperor may invade Russia only once in all human history. In estimating the probability of an event, we rely therefore not only on the frequency of the type of event in question but on our total knowledge of the situation, including our knowledge of the intentions and characters of whatever historical agents are involved. To think otherwise is to confuse history with dice-rolling or coin-tossing.

Believers in miracles regard miracles as the work of God, who is regarded as a personal agent. To assess the probability of a miracle, therefore, one must do more than consider how frequently they occur. One must consider whether there is a God, whether he is the sort of being who could be expected to do miracles from time to time, in what circumstances this could be expected to occur, and so on. If I believe in a personal God, and believe that God has the ability to intervene in nature, and that he is a being who has good reasons to intervene in nature in certain circumstances, then I will estimate the probability of a miracle in those circumstances much more highly than does Hume.

Anyone who judges miracles extremely improbable, as does Hume, bases the judgment not merely on objective statistical data, but on a variety of beliefs about other matters. Of course it is possible that Hume or others who judge miracles extremely improbable have objectively powerful evidence that God does not exist, or that God is not the kind of being who performs miracles, but it seems more likely to me that Hume is actually simply expressing his beliefs about these matters, and the judgment of probability made is therefore of the subjective kind. It seems or appears likely to Hume that miracles do not occur, but of course miracles may not appear nearly so improbable to someone else who holds different convictions about God. Anyone who actually believes that a miracle has occurred will of course believe that the objective probability of that miracle is 1.

I believe that the concept of probability that underlies Climacus' argument is also subjective. Climacus says that the believer must firmly hold to the notion that the incarnation is a paradox and is therefore improbable. However, since the believer thinks the incarnation has actually occurred, he cannot believe that the objective probability of the event is low, since the objective probability of an event that has occurred is 1. The meaning must be that the believer understands the event as one that will *appear* improbable to someone who holds certain beliefs. For example, someone such as Hume, who believes that miraculous events are in general improbable, will certainly make the same judgment about the idea of a divine incarnation. Anyone who is inclined to think that only events that can be rationally understood can occur, and who also cannot understand how God could become a human being, will think the event improbable. Anyone who is inclined to believe that genuinely unselfish love does not exist will find the idea of God suffering on behalf of human beings similarly improbable. All of this implies that the improbability of the incarnation must be seen as relative to the perspective from which it is viewed.

This corresponds perfectly with our earlier contention that the paradoxicalness of the paradox is itself a function of sin, which creates the "infinite qualitative distance between God and human beings."[40] If, however, the improbability of the paradox is a function of the subjective perspective from which it is viewed, why is the idea of viewing the paradox as probable wrong-headed, as Climacus plainly says? Why is it that the perspective of sinful human beings gains a kind of authority here as the defining perspective? Why shouldn't the believer assert that it is probable to her?

The answer surely lies in the fact that the B hypothesis assumes that human beings are in fact sinners. The perspective of sin is in fact the perspective that every human being occupies, at least prior to faith. And since the transition from sin to faith is not, for Climacus, a one-time event, but a transition that must continually be renewed, it remains necessary for the believer to define the content of her faith polemically, as that which necessarily is in opposition to the thinking of sinful human beings. The believer is not offended but the believer is the person who has confronted and continues to confront the possibility of offense. If faith loses its provocative character and no longer confronts our natural patterns of thinking as a rebuke, it has indeed essentially altered its character. Nevertheless, there is a sense in which the incarnation is no longer improbable to the believer, simply because it is for her something that has occurred. It is improbable only in the sense that she knows it appears unlikely or improbable to our sinfully corrupted patterns of thought. The event remains improbable in that it was not something we expected to occur.

Does the subjective improbability of the paradox imply that the quality of the historical evidence is no concern? It might appear so for the unbeliever, since the event will appear to him to be massively improbable. Whether this is so depends on how pervasive the corrupting effects of sin are on the intellect. However, I believe that the claim that evidence is of no value whatsoever to the unbeliever is not strictly implied by the requirements of hypothesis B, though I doubt that Climacus would admit this. The hypothesis requires that people be construed as sinful enough that they cannot arrive at the Truth apart from an encounter with the god in which they receive the condition. It is not obvious to me that one aspect of this process of giving the condition could not consist in giving the individual evidence that the god-man is indeed the god.

It is true that the giving of the condition is made possible by a life-changing relationship in which the individual becomes a disciple of the god. Coming to know the god and becoming his disciple is hardly reducible to a process of obtaining evidence. If I meet a person, even an ordinary person, and come to know that person, the relationship formed is far richer than the notion of accumulating evidence allows. However, this by no means implies that one could never gain evidence for one's beliefs about another person through the process of coming to know that person, and the same possibility would appear to hold in the case of coming to know the god.

Of course the individual's sinfulness may give him a strong tendency to dismiss any evidence provided, because the beliefs in question appear so improbable. But it seems possible that strong evidence might challenge this presumption of improbability. So long as we are careful to insist that the evidence alone could not produce faith in the individual, it seems compatible with the B hypothesis to assert that evidence might play a positive role in the process in which faith comes into being within the individual.

It also seems possible for evidence to have some value to the believer. Climacus' view to the contrary is surely rooted in his claim that the faith which is the result of the first-person encounter with the god does not rest on evidence in any form. He thinks that if such a faith is sufficient to overturn the subjective improbability of the event, it will surely not be troubled by flaws in the historical record.

This is essentially the same argument we examined in the previous section and is subject to the same reservations that I expressed there. Perhaps it is true that it is the experience of meeting Jesus that is decisive in altering the natural judgment that God would not become a human being. Thus the experience may be the decisive ground of faith, and the inconclusiveness of scholarly debate may be insignificant to the believer. However, this is compatible with claiming that it is important that there be evidence, at least for some people who are troubled by doubts of a certain kind. The evidence may not be of such a nature as to convince unbelievers, but it may be the kind of evidence that is recognized as sufficient when seen through the right eyes.

After all, it is surely possible for someone to doubt whether the experience of Jesus which is the ground of faith is veridical. If we have some reasons to think that Jesus really existed, really is divine, has a certain character, and so on, such information could be helpful in resolving such doubts. If I have an experience of someone who appears to be Mother Teresa, I will be much more likely to believe the experience is veridical if I have background information about the reality of Mother Teresa and about her character, than would be the case if I had never heard of Mother Teresa. Thus the traditional arguments for the reliability of the gospels, and the testimony provided in the gospels for the claim that Jesus is divine, including the miracles, Jesus' own claims to be divine, the profundity of Jesus' teaching, and especially the resurrection, could be of significance to a believer. They are not sufficient to produce faith, and perhaps not necessary for many people, but they may well be for others part of what one might call the normal process by which faith comes into being. They may also have value in confirming faith that is present and helping to relieve doubts and allay various objections.

There is little doubt, I think, that the claims I am making run strongly contrary to the intentions of Climacus, who simply can see no value in traditional apologetics. It is instructive to look at Climacus' treatment of what is traditionally cited as evidence. Climacus admits that the god must make his presence known in the world in some way, though he says that every "accommodation for the sake of comprehensibility" is of no value to the person who does not receive the condition, and is therefore "elicited from him [the god] only under constraint and against his will."[41] I do not see why this should be so.

As Climacus himself says, it surely makes no sense to suppose that the god is literally indistinguishable from any other human being and that there is no sign which points to his divinity. Of course the gospels meet this requirement in the case of Jesus by presenting him as an authoritative teacher, as a worker of miracles, and as someone who himself claims to be divine. If the god wills to reveal himself, and if this requires some sign or evidence of his divinity, then it is hard to see why the god should grant such signs only "under constraint and against his will." Even if we grant Climacus the claim that such signs will only be of value to people of faith, though I have given reason to question that claim, it does not follow that the signs are insignificant for those people who do indeed have faith.

Climacus says that miracles cannot help much, as a miracle (or "the wonder" as the Hongs strictly translate) does not exist immediately, but "is only for faith."[42] It is not clear just what this means. The statement could be read as saying that an event becomes a miracle by my belief that it is. However, this claim is absurd on its face, and in any case directly contradicts a principle Climacus firmly holds, namely that the apprehension of something cannot alter the nature of what is apprehended.[43] If he means that miracles will only be believed by those who have faith, this is possible, though not obvious, but that does not mean that the miracles lack evidential value for those who do possess faith.

Surely Climacus is right when he says that miracles and other evidence do not lead automatically to faith and that they can indeed lead to offense. If the gospels are accurate, many contemporaries of Jesus observed him perform miracles without becoming disciples, and in fact many seem to have been offended by him. However, this does not imply that the miracles are of no value to those people who did possess faith. Certainly, the traditional Christian view is that the "signs" Jesus did are valuable in this way. For example, Peter's first sermon on the day of Pentecost appeals to the "mighty works, signs and wonders" which God had done among the people through Jesus.[44] So far as I can tell, Climacus' deviation from this traditional Christian view and complete denigration of historical evidence is unwarranted, even given the basic correctness of his own view of faith and its genesis in the individual. One can of course resort to the claim that Climacus is not trying to present Christianity, but only his own imaginative construction, but this claim appears strained by his own repeated confessions of plagiarism and by his explicit mention of Christianity at the end of the book. His imaginative proposal is clearly intended to illuminate the logical situation of Christian faith.

CLIMACUS CONFESSES: IS HIS EXPERIMENT CHRISTIANITY?

At the conclusion of chapter 5, Climacus plainly tips his hand for the benefit of any reader obtuse enough to have failed to see that the logical and conceptual issues he has discussed are offered for their value in helping the reader understand the nature of Christian faith and its relations to various philosophical views. After a few more barbs at the Christendom which wants to "naturalize" Christianity by celebrating its "triumph," a triumph that amounts to the transformation of Christianity into its opposite, and a concluding defense of the Aristotelian principle of noncontradiction, the only defense against the confusion of the Christian with what is logically incompatible with Christianity, Climacus tells what he is about as plainly as an ironical humorist can. All the borrowing and allusions to the New Testament and other Christian writers has been intentional, and if Climacus ever writes a continuation, he intends to "call the matter by its proper name and clothe the issue in its historical costume."[45] What that will be is not difficult to determine, since "as is well known, Christianity is the only historical phenomenon that despite the historical—indeed, precisely by means of the historical—has wanted to be the single individual's point of departure for his eternal consciousness...."[46]

Climacus, in a comment that recalls the "proofs" of his hypothesis offered to the interlocutor at the end of the first two chapters, says that Christianity is unique in its linking of the individual's eternal happiness with history. Christianity is thus distinguished from philosophy, which presents us with ideas for contemplation, from mythology, which presents us with imaginative stories, and from ordinary history, which presents us with facts to be remembered. Christianity cannot be understood as a human creation; it has not "arisen in any human heart."[47]

Climacus even tips us off as to one possible reason for his literary trick. We have already seen in his discussion of faith and history a concern that Christianity, which presents the individual with a decision concerning his or her existence, not become the province of scholars. One can easily imagine a discussion of the issues that Climacus himself wants to consider, such as the nature of faith and its relation to history and to reason, and the difference between Christianity and idealism, becoming bogged down in a scholarly discussion of what theologian X and philosopher Y have said about the issues. However, "if in discussing the relation between Christianity and philosophy we begin by narrating what was said earlier, how shall we ever, not finish, but manage to begin, for history just keeps on growing."[48]

Climacus' admittedly whimsical device of converting the content of Christianity into a "thought-experiment" allows him to cut through this long-winded discussion and go straight to the logical heart of the issues. His high-handedness does, however, leave him open to a possible objection, one that some critics have been swift to raise, concerning the relation between his thought-experiment and Christianity. Does the thought-experiment really accurately represent Christianity? If not, does this not call into question whether the experiment can succeed in its purpose of illuminating Christianity? Once this question is asked, do we not need a scholarly inquiry into the essence of Christianity? If so, Climacus has not missed the clutches of the scholars after all.

Thus, some writers have objected that Climacus' version of Christianity is incomplete, since he says nothing about the resurrection of Jesus or eschatological issues. This kind of objection seems wrongheaded to me, for it rests on a misunderstanding of Climacus' game. He is not trying accurately to represent Christian theology, but only presenting us with a thought-experiment. Admittedly, the experiment borrows heavily from Christian teachings and is presented to illuminate Christian teachings, but it would be absurd to expect such an "invention" to embody the whole of Christian theology. All he needs to include in his thought-experiment are some features that are adequate logically to delineate Christianity from its neighbors. Incompleteness is therefore no objection. It would be a different matter if Climacus' project could be shown to embody something incompatible with Christianity, however.

It does seem then that to make a judgment on the thought-experiment one must have some views on what Christianity is, and this does mean that Climacus cannot totally escape the conclusions of scholarship. This does not mean that Climacus will get into a scholarly quarrel with anyone, however. The genius of his project is that it allows him to abstract features of Christianity that are so logically basic that they are very difficult to deny. Essentially, he assumes that there is *something* distinctive about Christianity when compared with pagan thought, and he tries to argue that this distinctiveness is linked to the fact that Christianity is rooted in a divine revelation rather than philosophical speculation, and to the fact that Christianity presents Jesus as a divine savior and not just a philosophical sage. Anyone who disagrees with these assumptions, anyone whose scholarship implies that Christianity is not essentially different from Greek thought and that Christianity does not present Jesus as divine and as the vehicle for God's revelation to humans, has a difficult task, historically speaking. It is hard to see how one could claim that such a view is what has historically been termed Christianity, though one could perhaps argue that this is what Christianity should *become*. A humorist and dialectician like Climacus will not get into the thicket of historical scholarship to argue with such a person, but Climacus stands ready to point out that this "advance" for Christianity, this "going further," looks suspiciously like a return to Socrates and Greek modes of thought.

CHAPTER
10

CHRISTIANITY IN THE CONTEMPORARY WORLD

Climacus ends his book with a "moral," and we would do well to ponder it in drawing our own conclusions about the book. The moral contains two straightforward claims and a barbed indictment. The first claim is that the projected hypothesis "indisputably goes further than the Socratic." The second claim is that the question whether the hypothesis is truer than the Socratic view "cannot be decided in the same breath." This second claim makes it clear that the first claim means only that the hypothesis manages to clearly differentiate itself from the Socratic view, not that it is necessarily truer or cognitively superior in some way. One cannot decide the truth question without deciding what one thinks about the essential components of the hypothesis: "a new organ: faith, and a new presupposition: the consciousness of sin, a new decision: the moment, and a new teacher: the god in time."[1]

The barb is thrown, not at the Socratic view per se, but at those contemporary representatives who were attempting to pass the Socratic perspective off as Christianity: "But to go further than Socrates, when one yet says essentially the same thing as he, only not nearly so well, that, at least, is not Socratic."[2] Christianity may be true or false, and it may well be something that we will want to reject, but intellectual honesty and integrity require that one not convert Christianity into something with which it is logically incompatible. This is a barb that is hurled not only against the Hegelians, who wished to identify God with human society and who saw the Truth in terms of our own discovery of our identity with the divine. It is directed against all the nineteenth-century theologies that in one way or another eliminate from their versions of Christianity those elements that logically differ-entiate it from pagan thought: faith, sin-consciousness, the moment, and most importantly, the incarnation.

THE IMPLICATIONS OF CLIMACUS' EXPERIMENT FOR CONTEMPORARY THEOLOGY

In chapter 3 we noted in passing that Robert Roberts has brilliantly shown how pertinent Climacus' attack here is against certain twentieth-century theologians.[3] A careful look at such theologians as John Cobb and Rudolf Bultmann reveal that in their thought Jesus is reduced in the final analysis to the status of Socratic teacher. Cobb, for example, construes the significance of Jesus in the following terms: Understanding God himself as the source of the creative transformation of the world, and salvation as a creative transformation in which the individual becomes open to growth, Cobb says that Jesus, more than any other human being, identified his own will with this source of creative novelty and thereby makes possible salvation.[4] For this reason Jesus is "the incarnation of the Logos in the fullest meaningful sense."[5]

It appears from this that Jesus is thereby given a unique status. However, a closer look reveals that this uniqueness, if present at all, is only quantitative and not qualitative. Jesus simply had a greater degree of a quality that many, even all, people can possess. Even Jesus did not always perfectly manifest this identification of his will with the source of creative novelty, and it is possible that there are others who manifested the same quality: "There might be someone of whom history has left no record who was constituted much as Jesus was, but that is idle speculation."[6] It is clear from this that Jesus is not essential for the individual to receive the truth; humans beings are not in error in Climacus' sense, and there could be many "Socratic" teachers who can help the individual transform himself, even if Jesus turns out to be the most effective one.

An even more interesting case, in some ways, is that of Rudolf Bultmann. Bultmann understands salvation as being freed from the past in such a way that one can face the future with openness as a responsible chooser. Instead of having an identity that is fixed by past decisions, possessions, and circumstances, the saved person is totally open to possibility. Bultmann, who has doubtless read Climacus, wants to hold that this radical openness to the future is a condition which is made possible only by an encounter with the good news about Jesus. However, as Roberts shows very convincingly,[7] Bultmann gives no credible account of why it is that the story of Jesus should be the only story that makes possible this state of radical openness to the future. Salvation as radical openness to the future has the strong ring of a "Socratic" truth, and there seems no plausible reason why other teachers than Jesus should not help the individual to "recollect" such a truth, however much Bultmann may deny that this is so. On such construals of salvation, or the Truth in Climacean language, it cannot plausibly be argued that the attainment of salvation depends on a relationship with the historical Jesus, understood as uniquely God.

Nor can it be argued plausibly that Climacus has misrepresented the character of Christianity on these essential points; that is, that faith or the incarnation are not really that significant to Christianity. The evidence for this is the way Cobb and Bultmann, who are after all professed Christians, twist and turn to try to maintain the uniqueness of Christ and the essential character of a relationship to Christ. The theologians themselves testify to the correctness of Climacus' claims on these points by desperately, albeit unsuccessfully, trying to meet his criteria for differentiating Christian from pagan thought. Given the recognition and the attempt, why the failure? The answer of Climacus would surely be that it is due to a misguided attempt to make Christianity plausible to its "cultured despisers" and eliminate the possibility of offense that is part and parcel of authentic Christianity, with its claims to rest on a revelation that comes in the person of God in historical human flesh.

Other theologians, most notably John Hick, Maurice Wiles, Michael Goulder, and Dennis Nineham,[8] and more recently, Thomas Sheehan,[9] have forthrightly conceded that traditional Christianity should be jettisoned and that the doctrine of the incarnation should be discarded as a myth. They are candid in admitting that this belief does indeed offend them. That Christianity should be uniquely and authoritatively true, resting on a savior who is uniquely God, is something they cannot swallow.

However, even these theologians, paradoxically, in some way wish to appeal to the authority of Jesus. That is, they do not simply straightforwardly argue for whatever Socratic truth they have latched onto, but try to show that the truth as they see it can be derived from *Jesus'* teachings. Sheehan, for example, claims that Jesus himself taught that God must not be thought of as a reality out there, but as a reality present in human experience and community; God is "God-with-us" and is present in the quest for justice and mercy. This presence of God constitutes the beginning of God's kingdom.

> The Father was not to be found in a distant heaven but was entirely identified with the cause of men and women. Jesus' doctrine of the kingdom meant that God had become incarnate: He had poured himself out, had disappeared into mankind and could be found nowhere else but there....Henceforth and forever God was present only in and as one's neighbor.[10]

Such a teaching is clearly "Socratic" in Climacus' sense. Far from presupposing that human beings are in error and require a divine savior, this teaching implies that human beings at bottom do possess the Truth. The interesting question is why, given the evidently Socratic nature of this truth, is it so important to Sheehan to trace this teaching back to Jesus. If Jesus was not the God-man, why does he possess any special authority? If the answer is that Jesus' authority derives from the truth and profundity of the teaching, then it is evident that in the final analysis the teaching stands on its own Socratic feet, and it does not matter what the historical Jesus taught. Nevertheless, writers such as Sheehan seem anxious to trace their views back to Jesus, and argue that traditional Christianity is somehow a distortion of his original message. Sheehan argues that the distortion began with Peter himself, who tried to hold on to the person of Jesus instead of Jesus' message.[11]

A similar pattern can be seen in several of the authors in *The Myth of God Incarnate*. One of the authors of this work argues, for example, that Jesus' original message was altered to include a myth of a divine savior by the Samaritan church.[12] But one may well ask, "Why does it matter what Jesus taught?" once it is conceded that Jesus was not divine and did not teach with divine authority? If a person thinks that Jesus was God incarnate and that our relation to him will determine our eternal destiny, then it would make some sense for that person to follow historical scholarship in determining exactly what Jesus taught, since Jesus is recognized by that individual as having divine authority (though Climacus would caution us that a living relationship with Jesus in the moment is the basis of faith, not historical scholarship). If, however, Jesus is a teacher who points us to a truth that is potentially embedded within each of us, why must we cling desperately to his authority? Such a view sounds once more like a case of "saying the same thing as Socrates, only not nearly so well," not nearly so well because what is said is burdened with deep conceptual confusion.

In a very interesting "Epilogue" to *The Myth of God Incarnate*, Dennis Nineham sees this problem and clearly voices it. How is it, Nineham asks, that his fellow theologians can deny Jesus' divinity but then go on to make extravagant claims about Jesus as a human being? If we deny the inspired authority of the New Testament and rely on the historical-critical method, can we really say that Jesus was morally perfect, a man whose concern was totally for others, a man whose life centered totally upon God, and so on? At best such claims would seem to be consistent with the historical record, but not really historically justified.[13]

In a brief response, Don Cupitt accepts the force of this warning and draws the consequences consistently.

> I acknowledge the limitations of our critical-historical knowledge of Jesus. However, the core of a religion does not lie in the biography or personality of the founder, but in the specifically religious values to which, according to the tradition, he bore witness. By these values I mean possible determinations of the human spirit whereby it relates itself to the ultimate goal of existence...[14]

Cupitt here straightforwardly acknowledges that the Christianity he is putting forward is a Socratic view. In effect, he is admitting that relying on Jesus' authority for his position is a mistake, a kind of hang-over of old ways of thinking.

One may well think that this point is unimportant. Isn't it merely a question of how a word is to be used, and shouldn't modern theologians be permitted their own sense of "Christianity?" Of course. However, if modern theologians are interested in contributing to clarity and responsible thought, they will be careful in how they use words. There are millions of Christians today who continue to use "Christianity" to designate a faith that implies that Jesus was uniquely God's son, a faith that rests on an authoritative, historical revelation, a view of Christianity which clearly makes it logically exclude Socratic perspectives on the Truth. Such a conception of Christianity has characterized the main body of Christian believers from the time of the New Testament onward. It is intolerable to have the same word designate positions that logically exclude one another. Hence if modern theologians call a view that is really Socratic "Christianity," the cause of clarity is hardly served. Those who continue to believe in what has heretofore been called "Christianity" will have to term their faith something else, and their relation to the tradition they are continuing is obscured. Traditional Christianity may be true or false, but one thing is certainly true, and that is that traditional Christianity and pagan thought are genuinely different.

The message of Climacus is therefore that Christian faith today is tied, as it has always been, to a particular cluster of concepts: "a new organ: faith, and a new presupposition: the consciousness of sin, a new decision: the moment, and a new teacher: the god in time."[15] Climacus is not denying, I think, that there is room for doctrinal development and new understanding of Christian teachings, but he is claiming that there are certain features that are essential to distinguish Christianity from pagan thought, ancient and contemporary. Genuine Christian thought rests on the assumption that human beings are sinful and that their salvation depends on a revelation to them by God, a revelation that must be accepted in faith and cannot be regarded as something to be transcended or surmounted. The heart of this revelation is God's own entrance into human history, an event which becomes the means by which God enters the personal history of individuals in every age, making a moment of decision both possible and necessary. The response of faith is not one that can be justified before a neutral, rational tribunal; it is rather one that necessarily goes against our existing assumptions about what is probable and which can only be believed when the individual, including the individual's past ways of thinking, is transformed by the encounter with the incarnate God.

COMMITMENT: A RETREAT OR AN ADVANCE?

Many thinkers would agree with Climacus that a Christianity that is tied to an authoritative revelation which revolves around an incarnate God necessarily conflicts with reason, though they may not agree with the sociological critique of "reason" that I have argued is implicit in Climacus' analysis. For thinkers such as this, one can only embrace Christianity through an act of commitment that is necessarily irrational. They see Climacus, or rather Kierkegaard, since Climacus' work is understood as part and parcel of Kierkegaard's own perspective, as recommending a repudiation of reason and a "retreat to commitment." Kierkegaard is here seen as tremendously significant, since he exemplifies and in many ways is the fountainhead for a strategy that has become pervasive in the twentieth century.

This retreat to commitment is not a blind embrace of irrationalism. Rather, Kierkegaard is seen as giving a kind of argument for the reasonableness of irrational commitment. Kierkegaard saw through the bankruptcy of the Enlightenment project of giving a rational justification for our ultimate life-choices, be those choices ethical or religious. Since no choice of this nature can be rationally justified, it follows that any choice is as justified as any other. Each individual must choose for herself, and this act of choice will then serve as a "foundation" for life, a substitute for the rational foundation the Enlightenment sought in vain.

Alasdair MacIntyre calls this the doctrine of "radical choice" and claims that it is exemplified in *Either/Or*, where the reader is presented with a choice between an aesthetic and an ethical lifestyle, with no objective way of deciding between them.[16] W. W. Bartley also credits Kierkegaard with being the originator of this strategy, and he specifically mentions the Johannes Climacus literature as among its sources. Kierkegaard maintains, says Bartley, "that the correctness of any system or way of life can never be proved. Any attempt to do so generates an infinite regress of proving; and thus a dogmatic presupposition is necessary. To adopt any particular way of life one *has* to make an irrational choice of some 'absolute presupposition' or revelation."[17] Bartley calls this argument the "*tu quoque* argument" and regards it as the inspiration for a host of contemporary forms of irrationalism.

Terence Penelhum, in *God and Skepticism*,[18] develops a perspective on Kierkegaard that is very similar, though developed with much greater care than one finds in Bartley, who freely attributes views to Kierkegaard that seem to have little textual basis. Penelhum sees Kierkegaard, along with Pascal, as accepting what Penelhum terms the parity argument. In *Philosophical Fragments*, he says, Kierkegaard uses the arguments of ancient skeptics to try to show that all our intellectual commitments regarding matters of fact are rationally unjustified and depend on faith, which is an act of the will. With regard to Christian faith, this act of the will is made possible by divine assistance and is not within our human powers. Nevertheless, the analogy between ordinary beliefs and religious faith is strong enough to show that the religious believer needs no rational justification for faith, since she does only what all human beings do with respect to other matters.[19]

Now it is certainly the case that Kierkegaard's writings, including the Climacus books, do attempt to show the limitations of human reason. The claim to think without assumptions or presuppositions, or to attain a final, systematic understanding of matters of fact flies in the face of human finitude and historicity. The Interlude in *Philosophical Fragments* does indeed emphasize the role of the will in the formation of human belief. However, critics such as Bartley nevertheless completely misunderstand what is going on in these texts. They assume that Kierkegaard is worried, as they are, about whether Christianity can be shown to be reasonable, and they therefore read him as trying to show that Christianity is as reasonable as any other view.

Such a view misses what Kierkegaard (and Climacus too on this point) is all about. He does not wish to show that Christianity is reasonable or that it is no more unreasonable than any other commitment. Rather he wants to show that Christianity is most definitely unreasonable, when analyzed from the perspective of a person who lacks faith or "the condition." The skeptical arguments in *Philosophical Fragments* are not directed at skeptical opponents of Christianity, who are regarded as doing Christianity a service by making the nature of offense evident. Rather, the target is apologists for Christianity, those who would make Christianity reasonable by showing its probability or speculatively reinterpreting its character.

For Climacus it is not the case that Christianity is "no more irrational than anything else." It is the paradox, and embodies within it the possibility of offense. Given its insulting claims about the sinfulness of human thinking, it will necessarily appear, in one sense, to be the height of irrationality. The arguments about the limitations of human reason are not intended to show "parity" between Christian faith and other commitments, and are not intended as a "you too" response to critics. Rather, they are an attempt to burst the bubble of rationalistic defenders of faith, defenders who are seen as pimps who prostitute what they are trying to save.

The really decisive epistemological point being made by Climacus concerns what I should term the perspectival nature of human reason. Human reason is not a neutral arbiter of religious truth, but always expresses the character of the reasoner. Reason is passionate; it embodies either the imperialistic urge to dominate that leads to offense or the humble recognition of my limits that leads to faith. The moral to be drawn from this point is not that one may commit oneself to anything, since all commitments are equally irrational, but that reflection on faith ought to be sensitive to its own engaged character. If I find Christian faith objectionable on rational grounds, that may imply something about Christian faith, but it may also imply something about me. Specifically, Climacus challenges me to reflect on whether or not my objections are an expression of the jolt which Christianity offers to my need to be autonomous and in control of my world. Does "postmodern man" find the idea of an authoritative, divine revelation intolerable because we have made some profound intellectual discovery? Or does Christianity seem unpalatable because it flies in the face of what post-Enlightenment people want to think about themselves, and, according to Climacus, what human beings in every age have wanted to think about themselves?

Nor should we forget that the perspectival character of reason implies that offense is not the only option for a thinking person. As we have interpreted Climacus, faith in Christ is not a blind leap, nor an embracement of a logical contradiction. It is rather a commitment to become a follower of Jesus which is made possible by an encounter with

Jesus that transforms the individual, including the individual's thinking patterns. Climacus does not see this transformation as grounded in evidence, though I have argued that he really ought to allow for the possibility that evidence might play a positive role in the process. Rather he sees belief in Jesus as something like a basic belief, a belief that the transformation makes possible. That, however, does not mean that the transformation and the belief that is part of its outcome are thereby groundless. What is needed for faith is not an arbitrary commitment, but an encounter with a living reality that can give me the ability to grasp the truth. Thus Kierkegaard responds to the Enlightenment critique of faith by a critique of Enlightenment thinking itself, but he does not thereby in postmodernist fashion jettison a realistic concept of truth.

SUBJECTIVITY AND TRUTH

A critic may respond that this description of the encounter begs all the interesting questions. How does Climacus know that the encounter is indeed an encounter with God and that the transformation is one that brings the individual into the Truth, or the Truth into the individual? As a question to Climacus, this query is misdirected, since he does not claim to be a Christian. We can, however, understand the question as a query to the believer, with Climacus as the believer's designated spokesman. How, then, does the believer know that the moment Climacus has described is a reality?

Here everything depends on the underlying epistemological assumptions. If one takes "knowledge" in the sense of classical foundationalism, then the believer cannot know these things. Here Climacus' skeptical admonitions are pertinent. If I limit myself to what is objectively certain, there is no body of evidence or philosophical argument that will provide a warrant for the truth of Christianity. The question is whether that is a problem for Christianity or rather one more indication of a problem with classical foundationalism. My Christian faith may be grounded in an encounter with the living Christ, but I cannot be expected to demonstrate that this encounter is a reality to an unbeliever, given the perspectival nature of reason and the inherent uncertainty which attaches to finite human experience.

The rejection of classical foundationalism does not, however, imply that "anything goes." Specifically, it does not imply that there is no such thing as objective truth or that there are no ways of getting in touch with that truth.

Kierkegaard has, I think, rejected what Gadamer has called the Enlightenment "prejudice against prejudice." He has, in agreement with many contemporary "postmodern" thinkers, come to terms with the finitude and historicity of human thinking. He does not, however, assume that finitude and historicity always cut us off from the possibility of truth, as many contemporary thinkers do. To assume this is not really to have abandoned the "prejudice against prejudice," because it is implicitly to assume that our "subjectivity" always acts as a distortion, a veil that clouds the truth. It is to fail to acknowledge the possibility that our subjectivity could enable us to grasp truth as well as block us from the goal. Like the radical critics of reason, Kierkegaard shows us the ways our subjectivity makes any final system of truth impossible. However, Kierkegaard goes the whole way and really takes historicity seriously. This means that the factors that block and distort our grasp of truth are historical as well and could be changed. Hence, even though "the system" may not be attainable, truth may be provisionally grasped. However, the crucial condition for this is not a retreat to objectivity, but a transformation of subjectivity, a personal change.

Alvin Plantinga, in defending what he has termed "Reformed Epistemology," has argued that knowledge is the product of my human cognitive mechanisms, when these mechanisms are functioning as they were designed to function in the environment in which they were intended to function.[20] Of course such an epistemological perspective is by no means metaphysically neutral; it presupposes that we know some things about human beings and their purposes. However, why should we think that any epistemological theory can be metaphysically neutral, or that we could even get started on an account of what knowledge is without assuming at least provisionally that we know some things? If this is the kind of epistemological perspective that underlies the question as to whether the Christian can know that his encounter with Christ is genuine, then the negative answer the classical foundationalist would give is by no means obviously right. I believe a positive answer can be given with a slight emendation of Plantinga's view.

The Christian who takes Climacus' view of faith will surely say that with respect to essential truth, our cognitive faculties are impaired by sin; they are not functioning as they were intended to function in an environment in which they were designed to function. Hence an important modification to Plantinga's definition must be made. Truth, at least essential truth, is the product of the restoration and healing of our cognitive faculties, which makes them able to function as they were intended to function in an environment in which they were intended to function. The restoration and healing is one that is made possible by the transformation of the knower through an encounter with Christ. In this transformation, the prideful attitudes of imperialistic reason are put to death, and the individual can begin to recognize Jesus Christ as God incarnate, the one who fulfills my deepest needs and hopes, including the needs and hopes of reason itself. Reason is fulfilled by coming to understand its own limits and discovering what it had futilely sought in its domineering manner all along. What is required for my cognitive mechanisms to function appropriately in this case is my own spiritual transformation.

Perhaps the word "mechanisms" is inappropriate here, implying as it does that the truth is the result of some machinery whirring along inside me. The truth is rather that the attainment of truth is inseparably bound up with my own spiritual transformation, and that is far from a mechanical process, but is on the Christian perspective achieved through a relationship. The term "mechanism" is inappropriate here for another reason as well, since the process in this case includes an important role for choice. The insights the encounter with Christ makes possible require attitudes that I can will to affirm or repudiate.

Human existence, as Kierkegaard understands it, neither guarantees nor excludes the attainment of truth. Kierkegaard affirms, with "postmodern" writers, the *hubris* of rationalisms of various sorts, and stresses the finitude and historicity of human existence. However, he also affirms, with traditional Christians and on this point the ancient Greeks as well, the possibility that in that finitude and historicity we may discover truth. With respect to the Truth, that discovery is one that is linked to subjectivity. We cannot discover the Truth apart from the spiritual transformation whereby we begin to embody the Truth.

Notes

1. ON READING KIERKEGAARD AND JOHANNES CLIMACUS

1. *Concluding Unscientific Postscript*, translated by David F. Swenson and Walter Lowrie (Princeton: Princeton University Press, 1968), p. 14 (*Samlede Værker*, 1st ed., 14 vols. [Copenhagen: Gyldendals, 1901–1906] vol. VII, 2). In future references to the *Postscript*, the first number will refer to the pagination of the old Swenson-Lowrie translation. All references to Kierkegaard's published writings will also include, as a second number in parentheses, the pagination of the first edition of the Danish *Samlede Værker* (volume number will appear first, followed by the page number). The new Hong translation of *Postscript*, as well as the other volumes in the *Kierkegaard's Writings* series, includes the pagination of this edition in the margins. Throughout this book I have freely modified translations or used my own, but I always supply an English page reference for the benefit of the reader.

2. *Postscript*, p. 245n (VII, 234n).

3. See, for example, Louis Pojman, *The Logic of Subjectivity: Kierkegaard's Philosophy of Religion* (University, Alabama: University of Alabama Press, 1984); Steve Dunning, *Kierkegaard's Dialectic of Inwardness: A Structural Analysis of the Theory of Stages* (Princeton: Princeton University Press, 1985); John Elrod, *Being and Existence in Kierkegaard's Pseudonymous Works* (Princeton: Princeton University Press, 1975); and Mark Taylor, *Kierkegaard's Pseudonymous Authorship: A Study of Time and the Self* (Princeton: Princeton University Press, 1975).

4. Louis Mackey, *Kierkegaard: A Kind of Poet* (Philadelphia: University of Pennsylvania Press, 1971).

5. This approach is well illustrated in discussions of Kierkegaard in two of Mark Taylor's recent works, though neither work is devoted solely to Kierkegaard. See his *Tears* (Albany: State University of New York Press, 1990), and also *Erring: A Postmodern A/Theology* (Chicago: University of Chicago Press, 1984).

6. Louis Mackey, *Kierkegaard: A Kind of Poet*, p. xi.

7. Besides Taylor's own work, the following books from the *Kierkegaard and Postmodernism* series illustrate the kinds of tendencies I have in mind: Louis Mackey, *Points of View: Readings of Kierkegaard* (Tallahassee: Florida State University Press, 1986); Sylviane Agacinski, *Aparté: Conceptions and Deaths of Søren Kierkegaard* (Tallahassee: Florida State University Press, 1988); and John Vignaux Smyth, *A Question of Eros: Irony in Sterne, Kierkegaard, and Barthes* (Tallahassee: Florida State University Press, 1986). A writer who differs from the above in some important respects but still situates Kierkegaard in the radical milieu of Derrida is John Caputo, *Radical Hermeneutics: Repetition, Deconstruction, and the Hermeneutic Project* (Bloomington: Indiana University Press, 1987).

8. See H. A. Nielsen, *Where the Passion Is: A Reading of Kierkegaard's Philosophical Fragments* (Tallahassee: Florida State University Press, 1983);

and Robert Roberts, *Faith, Reason, and History: Rethinking Kierkegaard's* Philosophical Fragments (Macon, Georgia: Mercer University Press, 1986).

9. Mackey, *Points of View*, p. 190.

10. See Henning Fenger, *Kierkegaard: The Myths and Their Origins* (New Haven: Yale University Press, 1980). P. 147 and p. 214 contain particularly good examples of this kind of debunking.

11. See Josiah Thompson, *Kierkegaard* (New York: Alfred Knopf, 1973).

12. *Works of Love*, translated by Howard and Edna Hong (New York: Harper and Row, 1962), pp. 213–30 (IX, 216–34).

13. *The Point of View for My Work as an Author: A Report to History*, translated by Walter Lowrie (New York: Harper and Row, 1962), p. 72 (XIII, 561–62).

14. See again *The Point of View*, pp. 64–92 (XIII, 556–75).

15. "A First and Last Declaration," in *Postscript*, p. 551 (VII, 546).

16. See Mackey, *Points of View*, p. 187.

17. Many books could be cited as illustrating this procedure, for example John Elrod, *Being and Existence in Kierkegaard's Pseudonymous Works*, and James Collins, *The Mind of Kierkegaard* (Chicago: Regnery, 1953).

18. Niels Thulstrup, "Commentator's Introduction," in *Philosophical Fragments*, translated by David Swenson, revised by Howard V. Hong (Princeton: Princeton University Press, 1962), p. lxxxv.

19. See Nielsen, *Where the Passion Is*, pp. 22–23.

20. See Robert Roberts, *Faith, Reason, and History*, p. 7.

21. *Philosophical Fragments*, p. 7; (IV, 177). This quote and all future quotations and references from *Philosophical Fragments* will be referenced to the new Princeton edition, *Philosophical Fragments* (with *Johannes Climacus*) edited and translated by Howard V. Hong and Edna H. Hong (Princeton: Princeton University Press, 1985). The first number given is to this edition; the number in parentheses is to the pagination of the first edition of *Sämlede Værker*, volume IV. The translations are usually my own; the English reference given is for the convenience of the reader. If no book is cited in a note, the reference is to *Fragments*.

22. P. 7 (178).

23. *Søren Kierkegaard's Journals and Papers*, 7 vols., edited and translated by Howard V. Hong and Edna H. Hong (Bloomington: Indiana University Press, 1967–78), entry #1575. (Subsequent references to the *Journals and Papers* will give only the entry number for the Hong edition.)

24. Published in English with the new Hong translation of *Philosophical Fragments*.

25. For a fuller account see my article "Kierkegaard's View of Humor: Must Christians Always Be Solemn?" *Faith and Philosophy* 4, 2 (1987), 176–86, and chapter 10 of my book *Kierkegaard's* Fragments *and* Postscript (Atlantic Highlands, N.J.: Humanities Press, 1983).

26. *Postscript*, pp. 459–62n (VII, 447–52n).

27. *Postscript*, p. 462 (VII, 451).

28. *Postscript*, p. 403 (VII, 391).

29. *Postscript*, p. 402 (VII, 391).

30. *Postscript*, p. 243 (VII, 231).

2. AN IRONICAL THOUGHT EXPERIMENT

1. Plato represents Socrates as posing this paradox and solving it by appeal to the soul's recollection of truth it possessed before birth, in the *Meno* (80d-81c). See any standard edition of Plato, such as *Plato: The Collected Dialogues*, ed. Edith Hamilton and Huntington Cairns (Princeton: Princeton University Press, 1961), p. 363.

2. The image of Socrates as a midwife is developed at some length in the *Protagoras* (149b-151d). See Hamilton and Cairns, *Plato: The Collected Dialogues*, pp. 854–56.

3. P. 13 (183). The reader is reminded that all references without other identification are to *Philosophical Fragments*, and that the first number refers to the pagination of the *Kierkegaard's Writings* edition, and the second number (in parentheses) refers to the pagination of the first edition of *Samlede Værker*.

4. P. 14 (184).

5. Pp. 14–15 (184).

6. Pp. 17–18 (187).

7. P. 19 (188).

8. In developing his thought-experiment, Climacus uses the definite article to speak of "the god" in a way reminiscent of Plato. In understanding the application of the experiment to Christianity, which will quickly become apparent as the point of the whole procedure, it will often be more natural to speak of God with no definite article. I will sometimes follow Climacus and use the definite article to keep the flavor of his thought-experiment in view, but in some cases, particularly where I am reflecting on the implications of his experiment for Christianity, I will switch to the more normal Christian terminology.

9. *Postscript*, p. 245n (VII, 234n).

10. P. 21 (191).

11. Pp. 21–22 (191).

12. *Postscript*, p. 246n (VII, 236n).

13. I shall not attempt to decide the question as to whether there are other religions, such as Judaism and Islam, which are similar to Christianity in posing the problem of a historical foundation for salvation. Climacus thinks that there is something unique about Christianity.

14. See for example the essay by John Hick, "Jesus and the World Religions," in *The Myth of God Incarnate*, edited by John Hick (London: SCM Press, 1977). Several later books of Hick's repeat this theme. Thomas Sheehan has developed a somewhat similar line of thought in his *The First Coming: How the Kingdom of God Became Christianity* (New York: Random House, 1986).

15. *The Point of View*, p. 13 (XIII, 523).

16. For those who want more on the relation between Climacus and Kierkegaard, I recommend chapters 1 and 2 of my *Kierkegaard's Fragments and Postscript* and numerous sections near the end of each chapter, particularly at the ends of chapters 11 and 12.

17. Act I, Scene v.

18. *Postscript*, p. 3 (VII, v).

19. Niels Thulstrup, "Commentator's Introduction," in the Swenson translation of *Philosophical Fragments* (Princeton: Princeton University Press, 1962), p. 152.
20. H. A. Nielsen, *Where the Passion Is*, p. 3.
21. P. 8 (178).
22. P. 8 (178).

3. CONSTRUCTING AN ALTERNATIVE TO THE
SOCRATIC VIEW OF "THE TRUTH"

1. Pp. 9–10 (180). That the highest human task is to gain true wisdom and knowledge, because knowledge is linked to virtue, is a theme in many Platonic dialogues, including the *Protagoras* and *Meno*. The most famous attempt to prove the immortality of the soul is of course in the *Phaedo*.
2. *Postscript*, p. 166n (VII, 178).
3. P. 15 (184–85).
4. See p. 12 (183), for example, where in the discussion of the Platonic view Climacus says that "eternal happiness is given...in the possession of the Truth that I had from the beginning."
5. P. 111 (272).
6. See Robert Roberts, *Faith, Reason, and History*, pp. 30–44.
7. See Albert Camus, *The Myth of Sisyphus and Other Essays* (New York: Random House, 1955).
8. P. 20 (190).
9. P. 14 (184).
10. P. 15 (184).
11. P. 15 (185).
12. See Bernard Williams, *Moral Luck* (Cambridge: Cambridge University Press, 1981), for a seminal discussion of the concept of moral luck.
13. *Apology*, 41D, *Plato*, edited by Edith Hamilton and Huntington Cairns, p. 25.
14. Pp. 16–17n (186–87n).
15. Pp. 14–15 (184).
16. P. 11 (181).
17. P. 18 (188).
18. P. 14 (184).
19. P. 20 (190).
20. P. 17 (187).
21. Pp. 17–18 (187).
22. P. 20 (189).
23. P. 20 (189).
24. *Postscript*, p. 452 (VII, 440).
25. P. 21 (191).
26. P. 21 (191).
27. P. 21 (191).
28. P. 22 (191).
29. P. 11 (181).

30. See M. J. Ferreira, "The Faith/History Problem and Kierkegaard's *A Priori* 'Proof'," *Religious Studies* 23 (1987), pp. 337–45.
31. P. 111 (272).
32. P. 111 (272).
33. *Postscript*, p. 332 (VII, 322).
34. P. 109 (271).
35. P. 22 (191).

4. THE POETRY OF THE INCARNATION

1. P. 23 (192).
2. P. 23 (192).
3. P. 24 (193).
4. P. 24 (193).
5. P. 33 (200).
6. P. 25 (194).
7. Robert Roberts argues in this way in his book, *Faith, Reason, and History*, pp. 51–52.
8. P. 32 (200).
9. P. 32 (200).
10. P. 28 (196).
11. P. 28 (197).
12. P. 26 (194).
13. P. 27 (196).
14. P. 29 (197).
15. P. 29 (197).
16. P. 33 (201).
17. P. 32 (200).
18. P. 33 (201).
19. P. 34 (202).
20. Pp. 35–36 (202–203).
21. P. 36 (204).
22. P. 35 (202).
23. P. 36 (203).
24. Many writers who are addressing the problem of the relationship of Christianity to other faiths in a religiously pluralistic world evidence this sort of embarrassment with respect to the incarnation. A clear example is found in John Hick, "Jesus and the World Religions," in *The Myth of God Incarnate*. Much of Hick's writings since this essay is along the same line.
25. I Corinthians 2:9. This Pauline passage is alluded to frequently in Kierkegaard's writings.

5. THOUGHT, PASSION, AND PARADOX

1. P. 37 (204).
2. P. 38 (205).

3. P. 38 (205).

4. Pp. 38–39 (206).

5. P. 39 (207).

6. P. 45 (212).

7. Climacus generally uses the Danish term *Forstanden*, which is properly translated by the Hongs as "the understanding," when referring to the faculty of human thought. It is of course well known that Hegel and some other German philosophers made a distinction between reason (*Vernunft*) and understanding (*Verstand*) and claimed that though the understanding cannot arrive at ultimate or absolute truth, reason could. It might be thought that the fact that Climacus uses the Danish term for the understanding is significant and that when he argues, as he does later, that human thinking cannot comprehend the absolute paradox of the B hypothesis that it is only the understanding that is limited in this way, not reason. I believe that this inference would be absolutely mistaken; a close reading of *Philosophical Fragments* as a whole leaves no doubt that Climacus thinks that human beings are completely unable to comprehend the paradox of the incarnation. It was in fact to preclude this misinterpretation that David Swenson originally translated *Forstanden* as "the reason." To signify my own agreement with Swenson on this point, I shall talk interchangeably about reason or understanding in discussing these issues.

8. P. 37 (204).

9. P. 37 (204).

10. P. 37 (204).

11. Pp. 38–39 (206).

12. P. 39 (207).

13. P. 39 (207).

14. P. 40 (207).

15. See David Hume, "Sceptical Doubts Concerning the Operations of the Understanding," section 4 of *An Inquiry Concerning Human Understanding* (Indianapolis, Ind.: Hackett Publishing Co., 1977), pp. 15–25.

16. See Immanuel Kant, *Critique of Pure Reason*, translated by Norman Kemp Smith (New York: St. Martin's Press, 1965), pp. 500–506.

17. P. 40 (207).

18. *Concluding Unscientific Postscript*, pp. 280–82, 284–85 (VII 271–73, 275–76).

19. P. 41n (208n-209n).

20. See Alvin Plantinga, *The Nature of Necessity* (Oxford: Oxford University Press, 1974) pp. 196–221. Plantinga's argument that the possibility of God's existence implies the necessity of God's existence is of course far more complex and ingenious than this bald statement of its import.

21. P. 42n (209n).

22. P. 42 (209).

23. P. 42 (209).

24. P. 42 (209).

25. P. 44 (211).

26. P. 43 (211).

27. Pp. 42–43 (210).

28. See my *Kierkegaard's Fragments and Postscript*, chapter 8, and my article

"Kierkegaard's Attack on Apologetics," *Christian Scholar's Review* 10, 4 (1981), 322–32.

29. P. 45 (212).
30. P. 44 (212).
31. P. 45 (212).
32. P. 45 (213).
33. P. 45 (212).
34. P. 45 (213).
35. P. 45 (213).
36. Pp. 45–46 (213).
37. P. 46 (213).
38. P. 46 (213).
39. P. 46 (214).
40. P. 46 (214).
41. P. 47 (214).
42. Pp. 46–47 (214).
43. P. 47 (214).
44. P. 47 (214).
45. P. 39 (206).
46. P. 47 (214).
47. P. 47 (214).
48. P. 47 (214–215).
49. P. 47 (215).
50. P. 48 (215).
51. Pp. 47–48 (214–15).

6. THE ECHO OF OFFENSE

1. P. 54 (220).
2. P. 53 (219).
3. P. 51 (217–18).
4. See Merold Westphal, *Kierkegaard's Critique of Reason and Society* (Macon, Ga.: Mercer University Press, 1987), p. 88.
5. P. 51 (217).
6. Pp. 49–50 (216–17).
7. P. 50 (217).
8. Pp. 52–53 (218–19).
9. P. 53 (219).
10. P. 51 (217).
11. See, for example, *Training in Christianity*, translated by Walter Lowrie (Princeton: Princeton University Press, 1944), pp. 62–63 (XII, 55–56), and *The Sickness unto Death*, translated by Howard V. and Edna H. Hong (Princeton: Princeton University Press, 1980), pp. 84–87 (XI, 195–99).
12. For examples of commentators who appear to take this line see Alastair Hannay, *Kierkegaard* (London: Routledge and Kegan Paul, 1982), pp. 106–108; Louis Pojman, *The Logic of Subjectivity* (University, Ala.: University of Alabama

Press, 1984), pp. 24, 100–102; and Herbert M. Garelick, *The Anti-Christianity of Kierkegaard* (The Hague: Martinus Nijhoff, 1965), p. 29.

13. Pp. 53, 108–109 (219, 270).
14. P. 49 (216).
15. P. 47 (215).
16. See particularly *The Sickness unto Death*, pp. 83–96 (XI, 194–207).
17. Pp. 53–54 (219–20).
18. P. 54 (220).
19. P. 54 (220).

7. REASON AND THE PARADOX

1. Pp. 55–56 (221–22).
2. Pp. 56–57 (222–23).
3. The Danish word *Discipel* seems almost perfectly captured by the English "disciple," and it is puzzling to me that the Hongs chose to translate it by "follower" in so many cases. The Danish term, like the English "disciple," is a biblical term, and the biblical overtones are surely intended in a work that is so full of biblical allusions and quotations. Also, the English term "disciple" has strong intellectual connotations; one can be a disciple of a teacher, as Plato is sometimes said to be a disciple of Socrates, and these connotations also seem very much present in the Danish text, written as it is in the idiom of philosophical idealism. In short, "disciple" has just the right ambiguity in that it can serve as a term for an intellectual follower but also as a term for a follower of Jesus. "Follower" lacks these rich connotations. Its one merit might seem to be that it is an existential term that suggests action, but this is actually a demerit, since it removes some of the ironical flavor of Climacus' work, which is one that tries to describe an existential commitment (Christianity) in the idiom of philosophical idealism.
4. P. 59 (224).
5. P. 62 (227).
6. See David Swenson's classic *Something about Kierkegaard*, revised edition (Minneapolis: Augsburg Publishing Co., 1945). Also see Alastair MacKinnon's "Kierkegaard: 'Paradox' and Irrationalism," in Jerry Gill, editor, *Essays on Kierkegaard*, and his "Kierkegaard's Irrationalism Revisited," *International Philosophical Quarterly* 9 (1969), 165–76. Classic essays by Fabro and Søe can be found in *A Kierkegaard Critique*, edited by Howard Johnson and Niels Thulstrup (New York: Harper and Row, 1962).
7. Actually, these writers and those to be discussed below often refer to Kierkegaard rather than Climacus, even though they are discussing the Climacus section of Kierkegaard's authorship. Not everyone acknowledges the distinction between the pseudonym and Kierkegaard himself as I do. To avoid awkwardness in my discussion I shall continue to speak of Climacus rather than Kierkegaard in referring to these treatments of Kierkegaard, even where the authors in question speak of Kierkegaard.
8. See Alastair Hannay's *Kierkegaard* (London: Routledge and Kegan Paul, 1982), pp. 106–108.

9. See Brand Blanshard, "Kierkegaard on Faith," in *Essays on Kierkegaard*.

10. Herbert Garelick, *The Anti-Christianity of Kierkegaard* (The Hague: Martinus Nijhoff, 1965), p. 28.

11. Louis Pojman, *The Logic of Subjectivity* (University, Ala.: University of Alabama Press, 1984), p. 136.

12. Pojman, p. 137.

13. See, for example, *Postscript*, p. 85 (VII, 73). The description of human life as a synthesis of temporality and eternity pervades Kierkegaard's writings. See, for example, the famous opening pages of *The Sickness unto Death*, edited and translated by Howard V. and Edna H. Hong (Princeton: Princeton University Press, 1980) pp. 13–14.

14. In *Concluding Unscientific Postscript* Johannes Climacus describes existence as a "striving," which involves a "self-contradiction" (P. 84; VII, 72).

15. P. 87 (250).

16. *Postscript*, P. 512 (VII, 504).

17. P. 62 (227).

18. For example, see *Postscript*, p. 183 (VII, 171). It may be that the designation of the paradox as the absurd by Climacus is a consequence of the non-Christian character of the pseudonym, or at least of the professedly non-Christian stance. It is worth noting that Alastair McKinnon's computer studies of the Kierkegaardian text have shown that references to the incarnation as the absurd come almost exclusively from the pseudonymous authorship, which represent how the incarnation will appear to a non-Christian, and are almost nonexistent in Kierkegaard's nonpseudonymous writings. See Alastair MacKinnon, *The Kierkegaard Indices* (Leiden: E. J. Brill, 1970–1975), particularly volumes III and IV.

19. P. 86 (249–50).

20. For example, Hegel says that nature is a contradiction. See his *Philosophy of Nature*, translated by A. V. Miller (Oxford: Clarendon Press: 1970), pp. 17–22.

21. *Postscript*, p. 459 (VII, 447).

22. P. 108 (270).

23. Pp. 108–109 (270).

24. P. 53 (219).

25. P. 101 (263). (My emphasis)

26. P. 101 (263–64).

27. *Postscript*, p. 504 (VII, 495).

28. See *Training in Christianity*, pp. 124–25 (XII, 117). (New translation will be titled *Practice in Christianity*.)

29. See Pojman, *The Logic of Subjectivity*, p. 123.

30. P. 39 (207).

31. This is just an illustration. I do not mean to suggest by this example that the materialist is correct; as a matter of fact, my sympathies lie with the dualist.

32. Pp. 46–47 (214).

33. P. 52 (218).

34. See *The Sickness unto Death*, pp. 83–96 (XI, 194–207) and *Training in Christianity*, p. 64 (XII, 57).

35. A good example of this reading of Kierkegaard is found in W. W. Bartley,

III, *The Retreat to Commitment*, second edition (LaSalle, Ill.: Open Court Publishing Co., 1984), pp. 39–49.

36. *Postscript*, p. 35n (24n).

37. See *Fragments*, p. 59 (224), and also *Postscript*, p. 514 (VII, 505).

38. P. 59 (224).

39. *Søren Kierkegaard's Journals and Papers*, vol I. (Bloomington: Indiana University Press, 1967), entry no. 10, p. 7.

40. P. 48 (215).

41. Pp. 47–48 (214–15).

42. P. 59 (224).

43. Pp. 55–56 (222).

44. P. 62 (227).

45. P. 62 (227).

46. Alvin Plantinga, "Reason and Belief in God," in *Faith and Rationality*, edited by Alvin Plantinga and Nicholas Wolterstorff (Notre Dame, Ind.: University of Notre Dame Press, 1983), pp. 16–91.

47. Plantinga, "Reason and Belief in God," pp. 78–82.

48. See pp. 59–60 (225–26).

49. Pp. 59–61 (225–26).

50. P. 60 (226).

51. P. 65 (229).

52. P. 58 (224).

53. P. 59 (225).

54. Pp. 66–71 (230–34).

55. Pp. 66–67 (230–31).

56. P. 68 (232).

57. P. 69 (233).

58. I thank Robert Roberts for calling my attention to Bloom's writings and this passage in particular.

59. Anthony Bloom, *Beginning to Pray* (New York: Paulist Press, 1970), p. xii.

60. P. 104 (266).

61. Louis Pojman makes this charge, for example, in *Religious Belief and the Will* (London: Routledge and Kegan Paul, 1986).

62. The following passage is crucial here: "If the teacher (the god) is to be the occasion that reminds the learner, he cannot assist him to recollect that he actually does know the Truth....That for which the teacher can become the occasion of his recollecting is that he is untruth....To this act of consciousness, the Socratic principle applies: the teacher is only an occasion, whoever he may be, even if he is a god" (p. 14 [184]).

63. See especially the second section. The following quote is very typical: "The decisive mark of Christian suffering is the fact that it is voluntary, and that it is *the possibility of offence for the sufferer*" (italics Kierkegaard's) (*Training in Christianity [Practice in Christianity]*, p. 111 [XII, 104]).

64. *Sickness unto Death*, p. 83 (XI, 195).

65. *Postscript*, p. 51 (VII, 39).

8. BELIEF AND THE WILL

1. P. 72 (235).
2. Pp. 87–88 (251).
3. For an example, see David Wisdo's essay, "Kierkegaard on Belief, Faith, and Explanation," in *International Journal for Philosophy of Religion* 21, 2 (1987), 95–114.
4. P. 73 (236).
5. P. 74 (237).
6. See H. A. Nielsen, *Where the Passion Is*, pp. 129–33.
7. H. A. Nielsen, *Where the Passion Is*, p. 130.
8. H. A. Nielsen, *Where the Passion Is*, p. 130.
9. P. 74 (237).
10. P. 74 (237).
11. P. 75 (238).
12. *On Interpretation*, 21b-23a. See *The Basic Works of Aristotle*, edited by Richard McKeon (New York: Random House, 1941), pp. 54–60.
13. P. 75 (238).
14. P. 75 (239).
15. See H. A. Nielsen, *Where the Passion Is*, pp. 130–39.
16. Pp. 75–76 (239).
17. P. 76 (239).
18. P. 76 (240).
19. See *The Concept of Anxiety*, translated by Reidar Thomte (Princeton: Princeton University Press, 1980), pp. 85–91.
20. H. A. Nielsen, *Where the Passion Is*, pp. 135–36.
21. P. 79 (243).
22. P. 77 (241).
23. Richard Taylor, *Metaphysics*, second edition (Englewood Cliffs, N.J.: Prentice Hall, 1974), pp. 67–68.
24. Richard Taylor, *Metaphysics*, p. 68.
25. P. 80 (243).
26. Louis Pojman, *Religious Belief and the Will*.
27. See Pojman, *Religious Belief and the Will*, pp. 143–48, for a fuller account of the following distinctions.
28. Pojman, *Religious Belief and the Will*, p. 179.
29. Pojman, *Religious Belief and the Will*, p. 192.
30. Pojman, *Religious Belief and the Will*, p. 158.
31. Pojman, *Religious Belief and the Will*, p. 189.
32. Terence Penelhum, *God and Skepticism* (Dordrecht, Holland: D. Reidel Publishing Co., 1983), pp. 81–82, 114.
33. David Wisdo takes exactly this line in his article, "Kierkegaard on Belief, Faith, and Explanation," in *International Journal for Philosophy of Religion* 21, 2 (1987), 95–114.
34. See Pp. 86–88 (250–51).
35. P. 83 (247).
36. P. 84 (247–48).

37. P. 81 (244).
38. P. 81 (244).
39. P. 81 (245).
40. P. 81 (245).
41. Robert Roberts says this in *Faith, Reason, and History*, pp. 109–17. Roberts thinks that Climacus' arguments in the Interlude may be ironical, and that Climacus may be pulling our leg, forcing us by his outrageous claims to think things through for ourselves.
42. Pp. 81–82 (245).
43. P. 82 (245).
44. P. 82 (245–46).
45. P. 82 (246).
46. P. 84 (248).
47. P. 82 (246).
48. P. 84 (248).
49. See *Concluding Unscientific Postscript*, p. 299n (VII, 290n). Also see *Fear and Trembling*, translated and edited by Howard V. and Edna H. Hong (Princeton: Princeton University Press, 1983), pp. 5–7 (III, 57–59).
50. *Fear and Trembling* develops this polemic about going further at length, not only with respect to faith, but also with respect to the doubts of the skeptic. Besides the section cited in the last note, see also pp. 121–23 (III, 166–68).
51. P. 85 (248).
52. P. 84 (248).
53. P. 83 (246).
54. P. 62 (227).
55. See, for example, the stress Climacus puts on a first-hand encounter in which the condition of faith is received from the God (70; 233).
56. P. 14 (184).

9. FAITH AND HISTORY

1. Pp. 89–90 (252–53).
2. P. 92 (255).
3. P. 93 (256).
4. P. 93 (256).
5. P. 97 (260).
6. P. 94 (257).
7. P. 95 (258).
8. Pp. 97–98 (260–61).
9. P. 98 (260).
10. P. 94 (257).
11. P. 95 (258).
12. Pp. 96–97 (259–60).
13. P. 96 (259).
14. P. 96 (258).
15. P. 99 (262).
16. P. 99 (262).

17. P. 99 (262).
18. *Postscript*, pp. 184–85n (VII, 172–73n).
19. P. 99 (262).
20. P. 99 (262).
21. P. 100 (262).
22. P. 106 (268).
23. P. 104 (266).
24. P. 104 (266).
25. P. 104 (266).
26. For some excellent examples of how theologians do this, even though they intend to remain fully Christian in their view of Jesus, see Robert Roberts, *Faith, Reason, and History*, chapter 1.
27. *Fear and Trembling*, p. 55 (III, 105).
28. Pp. 13–14 (183–84).
29. P. 109 (271).
30. *Postscript*, pp. 498 and 507–508 (VII, 489 and 499–500).
31. P. 104 (266).
32. M. J. Ferreira, "The Faith/History Problem and Kierkegaard's A *Priori* 'Proof'," *Religious Studies* 23 (1987), 337–45. I realize that Ferreira's argument here presupposes a particular theory of identity for historical figures, and that if one adopted some rival theory, in particular some austere version of a causal theory, this argument may not hold. However, I find Ferreira's view extremely plausible, and I am inclined to think that any theory of identity that would have as an implication that I could meaningfully refer to a figure about whom I knew nothing at all would carry a heavy burden of proof.
33. See Alvin Plantinga, "Reason and Belief in God," in *Faith and Rationality*, edited by Alvin Plantinga and Nicholas Wolterstorff (Notre Dame, Ind.: University of Notre Dame Press, 1983), pp. 46–47, for an account of what it is for a belief to be properly basic.
34. I do not wish to deny here that in a wide enough sense of "evidence" this encounter which I describe as the ground could itself be viewed as evidence. In saying it is not evidence I mean first that it is not a propositional belief which has any logical relations to faith, and secondly that it does not form the basis for any process of inference by which the individual arrives at faith.
35. The following remarks are inspired by some points made with respect to religious experience by William Alston, "The Place of Experience in the Grounds of Religious Belief," unpublished paper delivered at a conference at Gordon College on "The Future of God," May 26, 1989. I do not claim that Alston would endorse this use of his distinction.
36. See my "The Epistemological Significance of Transformative Religious Experience," in *Faith and Philosophy* 8, 2 (1991), 180–92.
37. P. 104 (266).
38. Pp. 94–95n (257–58n).
39. The following well-known passage lies at the heart of Hume's argument: "A miracle is a violation of the laws of nature; and as a firm and unalterable experience has established these laws, the proof against a miracle, from the very nature of the fact, is as entire as any argument from experience can possibly be imagined" (*An Inquiry Concerning Human Understanding* [Indianapolis, Ind.:

Hackett Publishing Co., 1977], p. 76). See pp. 72–77 for the thrust of Hume's argument.

40. See my discussion in chapter 7.

41. P. 56 (222). I am tempted to translate this passage in the following manner: "Every accommodating aid in understanding cannot genuinely help the one who has not received the condition, which is why it is extorted from the god only unwillingly."

42. P. 93 (256).

43. See the discussion of the necessity of the past in the Interlude, pp. 79–80 (243).

44. See Acts 2:22.

45. P. 109 (270).

46. P. 109 (271).

47. P. 109. This is one of many allusions to I Corinthians 2:7–9 in Kierkegaard's authorship.

48. P. 109 (271).

10. CHRISTIANITY IN THE CONTEMPORARY WORLD

1. P. 111 (272).

2. P. 111 (272).

3. See Robert Roberts, *Faith, Reason, and History*, chapter 1.

4. See John B. Cobb, Jr., *Christ in a Pluralistic Age* (Philadelphia: The Westminster Press, 1975), pp. 139, 142. Also see "A Whiteheadian Christology," in *Process Philosophy and Christian Thought*, edited by Delwin Brown, Ralph E. James, Jr., and Gene Reeves (Indianapolis: Bobbs-Merrill Company, 1971), p. 392.

5. *Christ in a Pluralistic Age*, p. 140.

6. *Christ in a Pluralistic Age*, p. 142.

7. Besides *Faith, Reason, and History*, pp. 34–37, see also Robert Roberts, *Rudolf Bultmann's Theology* (Grand Rapids, Mich.: Wm. B. Eerdmans, 1976), chapter 3.

8. See *The Myth of God Incarnate*, edited by John Hick (London: SCM Press, 1977).

9. Thomas Sheehan, *The First Coming* (New York: Random House, 1986).

10. Sheehan, p. 61.

11. Sheehan, p. 124.

12. Michael Goulder, "The Two Roots of the Christian Myth," in *The Myth of God Incarnate*, pp. 64–85.

13. *The Myth of God Incarnate*, pp. 186–203.

14. *The Myth of God Incarnate*, p. 205.

15. P. 111 (272).

16. Alasdair MacIntyre, *After Virtue*, second edition (Notre Dame, Ind.: University of Notre Dame Press, 1984), pp. 39–47.

17. W.W. Bartley, III, *The Retreat to Commitment*, second edition (LaSalle, Ill.: Open Court Publishing Co., 1984), p. 42.

18. Terence Penelhum, *God and Skepticism* (Dordrecht, The Netherlands: D. Reidel Publishing Co., 1983), pp. 75–84.

19. Penelhum, *God and Skepticism*, pp. 114–15, 81–82.

20. Alvin Plantinga, "Justification and Theism," *Faith and Philosophy* 4, 4 (1987), 403–26.

Index

C. STEPHEN EVANS, Professor of Philosophy and Curator of the Howard V. and Edna H. Hong Kierkegaard Library at St. Olaf College, is the author of *Søren Kierkegaard's Christian Psychology* and *Kierkegaard's* Fragments *and* Postscript: *The Religious Philosophy of Johannes Climacus*.